THE SCOTLAND
OF OUR FATHERS

CARNOCK HOUSE AND GARDEN, STIRLINGSHIRE

THE SCOTLAND OF OUR FATHERS

A Study of Scottish Life in the Nineteenth Century

BY

ELIZABETH S. HALDANE

WITH 24 ILLUSTRATIONS
AND MAPS

LONDON
ALEXANDER MACLEHOSE & CO.
58 Bloomsbury Street
1933

PRINTED IN GREAT BRITAIN BY ROBERT MACLEHOSE AND CO. LTD.
THE UNIVERSITY PRESS, GLASGOW

PREFATORY NOTE

Ostendamus quos sibi Caledonia viros seposuerit
(Let us shew the manner of the men that Scotland has set apart for herself)

The speech of Galgacus on the Mons
Graupius in the *Agricola* of Tacitus

ON the social side the last century has been little dealt with, compared with its predecessor, perhaps because it is so near, and it is difficult to judge of periods too near, but perhaps also because the eighteenth century was so exciting. From being a dead and backward country Scotland then pulled herself together and began to declare herself a Nation, to develop her resources, and produce great men of action and letters.

What are we to say of the next century? It had a great inheritance, and it had in the beginning a literature of which it might be proud. Then it plunged into the vortex of the Industrial Revolution. Scotland won power for its people, it became rich beyond its dreams, it developed all the powers that science provided for its use. It took its place proudly beside its rival across the border. It held its head high and its great men left it to become rulers of Great Britain and of the Empire.

But as a nation has it lost its soul? Has the search for money and power dimmed its sight? So people tell us. They say we are now but a Province—an important Province—but no Nation. Our population

is decreasing, our trade is decreasing and our great men
are no more.   They tell us we are suffering for our
neglect of our duty and our self-sufficiency in the years
gone by.   They tell us that the Religion that was our
stand-by is dead, that Secularism has taken its place
because our church was not faithful to its standards and
let its precious heritage slip from its hands.   They tell
us that our vaunted education has become atrophied,
that we produce machines calculated to pass examinations but devoid of life and its adaptive powers.   They
tell us that physically we are a town-bred people who
have lost hold on nature and the health nature gives.

It is to combat these assertions that this book is
written.   We cannot deny them all, for some of them
are true.   But we may try to show from our past history
that though we have had a time of " fallow " such as
all nations sometimes have, we have also got it in us
to do great things still, we know not how or by what
means.   In the present century we have been pressed
down by the losses of War and by Trade Depression
more than others.   We are standing up again to act as
we did two hundred years ago when things were blacker
still.   We are forming Societies for developing our
trade.   We are determined to reform our government
in so far as that is necessary.   Administratively we want
to do for ourselves in certain directions even if our re-
collection of a Parliament in days gone by does not make
that one of our desires.   We want to be National only

in so far as that enables us to be International, and we cannot be International without first being a Nation.

It may be said that this book falls between two stools : it may be considered insufficiently informative on the one hand, or, especially when it dips into theology or statistics, too solemn on the other. But further information can be got elsewhere and dull parts may be skipped. Then again it deals with dates remembered by many as well as by the author, and her remembrances are sure to be capped by others claiming to be more accurate. This last is undoubtedly true, for much is written as personal experiences or else learned through the ' Fathers ' of the writer, and all such remembrances are fallible. Also but the fringe of a great subject has been touched. A certain amount of repetition has been difficult to avoid.

Great assistance has been given by kind friends who, however, must not be implicated in any accusation of inaccuracy, for they have mainly supplied material, books, manuscripts and pictures. Some of them must be mentioned :

There are first the ever helpful Librarians of The National Library of Scotland, the National Central Library, The County Library of Perthshire (Auchterarder Branch), The Public Library of Westminster and that of the Royal Horticultural Society. Of individuals there are : Sir Thomas Middleton, The Earl of Crawford and Balcarres, Miss Christie of Cowden, Dr.

R. H. Makgill, Mr. Robert Waterston, Mr. J. A. Butter-
field, Mr. Wm. Cuthbertson, Sir Leslie Mackenzie, Sir
Arthur Hill, Mr. John Smyth and Miss Ritchie of
Prestwick. Professor Ernest Barker of Cambridge has
been good enough to read the larger part of the proofs.
Then there must be mentioned certain officials at the
Public Offices and the writer's Publisher, all of whose
patience and kindness have been great.

ELIZABETH S. HALDANE.

CLOAN, AUCHTERARDER,
September 1933.

CONTENTS

ILLUSTRATIONS

MAPS AND PLANS

The Frontispiece is from a drawing by Miss Mary Wilson, reproduced from *Scottish Gardens* by Sir Herbert Maxwell, by permission of the publishers, Messrs. Edward Arnold & Co.

The illustration of the Paisley Encyclopaedia Club is reproduced by permission of Messrs. Alex. Gardner Ltd.

CHAPTER I

INTRODUCTION

It is difficult to write about a century with such tremendous upheavals as the Nineteenth, even though we are only dealing with a restricted area. The beginning of the century differs enormously from the end in social outlook and social conditions. Then in Scotland there is another difficulty, for East, West, North and South seem to have differences greater than one would expect in a country comparatively so small. When we are dealing with the present century these differences may not be so great, for communication is so much easier and every day it becomes easier still, now that the medium of air is added to those of sea and land, and any part of the country can be reached in a very few hours. But those who love the old order of things, even though they would not for a moment wish to revert to it, and who remember that the present can only be properly understood by the past, may find this brief survey of old conditions, partly remembered and partly heard of, not wholly uninteresting.

We Scots seem to have come to a rather crucial stage in our history, for there is a feeling that whatever we may believe about the sense of nationality and its dangers when taken in a narrow and selfish spirit, we

A

should certainly lose something of intrinsic value if we lost that sense altogether, since we know that, small and struggling nation as we are, our nationality has sustained us through many difficulties and helped us through our endeavours to make the best of hard conditions. From a pecuniary point of view Scotland has been well treated by her wealthy and powerful partner, but as old Lord Balcarres said in the eighteenth century when complaining of the Union having taken sons of the best Scotch nobility to London, leaving the daughters deserted and solitary at home, ' a pound of gold is not worth a pound of ancestry.' So sometimes we feel that we should, for instance, have made more progress in our education had we been left to work it out in our own way without the impersonality of those dim and distant figures ' My Lords ' looming from afar in London ; that not only might we now be free to work under educational regulations such as those governing Adult Education in England, but also that, for instance, equal provision might be made for preserving our ancient Records, and we might have something better for our Government offices than deserted commercial buildings which cannot be said to house them with much dignity. Our present system calls on one Cabinet Minister to deal with subjects dealt with by several Ministers in England, and all Scottish matters have in the first place to be scrutinized by the Scottish Office before receiving Treasury sanction. All this appears to the ordinary Scot to involve delay, and he would rightly or wrongly like to be in more direct contact with the spending authorities. Doubtless these things are in our own hands, but we should bring our minds to bear on them.

Parliament in Scotland has never had the significance to the people that it has had in England, but good government is a different matter, and surely it may be carried on without a separate supreme legislative body, since the countries are too closely intertwined for this to be essential.

.   .   .   .

North Britain, as it was called after the Union, has made a mark in history quite incommensurate with its size and population. From this time onward it claimed to be an eighth of Britain (a claim far from justified now) and on the strength of this claim it made quite a favourable bargain. For in 1707 it was a poor country, and it remained a poor country for many years afterwards. Its agriculture was at a desperately low ebb and industrially it hardly existed. The strange thing was that Scotland managed to play so great and even so tiresome a part in history, so far as England was concerned, for while the population of Scotland at the time of the Union was estimated at something over a million (about an eighth of the English) her wealth was but a fortieth. Hence she did well by having forty-five members in the British House of Commons, even though by population she was entitled to eighty-five. The discrepancy between population and wealth has always been her bane. Her people were scattered about in villages or crofts, for Glasgow was still a

small town of something like 12,500 inhabitants.
Edinburgh was not more than about double that
size.

During the next 150 years, and indeed to the end of
the last century, Scotland's progress was carried on
consistently. Her population increased from one million
to over four and a half, and her riches also increased.[1]
Glasgow, from being a pretty country town, finally became an enormous and wealthy city of over a million
people. Industry and commerce progressed even faster
than agriculture. The Highlands alone have become
more and more depopulated till now the rate of decrease
in the ten western counties is calculated at 5000 a year.
Emigration to Canada and elsewhere has taken away
many. Even early in the present century it was estimated as being over 42,000 a year, though now of
course that has ceased ; but the great exodus of
population has been into towns.

It is clear that we must, unlike the general ideas of
the traveller, consider Scotland as largely composed of
a town population. Since the century began there has
been a constant increase of those living in town at the
expense of country dwellers, and now nearly 70 per
cent of the population are town dwellers. The urban
population numbers 3,361,364 and the rural 1,481,170.
Scotland is also in great measure an uncultivated
country, for only about a quarter of it is under culti-

[1] In 1931 the population of Scotland was 4,842,554, about 40,000
less than ten years before. The population of Glasgow is provision-
ally estimated in 1933 as 1,102,065.

vation. Hence it is a country in which solitude can be readily found and even in the cultivated areas the population is sparsely distributed.

Of the rural part of the country a large amount is set aside for sport, which brings, or has brought, a certain amount of wealth, but also depopulation. It is uncertain how long this can continue, probably not for very long; but it arose during the century we are considering with the growth of deer forests, succeeding the time when sheep farms were very valuable, and the still earlier time when they took the place of a crofter population.

Not until recent years, and since the end of the period about which we are writing, has there been a check in the material progress of Scotland. The drain southwards during recent years has been ominous. Not only has the population of Scotland decreased, but trade has drifted south, and hence unemployment is higher in Scotland than in the whole United Kingdom and there is anxiety as to where this is to end.

Whether or not it helps us towards understanding why these things should be and whether they can be checked, it is worth while considering what has been the history of the Scot in relation to his surroundings and trying to discover the rock out of which he has been hewn—that is to say, the material and spiritual conditions which existed a century or more ago, and the developments which emerged from them. It is also worth while considering the form taken in the past by education—taking education in the widest sense, as not only book learning but also social conditions, amusements for mind and body, forms of expression, songs and so on. It is interesting likewise to recall the food the Scot took and even more the drink he obtained, and generally the social customs that have existed and are now past. We shall find a different way of spending leisure as well as of undertaking work, changes being brought about by increased and altered methods of transport, by smaller families taking the place of large, by town life taking the place of rural life, and by constant movement abroad of the best part of the population, leaving the less competent and older behind.

There is in Scotland one special factor which has operated in its life longer than it has done in most countries. In Scotland the Church has dominated the life of the country in a remarkable way—the civil life as well as the spiritual—so that it has left its mark to this day. No doubt things have changed greatly in this respect ; the number of persons attending church has certainly decreased a good deal since the urbanization of the country has taken place ; but we shall find that religion has fundamentally influenced Scottish character even where there has been a vigorous effort to disclaim it.

In estimating the character of her people we have to remember there were other things that influenced Scotland as well as her religion. In effecting a union with England she preserved not only her Church, but also her law and the feudal tenure of land, and that meant a good deal. In former days Scottish sympathies had been more with France than England. Every Scottish traveller in France recognizes in her châteaux not the castles of England but those of his own country, with their turrets and corbels or crow's steps. He finds too that many of the words in ordinary Scottish use are French in origin. He eats a ' gigot ' of mutton, a ' bursary ' is gained by his child, he uses 'ashets' and 'carafes.' He ' convenes ' his meetings and ' homologates ' the proceedings ; his wife used to wear ' jupes ' and have her ' aumries '. His local dignitaries, his provost and bailies, and the dog Latin used in educational circles, savour more of the Scots Colleges in Paris and Rome than of the universities of England. There has been in Scotland also, in spite of her poverty and lack of the amenities of life, a sense of oneness with a larger culture such as enables a Scot to take his place happily and unselfconsciously in foreign society as one who can enter into the feelings and sentiments of lands not his own. This power has been of the utmost use in guiding his destinies. So often it happens that the Scot has felt more at home on the Continent than in England. Louis Stevenson tells us how the difference operates : it is subtle but real. The Scot ' has had a different training ; he obeys different laws ; he makes his will in other terms, is otherwise divorced and married ; his eyes are not at home in an English landscape or with English houses ; his ear continues to remark the English speech ; and even though his tongue acquires the Southern knack, he will still have a strong Scots accent of the mind.' The Scotsman, he tells us, is vain, interested in himself and others, eager for sympathy, while the egoism of the Englishman is self-contained. What is worst of all to the ardent but terribly self-conscious Scot, he is apt to be, as Stevenson says, put in the attitude of a suitor or poor relation !

And he seems to escape from all this when abroad—abroad indeed anywhere, and hence he travels more than most men : more perhaps than any small nation, leaving his poor land with sorrow but still with alacrity, till the time comes for him to return to it to die or to leave to his countrymen hard earned riches because they are his countrymen. Nationalism has its dangers, but it keeps a certain pride of life that is a valuable possession. It no doubt also leads to a sort of provincialism and narrowness when unchecked.

At one time it seemed as if France would have made a better ally for Scotland than England because the two had so many points of contact. Both were clear and logical in their reasoning ; they could not away with the casual and almost slipshod methods of the English. Both were severely practical and thrifty ; both had the intense feeling for family life that seemed lacking in England. Both preferred to keep their children at day schools rather than send them to boarding schools, not only because it was economical to do so but also because they wished to know their children in their normal lives and help them in their learning ; for both valued learning in itself and not only as a means to something else : Scottish children, too, were older for their age, more thoughtful and less polished and urbane, than the English. But of course an economic alliance with

France of a permanent sort was unthinkable. The two countries were separated by nature as well as by language, and above all by religion. It became more and more evident that England was the natural ally as communications improved. In old days it was probably safer and certainly cheaper to cross the sea than to cross the border, so that students went to Leiden or possibly to Paris: now it is otherwise. Indeed, it is now possible to ask why should this small country with a population less than Lancashire stand apart? Why should not Westminster govern both? She could have her Departments for Education and Health and so on, but her law might gradually assimilate itself to that of England, especially as she makes her final Appeal to the House of Lords. Her Church, of course, could not be touched, but the Imperial services of Army, Navy and Air are already the same.

All this sounds true, but the Scot, despite the fact that he sees business everywhere being rationalized and made more efficient and economical by being amalgamated, and even agrees that he might gain by the process, is conscious that there is something above even efficiency and economy, something which can only be expressed in higher terms. Therefore he feels that he must do for himself and follow his own traditions, for he believes that he has a tradition to follow. All he wants is to know that his affairs are not relegated to an uninterested Assembly but are being dealt with as effectively as those of the rest of the Kingdom.

.   .   .   .

It is none too easy to crowd one's impressions of a century of growth such as that made by the century we have left behind into one arithmetical period. The nineteenth century grew so evidently out of the last portion of the eighteenth and the Revolution that took place then—a Revolution of a social and industrial as well as a political nature—that it is hardly possible not to refer to that time of lively progress. Then again we should take leave of the nineteenth century only on the outbreak of the Great War, which was to effect an even greater change in the world than did the French Revolution and its repercussions. On the other hand, at the end of last century at any rate there has been a clear break made by new modes of living, new modes of locomotion by air and land, new views of social and family relationship (for this began before the War), and generally what the Germans call a new 'Weltanschauung'; so that we can talk of a nineteenth century point of view with some meaning as being something which more or less characterized a definite period or time.

.   .   .   .

The first thing we have to note in thinking of Scotland is how the four or five million people who inhabit it are distributed through their 33 counties and 874 parishes.

When we look at a map of population such as the one reproduced at the end of this book, we see vividly how that population is distributed. In London we should find the same sort of population crowded into one small county with parts of others adjoining. In Scotland it would appear that there are great tracts practically uninhabited. We get as a matter of fact more than half of Scotland with but a fraction of her population, hardly one-tenth, and then we have a great midland valley—perhaps one-fifth of the area —containing at least three-quarters of the population. Thus the development of coal and iron has transformed the country, and changed the problems that confront it from those that concern the rural dweller to those that face the townsmen. All this change cannot occur without a great transformation being effected throughout all the country, not merely in the industrial parts of it. Indeed, wherever men live they are affected by the transformation. All sorts of goods, even meat and milk, pour out from Glasgow to the remotest Hebrides. A more precious commodity still, men and women, pour back to swell the already large population. Tourists also pour in to look and enjoy, but not to dwell. The extent of the tourist range increases year by year, and it seems as though it will not be very long before the quiet tracts now occupied by grouse moors and deer forests will cease to be isolated and will become the playgrounds not only of the wealthy as before but of the ordinary people, the flyers, motorists, bikers and hikers. But we must remember that it will also be the breathing place for the Scottish town dwellers, and they love the land they have left. Therefore the duty of guarding its beauty—a beauty which is the great asset of the country—must be religiously observed.   Once lost it can never be re-covered.

Sometimes one wonders when passing through the endless rows of miners' cottages, or the iron-workers' squalid streets, and feeling horrified by the ugliness they present, whether we might not have had a different country, a country of beauty such as it was before so-called industrialism entered.   Whether industrial-ism might not have been what the name to many of us implies—a thing of beauty, not of hideousness. Whether Ruskin was not right and the object of our rulers should not have been the ' multiplication of human life at the highest standard' rather than the search for ineffectual wealth, mere exchangeable value. Had we thought of the relations of master to servant and employers to workmen and not of bosses to ' hands,' had one thought of the State in relation to the good living of its subjects and not merely to riches, we might not have come to the pass we have. But as it is, whether wrongs are righted by violent means or by peaceful, we have to face the future with courage and try to undo what has been wrong and do what seems to be for the best.   One thing is clear and that is that we have not sinned alone : only the natural beauty which we inherited seems to make our sins the greater.

To take but one example of the change in point of view that has come over the world in respect of the appreciation of beauty, let us think of the different estimation in which the scenery of Scotland was held a century and a half ago, before the wave of Romanticism had passed over Scotland. It was indeed a somewhat belated Romanticism, for it began much earlier in France and Germany. In the eighteenth century both England and Scotland were for the most part severely classical and unromantic. Scotland indeed, with its Moderatism in the Church and orthodoxy in all matters of importance, might well be termed pedantic. But when the Romantic spirit broke over the island she had more than her share with her Burns and her Scott as well as the smaller but still important fry. Scott taught the world to find a new meaning and interest in his country, and between his influence and that of Carlyle, who brought German romanticism to the knowledge of the English-speaking world, the effect was immense. Whether it was the English Lake School or native feelings that made what had been termed ' unpleasant ' into a matter to be not only admired but raved about, it is difficult to say. But Southey, a ' Lake ' poet, on his journey to Scotland shrank from the ' savage and terrible ' grandeur of Glencoe and preferred cultivated land to barren heaths. This, however, is not by itself conclusive evidence.

We all know how Scottish scenery was regarded in the eighteenth century from the records of the immortal Boswell and his Johnson when they made their famous Tour through the Highlands—those melancholy Highlands even when mitigated by the hospitality, and even politeness, of their inhabitants. For despite the unanimous condemnation of Johnson, Gray, and the good

John Wesley (who used to speak of ' horrid mountains ') we must recollect that there was for all of them
some compensation in the kindliness of the people.
But of course when Gray saw in Perthshire ' a wide and
dismal heath fit but for an assembly of witches ' one
must remember that the physical sensation of coming
into such regions may well have influenced the æsthetic,
and to this day if we were in fear of unknown dangers,
and in totally uncharted surroundings of an alarming
kind, our appreciation of beauty might be less intense.
To the uneducated traveller even now the terrible
dominates the sensations ; and often enough the appreciation of wild and unknown beauty is artificial. The
soldiers of Cumberland were ' sick daily ' in their minds
as well as bodies at the sight of the bleak and barren
mountains. John Wesley felt not very differently.

It is evident, however, that the sense of beauty had
begun to be felt even before the enthusiastic age. In
Susan Ferrier's writings, early in the nineteenth century, we have it in a very moderate and distilled form.
Her descriptions of the beauty so unappreciated by her
Lady Juliana are mostly of lovely reflections in lakes
which might as well have been in England : on the
whole we are left with an uncomfortable feeling about
the great wild mountains in which the English heiress—
poor soul—was enclosed. Southey says that the
English lakes will appear to advantage after the Scotch
—more than is gained in magnitude is lost in beauty.
The leaves of the birch are too small, too ' twinkling ' to
mass together in any point of view. A greater Scot than

Miss Ferrier, John Galt, hardly mentions the scenery. Still we are told that at the time Susan Ferrier wrote such scenery was in fashion—no doubt owing to the influence of the poetry of Scott and Burns. We are also told that the scenery might have charms for Ossian though none for the Lady Juliana ; but by this time the southern invasion had begun and Juliana had heard of the well-regulated visits of her fashionable friends. By 1819, Southey says, the Trossachs had been made famous by Scott. As the century advanced the fashionable friends multiplied, to the great benefit of the Scottish people financially and, above all, of the needy lairds who found almost to their surprise the possession of a good moor or extensive deer forest a source of wealth. Railways and wealth both contributed to this new invasion from ' furth the border,' and it resulted in marriages that were satisfactory on both sides.

The Royal Residence at Balmoral did something also to help in popularizing Scotland and bringing wealthy Englishmen to appreciate the benefits of moors and deer forests in autumn. The shooting season came opportunely when Parliament was up, and no longer were ' cures ' at Bath required for those who led a healthier life at all times.

Perhaps we cannot wonder at the English travellers having rather a dreary impression of Scottish scenery in the Lowlands before the improvements at the beginning of the nineteenth century took place. They must have missed the stately churches and well-built farmhouses when they gazed on the unenclosed lands and tree-less landscape which impressed every traveller from the south. The stone dykes, where dykes existed, cannot to them have taken the place of trim hedges, and in Johnson's time there was not, he says, a tree to be seen that was not younger than himself. Then when the mountainous areas were approached the rocks 'towered a horrid nakedness,' or as Goldsmith said ' the hills and rocks intercept every prospect,' and there was gloomy desolation.

Even when we come to Wordsworth, though he was of course struck with the natural beauty of the High-lands, he deplored ' the appearance of equality in poverty through the long glens of Scotland, giving the notion of savage ignorance—no home better than another, and barns and homes all alike.' A new well-built house delighted his sister Dorothy. Much as she admired the Highlands she rejoiced in a comfort-able white house surrounded by green fields such as she knew in Cumberland. She writes in 1802 that she and her brother hardly saw a thoroughly pleasing place in Scotland which had not something of the wilderness aspect. And the wilderness aspect was not admired by the gentler school of Lake poets. She explains her feelings by the sights she saw, the sea and the high mountains and the unenclosed hills, the scattered huts, the imperfect culture of the fields and so on. The personal element came in as it had every right to come, but in a form in which it had not come to the Scots who in their battle with natural forces had not been able to grapple with more than the essentials of living, leaving the amenities to be dealt with later. Wordsworth loved not only the hills but the quiet loveliness of the valleys and their well cared for farm-houses. He thought the hard living of the Scottish people, and the gloom of their religion, prevented them from adorning their houses.

It certainly seems to us strange that more attention was not paid to the amenities of life, but as the century advanced things improved. It was not realized what might be done with the conditions that existed, as is evidenced in Dr. Johnson's time by the longing expressed by the wife of Macleod of Macleod to be able to have a garden at Dunvegan Castle in Skye, the situation of which she considered an impossible one for any such scheme. As a matter of fact not only is there now a lovely garden, but plants are growing in it which are almost tropical and which it is found impossible to propagate on the mainland or on most of it. No doubt the possibility that expenditure might be increased prevented many lairds from experimenting in beautifying their surroundings, but where this was done the trouble was well rewarded.

It was much the same with farming, and fine woods were cut down and only replanted when the planting craze took place, which was in the happy time of rejuvenation in Scotland. There are districts in the northwest of Scotland such as those of East Buchan and the Outer Hebrides where trees will not grow, but there are, as we now know, great tracts where they do grow excellently when the right kinds are planted in the right way.

B

But in the early eighteenth century old timber was non-existent, except for a few stray trees round a gentleman's house, or yews in his burial place. Yet our coalfields and peat bogs show that wood must at one time have been abundant, and there are remains of the great Caledonian Forest. Then vegetables were hardly grown in the eighteenth century until turnips were discovered and properly cultivated. They were at first used as dessert at gentlemen's tables as we read in the Life of the Lord Aberdeen of the day, whose English wife was regaled by them. There were practically no apples in common use and cabbages represented the best of the truly named cottage kailyard. The introduction of plenty of ' berries '—gooseberries (grossets), currants and raspberries—effected a transformation in people's ideas of food. Why in a country where raspberries grow wild they were not developed earlier it seems hard to understand. But apart from kail for brose, vegetables and even wild fruit were not used as they ought to have been by the poorer people. Mushrooms, termed ' puddock stools,' are hardly touched to this day. The advantages of fruit and vegetables were not realized, or we might have had a healthier population.

The beginning of the century was a grievous time for town and country dwellers alike, for wages were small and food dear. But still there was a new spirit in the air. Great houses were being built in the country, taking advantage of the cheap labour, and new roads were being made—which was far more important. New bridges, redeeming an old disgrace, were now also being built. Indeed, though, as often happens, it was long before the good of this movement reached the workers, this new spirit pervaded the whole country. Politically, the old bad days of English domination, though it was exercised through a great Scotsman, Dundas, Lord Melville, were passing ; and way was being made for the Reform which culminated in the Act of 1832. Economically, a new country arose, covered with fields carefully fenced in and with woods planted for shelter (they were but young woods then) and with every aspect of coming prosperity. The industrial belt was dark and smoky, but that meant trade and occupation. From the docks of the Clyde vessels issued forth to foreign lands, taking with them the products of Scotland and bringing in corresponding imports. All promised well, though the common people were not content with their share of the general prosperity.

CHAPTER II

HOW THE PEOPLE LIVED

By the beginning of the nineteenth century the Scottish houses had developed into something not very different from what we now know, only they were built on a simpler scale, and, as far as the working people's houses were concerned, it was a very much simpler scale. The great castles were as of yore, but they were few, and many had fallen into ruins after they ceased to be needed for defence. The old-fashioned type of laird's house which was a sort of keep, tall and gaunt with small windows and crow's steps, and possibly adorned by a turret or several turrets, had for the most part developed into pleasant plain houses that looked you straight in the face without mystery and were very likely ' harled ' white, with deep-set windows and picturesque gables, again adorned with crow's steps. They were many of them, soon, alas, to be demolished in favour of pretentious buildings ' in the Gothic style.' It was fortunate when the plainer Georgian style was adopted. Of these houses Catherine Sinclair, a far-seeing observer, writes in 1840 : ' The moment any Scotch proprietor lays the foundation of a new house he may consider himself a bankrupt because he never leaves himself a sufficient income to inhabit it and he never seems able to stop

TYPICAL LAIRD'S HOUSE

SHOWING THE LOUPIN'-ON-STANE AND DOOCOT

while a stone remains in the quarry.' There have been many evidences of this passion for building, and the erections were difficult to keep up, inconveniently arranged, and famous collectors of dirt. The simple and almost primitive mode of living was departed from when the rush of unexpected wealth reached the landlord during the French wars or just after them. At that time—that is about 1820 and onwards for half a century —rents were high for arable ground, and there had also been a really amazing increase of wealth throughout Scotland owing to the advent of industries and the consequent development of coal mines and ironworks ; the shipbuilding on the Clyde exceeded that of almost any other country, and money poured into coffers that for so long had been woefully empty. It was at this time that Scotland became rebuilt. In the towns there arose districts of substantial well-built stone dwellings of good architecture (owing to the influence of the Adams and other competent architects) and in the country a succession of country houses of the type which we know so well through the unfortunate Abbotsford. It was simple for the industrialists to build such houses, or to purchase and improve estates whose owners could not afford to preserve them, and, when free of the burden of entails, were unable to sell. But the rural lairds very often, as the saying was, ' built themselves on the outside of their houses.' Anyhow these large houses were no blessing a hundred years later, when another and much greater war devastated Europe. Still the building of them gave employment at the time and the low rate of wages encouraged large schemes of improvement.

The melancholy thing was that the industrialist took no thought of the people who were his servants and workers, because he did not realise how important this was to his permanent success. Villages became towns, as we read of in Galt's *Annals of the Parish* ; men and women poured into the towns because there was but poor living in the country ; and no proper provision was made for their housing or health in the new quarters. This process no doubt began in the eighteenth century as a result of the Union, for directly trade with the Colonies was permitted the commercial centre of Scotland moved from the East to the more convenient West and developed largely there. Hence Glasgow and its surroundings grew fast, and gradually the rural part of Scotland became less populous. This process has gone on till the present day, when over two-thirds of Scotland's inhabitants are town dwellers. At all times there have been great tracts of uncultivated country in Scotland, and this can never be otherwise owing to the conformation of the land : even now, as has been said, it is estimated that only a quarter of it is under cultivation. Towns have indeed been made sanitary, and the distinction between town and country, once so marked, is every day becoming less clear, for the country is becoming urbanized as the town is gaining in healthiness and amenity. But this is a later growth, and it was not so last century, though town dwellers usually had easy access to country walks. The Scottish towns have had special difficulties of their own to contend with, not only because of bad building, but also because of solid building such as is difficult to destroy and replace, as has been done so much in brick-built England. The consequence is that town conditions in England were seldom so absolutely bad as in Scotland, though no doubt the Scottish houses were warm. Of course a great deal of this evil was inherited from the long apprenticeship to poverty served by the Scot. He had undoubtedly less of the tradition of decent living which the Englishman or Englishwoman possesses. Those who undertook housing work for the poor in both countries forty or fifty years ago know well the difference that existed then, and the difficulty that they encountered in establishing in Scotland even the standards that now prevail. One-roomed ' houses ' were by no means resented and to the end of the century they abounded even for large families who might in addition take in a lodger. The insect creation also abounded in both countries, but it was less resented in Scotland and when present in the children's heads it was not objected to since it was considered a sign of health ! In the great ' lands,' now divided up, but once inhabited by an aristocracy who probably lived in conditions not so very different, the difficulties in making healthy dwelling places were considerable. The striking thing was that in these unpromising conditions much intelligence and education was to be found. The mode of living clearly resulted from the French tradition of great houses let in flats rather than those that are ' self-contained.'

In Scotland all living is (and has perhaps always been) simpler than in the neighbouring country, though of course there are great houses which have weathered every storm and where life is indistinguishable from that of the great houses elsewhere. They are, however, few, and as in Scotland properties are mostly large they are more isolated than in England. Owing to the system of land tenure the comfortable manor-houses close by the village did not exist. The villages themselves were usually isolated units, excepting in some special cases, and the mansion-house was often so surrounded by its ' policies ' that its avenue separated it from ordinary habitations by a mile or more. This idea of separation seems to have grown at the date of the new buildings, for occasionally the old house was situated on or near the main road, and either the road was diverted or the house pushed back. This seems one of the unfortunate influences of the advent of wealth, when high stone walls were also built to enclose the private policies and gardens, for what reason one cannot imagine ; certainly they tended to separate the richer people from the poorer. Another curious characteristic of large Scottish houses was that the gardens were very frequently placed a long way from the ' big house,' to the great inconvenience of the present-day garden-loving population and also of the cook. The reason of this is also difficult to divine, though, of course, gardens were not the object of interest in old days that they are now, and most of them were made where had been the uninteresting kailyard of old days which had to be

kept out of view. Also early last century, and at the
end of the previous one, when planting came into
vogue, the master of the house perhaps liked to show off
his woods on the way to the garden. On occasion of the
long visits of olden days when horses had to be ' baited,'
older people can recollect the walk to the garden as a
diversion after luncheon ! Besides the garden there
was usually a small private burying ground, with or without a little chapel attached, though the latter was often
a ruin. The Scots have a love of laying their dead near
them and in their own land. It is not that they tended
their churchyards, for most of them were neglected,
though they were always objects of interest and venera-
tion. Scottish burial grounds were not ordinarily consecrated, and this might influence some of those of
another faith who desired a consecrated ground, but
this is no sufficient explanation. It rather seems due
to a curious sort of pride that liked to keep ' the Family '
by itself.

If towns were huddled together without thought of
planning or health, country villages were only better
inasmuch as the conditions of air and sunlight were
better. When the big mansions were rebuilt, ornamental cottages of the same style of architecture were
often erected also. They were, however, built more with
a view to appearance than comfort, and if used as lodges
were usually divided into two buildings, one on either
side of the entrance gate. In Scotland where, owing to
the short days in winter and the absence of sunlight generally, every opportunity of procuring it should have been

seized upon, both cottages and mansion-houses were frequently made to face north and placed in the bottom of valleys where the hills on either side no doubt sheltered them from the blast, but most certainly from the sun. Houses were frequently built with their backs on a bank so that no through ventilation was possible and damp ensued : this might have been done with some idea of economy, for one can see no other valid reason. Then the windows were often badly designed for light and air. No doubt the window-tax, a pernicious tax which lasted till 1851, affected the windows of the smaller houses. This annoying tax produced much altercation as to what constituted a window, e.g. whether one of zinc plate did so, and necessitated much domiciliary visitation. It also had a bad effect on building, for in Edinburgh it was discovered that a whole row of houses had been built without one window in the bedroom story of any house ! There was great gratitude accorded to Lord Duncan and Lord Halifax for getting the tax removed.

The ' midden ' in old days was usually close to the house, just as is seen in French farmhouses and cottages to this day. Indeed the likeness between the two countries in respect of outward form is still remarkable, as every Scottish traveller in rural France knows, and sanitary arrangements are equally peculiar. The intelligence of the inhabitants in both cases seems to be incommensurate with their outward conditions ! Fixed baths were very rare in large houses and it is only of quite late years that they have been introduced in small villages and cottages : there were none last century, and the weekly bath of the English working-man visitor was a cause of intense surprise. The lack is often due, of course, to bad water supply, but not always, for bad water supply in the village is doubtless common in England as well as in Scotland. Scotland can certainly boast of having nearly the same proportion of public baths as England ; but in Scotland there is less concern over their supply. The miners' wives resented the establishment of pithead baths and believed it was taking from them their long-recognized privilege of seeing that their husbands were well washed down at the kitchen fire ; for last century the living-room or kitchen was always a sleeping-room also, and baths when taken by grown-ups or given to the children were always carried out there because of the warmth of the fire.

There has never been the same pride taken in the outward appearance of the cottage in Scotland as in England, either by the occupier or the laird. In England the Squire and his wife really care to see pretty, prosperous-looking cottages on their estates, and make a point of visiting the people. Possibly the sort of visiting which took place in England might not be popular with Scottish cottagers. Here again there is a strong resemblance to French peasants who will never brook interference with their houses or affairs : their homes are indeed their castles.

The Scottish working people were never peasants ; they did not pass through the stage passed through by the French before the Revolution. They lived, it is true, like the French under a feudal system or, in the Highlands, a clan system, and they respected their superiors as heads of their land system or class. The laird bore the name of his property and was spoken to as such without prefix ; to have done otherwise would have been impolite. Even the ' Law Lords ' or judges lost their own names in that of the land which they were supposed to own, though their wives carried on the name they originally bore, to the great puzzlement of hotel-keepers abroad who valued their reputation. But the common people were always their ' own men ' and ready to speak to their superiors as intrinsically their equals. They had very likely attended the same school and this tradition of respect along with the sense of equality remained as a permanent possession. The writer cannot for instance forget the respect given even to an unfortunate Highland chief, a man of much dignity of demeanour, who through his own fault had landed in a poor-house. Not only was he spoken of by his territorial title, but he was buried by his clan with all honour, in his own family burial place, though it meant a long journey by water as well as by land ; in his lifetime he was quite certain that this would be the case and it was a source of happiness to him to think of it.

The English visitor always missed the pretty gardens which surrounded the English cottages and the greenery that embowered them. A potato patch did not take the place of a flower garden, and even farm gardens in Scotland were severely utilitarian. All this no doubt arose partly from the tradition of poverty, but partly

too, from the lack of æsthetic education, which might
have been added to the classical and somewhat pedantic
education which has always characterized the Scot.
And the absence of amenities was also visible within the
home. Boys and men entered without removing their
caps, and the table did not probably have a white cloth
or other suitable covering even when poverty did not
reign. The food in the country might be simple and
good but it was far from elaborate, and the old tradition for Sunday fare was to set a ' singit ' (singed)
sheep's head to boil and leave it there during church
hours. For it takes a deal of boiling, though we must
remember Bailie Nicol Jarvie's dictum that if too long
boiled a tup's head was ' rank poison ' ! Too much
stress was not laid on either the cooking or the serving
of the food, and the English tradition of a solid Sunday
dinner and roast never existed. Cooking on Sunday
was a matter of economy in labour.

The mother of the family, though she was held in
high respect, did not expect her boys to help her in
preparing and handing food : she did not even as in
England make the men or boys brush their own boots.
In fact in the ordinary things of life she did not apparently have the same deference as the man, though her
influence may have been more truly supreme. In
towns it was not the recognized thing that the man carried or wheeled the baby on Sunday walks as it was in
England : if he did so by any chance he was jeered at
by the onlookers : the man ' took the vows ' for his
child at christening, leaving the mother out, and there

are no godparents in Scotland. Perhaps it was a good thing to remind him that he had responsibilities ! In the writer's remembrance the man always walked a few steps in front of his womankind in going to church, and he had an absolute say which church was to be attended. The young bride might give a longing look at the ' Frees ' or ' U.P.s ' as she passed, but if *he* had been an ' Auld Kirker ' to the Auld Kirk they went. In the ' big house ' even an indoors male retainer would refer to the views of his master if an order were given by the mistress, and the laird was always esteemed above the lady by outside servants. All this might indicate a more elementary civilization; and certainly the absence of any joint control of the household meant living in a more elementary way. The comparison with French life does not here hold good, for in France the woman, though she does not take part in political life as a rule, nor very much in any sort of public life, plays a great and leading part in the family and its affairs. She absolutely manages internal matters and often outside business too. But there is one respect in which the two traditions agreed, and that is the way in which the children and the family generally held together. It always struck a good Scot as strange when he went to England to see how little family responsibility told on the individual. In Scotland the remotest cousin who got on the rocks had a helping hand held out to him, and both his honours and his disgrace were taken as something to the honour or disgrace of the family. Then there was both in France and Scotland a keen family feeling which objected on principle to sending boys and girls to boarding schools, so that they were brought up under artificial conditions and with a segregation of the sexes. The good old customs were breaking down under English influence before the century ended, but the feeling of old was that family life was best for the family, that boys and girls should, anyhow if dwelling in a town, live and learn together, and that the parents should keep in close touch with them and delegate their duties to no one. Among families living in the country there were often tutors and governesses when these could be afforded. On the whole, until later years when the richer parents broke the tradition, day schools prevailed in Scotland as they still do in France. Mixed schools of boys and girls together, of course, never existed in France, as they did, and to a great extent do, in the grammar schools of Scotland.

As regards Christian names there was always in Scotland a regular ritual. The eldest son was invariably ' named for ' the father's father, while the eldest girl was named after the mother's mother and so on. If a child died in infancy, as children so often did in the last century, the next infant was frequently given the same name in order to perpetuate it ; and this made baptismal investigations (before registration came into vogue) puzzling. The only exception to the regular rule was when the male child was the first to be baptized by a new minister, in which case he invariably received the latter's name. The result of this continual family naming was that there was a superabundance of

Johns, Jameses, Margarets and Jeannies. 'Fancy names,' i.e. those not in the family already, were hardly to be found in the village schools of last century.

To return to the housing of the people, there was one thing which was not cured in Scotland till well on in the century, and that was the dirt of the inns. There was not the same idea of what was fitting in a Scottish change-house as there was in an English one, and neither sheets nor food were immaculate. Travellers are always complaining of the butter being full of hairs, and disgusting. It was at one time considered unlucky to 'wash the kirn,' and according to the writer of the *Cottagers of Glenburnie* the hairs were supposed to help the butter to set ! One reason for the poverty of the inns probably was that the custom of gentlefolks in travelling was to stay with their friends whose boundless hospitality was well known. Hence the change-houses or inns were frequented by a very humble population. There was indeed no custom such as would serve to support the cheerful inns described so vividly by Dickens, and the roads being few and bad there was no constant flow of post chaises and coaches making a stop for meals or for the night. The best of the change-houses and the worst are described by Scott in his novels. To tell the truth it is only quite recently that the beds of Scottish inns have ceased to resemble boards, though they have for a long time past been clean.

Few things have made such a difference to modern Scotland as the improved communications by road and

rail. If we look down from an aeroplane we can see the
wonderful system of omnibuses that have now supple-
mented and in some places superseded the railways.
And yet railways are only a hundred years old, for the
first Scottish railways date from about 1832, while
charabancs are in their infancy. The difference railways
made to the rural population of Scotland in the last century is inconceivable. The Highland and Western Highland railways crept up bit by bit through mountains and
gradients hard to engineer. Before their existence, in
the middle of last century, the long cold journeys in
open coaches, often taken in desperate weather, were
things that could never be forgotten. It was a relief
sometimes to walk up the hills, and that form of exercise
was encouraged. But even coaches implied decent roads,
and people congratulated themselves on not having to
ride on horseback as in the century before. To our
modern ideas the marvel was that news spread as it did
from man to man. Early in the nineteenth century the
postman who brought letters to a village usually rested
a night before he returned, but carriers of goods, if
slow-going, were frequent enough.

For the first forty years of steam traffic it cannot be
said that trains were punctual ; conversations at Highland stations were lengthy and the lines were often
single, which always caused delay. The block system
was only made compulsory in 1889, and before that
the signal was merely kept at danger for a certain time
after one train passed and before another was allowed
to succeed it. When racing between two contending

c

companies (North British and Caledonian) occurred, it was rather alarming, though accidents were not as numerous as one might have expected. But what made most difference to Scotland was the development of transit to the South. About the middle of last century there was an excellent service from Edinburgh and Glasgow to London both by night and day, taking not more than ten hours en route. It mattered not that the 'Limited Mail,' carrying, as its name implied, the mails and a limited number of passengers, arrived in London at an unearthly hour in the morning, or that on the day train the twenty minutes allowed for the half-crown dinner at Preston or York seemed to fly too fast. The third-class passengers may be said to have 'travelled hard,' for of cushions there were none, backs were carried only half-way up and oil lamps divided between two compartments shook wildly with the motion of the train. But the cushions of the first-class carriages made excellent beds when drawn forward, and up to the early sixties passengers had the consolation of knowing that their luggage was in no remote goods van, but safely strapped on the top and covered by tarpaulin. For better or worse London and England generally came into close touch with Scotland, and English customs and English speech tended to dominate the Scottish in the upper grades of Society. It was extraordinary how little it affected the lower, even when they began to travel. It was however at this time, and no doubt very much through the good communications, that English schools came into fashion with better class Scottish parents, and the Episcopal Church, partly as a consequence, took a new lease of life and became the popular Church for those brought up in the upper ranks of Society; but again this did not affect those of a lower social grade and there were naturally patriots who held to the old customs.

In every account of Scotland we read not only of old customs passing away but of the use of Scottish language disappearing. Cockburn speaks of the loss of the Scottish accent and idiom owing to the habit of reading English books and of English intercourse. ' We looked upon an English boy at the High School as a ludicrous, incomprehensible monster,'[1] and no Englishman in his boyhood could have addressed the Edinburgh populace ' without making them stare, and probably laugh . . . Scotch has ceased to be the vernacular language of the upper classes, and with increasing communication it will have to be treated as a dead language and we shall lose our enjoyment of much fine literature. . . . Above all, we lose *ourselves* and become a poor part of England.'

It is true that a great part of Scottish or any nationality rests in the tongue it speaks, and the loss of the individuality of Scottish speech means a closer attachment to the greater nation. The fact, however, is that much of the Scots tongue still remains nearly a century after Cockburn wrote; the accent is recognizable in every Scot brought up in Scotland and the words come back to the older folk even when forgotten in youth.

[1] Cp. Borrow's *Lavengro*, and his account of the time when he attended the High School.

As Francis Jeffrey, who was homesick whenever away from his native land, says (in 1833): 'I pine hourly for shade and leisure and the Doric sounds of my mother tongue.' And he even 'cried plentifully'—this stern reviewer—as he read *The Gentle Shepherd*.

The Scot had originally hated the Union because it gave him the sense of being in touch with a people more civilized and forward than himself, and this produced a certain artificiality or lack of naturalness when in contact with them which never quite left him. This inferiority complex (as the jargon now goes) made him endeavour to mould his ways and speech to those of his rich and prosperous neighbour even after he was himself equally rich and prosperous. We have the testimony of Scottish writers to the effect that they always had this feeling when first they came into touch with Englishmen, despite their secret sense of superiority! And though it was true that Lord Brougham described the Scottish language as a ' pure and classical language which must on no account be regarded as provincial dialect any more than French was so regarded in the reign of Henry V, or Italian in the time of the first Napoleon, or Greek under the Roman Empire,' it was also true that English teachers of elocution like Thomas Sheridan were asked to give lessons to Scottish lawyers, clergy and professors, since it was fashionable to have an English accent in speaking or preaching and to write without those Scotticisms that caused English critics to deride. There is, however, this to be remembered, that the northerner, when he

went south, had certain advantages in his speech, hard
as he often tried to modify it. The Scots tongue seemed
to give confidence to those he dealt with and the Scot
kept his feet in his country if his head was in the
capital. He had been accustomed to simple if not parsi-
monious living, and often just managed to survive
during the first hard months or years of his stay in the
prosperous and lavish south. Hence he got a reputation for parsimoniousness. But it must never be forgotten in speaking of Scottish thriftiness that the Scot
had been accustomed to give generously when he had
it in his power and was persuaded of the object being
good, for he paid for missions and churches and
hospitals with no mean hand; and if he was a dis-
senter his church life had always to face the duty of
supporting itself. Therefore his national Church in
London, he was proud to boast, always headed the
list on Hospital Sunday.

The connection with England had a good side, of
course, from another point of view, for it brought
many of the amenities of English life into Scotland.
Before communication with England was what it became, cooking was of the simplest, though at its best it
was excellent. Scotch broth, mince collops, good black-
faced mutton, and singed sheep's head and haggis were
amongst the staple foods in a ' comfortable ' home.
Hours were early; in quiet homes dinner was at
5 o'clock until the middle of the century, and afternoon
tea only appeared in the towns about 1860. Before that,
wine and biscuits were handed round at the afternoon

call. Even the judges, however, succumbed by the sixties to 'kettle drums' and had cups of tea in their robing rooms. Now late dinners *à la Russe*, known by Scotsmen at first as 'dinner behind your back,' came into vogue, and instead of the far too numerous courses, and far too heavy viands, and far too much good French claret and other wines, a slightly more reasonable number of courses was served and appetite was more easily satisfied. Two soups, two fishes, two entrées, and then the main roast followed by a game course and sweets of various sorts still formed the normal dinner for a party of eighteen or so, a usual number for an Edinburgh dinner in the latter part of the century. For the first time, too, flowers upon the dinner-table and in the sitting rooms came into vogue in a way they had never done before, and the flower-gardening instinct which originally came from England developed in Scotland by leaps and bounds. A few rich men had before this made Italian gardens after returning from the Grand Tour, but that was all. In early days wax flowers under a glass case or closely packed everlastings in a vase were all that appeared in the way of floral decoration; sending wreaths to funerals was a development that came later still.

Mrs. Story, the wife of a famous Scottish divine, writes an entertaining book describing Edinburgh life in the thirties. She tells of the great dinner parties that were then in vogue and of the difficulty of remedying the evil effects on the uncovered mahogany tables of spilt wine and hot dishes; and how two Highland porters were got in to help in the salvaging task. Married women all wore caps and in the evening a sort of turban was much affected : it was of gold gauze finished with gold fringe and tassels. If a dinner party were in prospect the cook and waiters had, of course, to be secured from outside, and no trumpery economies were observed. The dinners were larger and more lengthy than those which came later. The huge roast of meat at one end and a gigantic turkey at the other end had to be carved by the male guest of honour on whom a serious responsibility rested. The elaborate sweets were the spoils of the children behind the scenes, before they were allowed to come in to dessert. For till the seventies dinners were early enough to allow them to do this, and to suffer the agonies of being dressed for the occasion and the dubious pleasure of receiving a little fruit and wine from their parents or their guests.

The formal and ceremonial side of life in Scotland was carried on longer than in England. Grace was always said before meat and often in a lengthy way ; the short English form was not approved of, especially if the fare were bountiful. The writer remembers the indignation of a gardener, also an elder in the church, at the ' Englishy ' butler's skimp traditional grace on the occasion of a solid supper. ' Sicna grace for sicna supper !' as he laconically observed. Morning and evening prayers were usual in all well-regulated homes, and in the larger country houses prayers were conducted with due propriety. Before the ceremony the domestic staff stood to attention, the men and women carefully ranged as to rank. No door bell ever rang on a Sunday, for if it had a visitor would not have been admitted. The ' family ' often had a special ' loft ' in the church which had a fireplace of its own, and there were sometimes special prayers for ' the family that is in high distinction among us,' and on the entry of that family, if that of a principal heritor, a special bow was often accorded to the said heritor by the minister. But all this only happened in the church by law established and not in those that had seceded. On the death of a heritor his pew was draped in black for a year or more and sometimes the pulpit also adopted this sombre hue.

As to the dresses of the young ladies, there were crinolines in vogue for a period of twelve years. They merged into half-crinolines and then bustles. Side curls were worn following the example of the Empress Eugénie, the beauty of the age, and the long curls likewise often worn were for some reason called ' Follow my Leader.' Croquet and archery served as amusements for the ladies in the country till more strenuous games were introduced ; newspapers were usually left to the gentlemen, who expected to have them, but of course there was plenty of light literature to read, though not many illustrated magazines. There were naturally many customs which were gradually introduced from London. Marriage ceremonies in old days were inordinately long owing to the custom of having wedding breakfasts and lengthy speeches. In less distinguished circles weddings were mostly in the evening, for there has never been any restriction as to hours of marriage in Scotland. The actual ceremony was usually quite short and informal, since there was no definite service laid down for it. The bride usually came supplied with certain ' plenishings,' including linen, for she had to be well supplied with ' napery ' all carefully marked with her initials and maiden name. To do this in ink would be thought disgraceful : it must either be woven in, or sewn in thread, usually in fine cross-stitch.

Funerals were also made less formal and expensive as the century wore on. Originally they played a great part in Scottish life, for the Scot likes to dwell on death, and its accompaniments interest him. A century, or even half a century ago, a funeral was an occasion for the reunion of friends and relatives and it took upon it rather a festive character. The plumed hearses and beautifully decked-up black Belgian horses and attendants with their weepers did not entirely cease even when the century ended. The male mourners, of course, wore hatbands of crape as well as weepers, and in the country at least there was a bow of crape behind the hat. Tall hats were *de rigueur* and, when possessed, surtout coats such as the elders wore with their white ties on Communion Sundays. A funeral was an entirely male occasion ; the service took place in the house and there was no service at the grave. The coffining, ' kisting,' or ' chesting,' was attended by an elder as is the case now in the country. This ceremony dates from the time when woollen material had to be used for dead clothes, according to an Act of Parliament passed just before the Union in 1707; in order to encourage the industry some authorized person had to see that the law was carried out, and the custom continued though the Act was repealed in 1814. At all times it had been considered essential that male relatives, even to a remote degree of consanguinity, should be invited to funerals, and any failure in doing so caused deep resentment, not to say quarrels. In any respectable family the dead clothes were always placed carefully in a drawer ready for use and the shroud was of a particular pattern.

As the Scot was interested in funerals and the trappings of death, so he liked to wear mourning for an unconscionable time. Of course this was a Victorian custom everywhere, following the example of the great Queen, but it was accentuated in Scotland. For a parent there was mourning for two years, crape for one year and ' half mourning,' i.e. black but no crape for the second year ; for a brother or sister, twelve months, and so on ; it was all regularly laid down ; a widow wore her mourning perpetually, though the deep crape, reaching nearly to her waist and terribly expensive and extravagant, gradually diminished in depth till after some years it disappeared altogether. The white bonnet strings and cap placed under the bonnet followed suit, though in old days it continued during life as did the becoming day cap with its long white streamers. Notepaper for a widow left small space for writing, but the black border diminished according to decrease in propinquity, till it was left at ' complimentary mourning' or Italian border for very distant connections.   Men merely had their hatbands and neckties to consider after the white weepers of the funeral day and Sunday were dispensed with.   The black bows of crape on the tall hats were also limited to the funeral day, though they might reappear for a few Sundays thereafter.

The minister on all occasions in the pulpit wore his black Geneva gown and bands and usually black gloves : the precentor inherited the gown when it lost its first lustre but, of course, did not wear bands.   He occupied a desk in front of the pulpit.

Christenings in old days were held in the church when the minister could get the parents to attend and induce the father to take his vows before the whole congregation.   But this task was a difficult one and in later times was not strictly enforced, so that the baptism of the child was more often performed at home.   The old custom of the parents giving the first person they met a gift of bread and cheese or sweets and cake is supposed to be a relic of heathen days : it was formerly usual but tended to become less common as the century advanced.

The Scot is by nature litigious ; he is argumentative in any case, and if there is any occasion for a ' ganging plea ' he is too ready to take advantage of it and face the consequences, which are often serious financially.   Scott understands this characteristic absolutely, as we know from his tales of Dandie Dinmont and poor Peter Peebles.   Burns knew it too, and that it is not a new characteristic is evidenced by what is said of it long ago by David Lyndsay of the Mount.   Cases may come before the Sheriff Substitute, be appealed to the Sheriff Principal, from him to the Court of Session and the ' Inner House,' and finally they may even reach the House of Lords.   Thus there is the possibility of a long and exciting run, but unfortunately also of much expenditure of money, and besides that, such litigation often enough caused bad blood between neighbours for generations.   Poverty is no specific against it, for the Scottish system, so well described in *Redgauntlet*, allows a poor man to go to law by means of pleading poverty or getting the help of one of the ' Poor's Lawyers.'   This is a good old custom, followed in the South generations later, though it was not appreciated by Alan Fairford, whose private affairs were interrupted by these unwelcome duties !

It was only in 1855 that the Inland Revenue duties between Scotland and England were equalized.   Before that time the excise officers were ever on the watch at the English frontier, for whisky was liable to extra duty when taken to England, and gradually whisky came into vogue there, though at first it was little drunk south of the Border.   In Scotland a ' spelding ' or dried salt haddock was in former days often placed beside the glass of ale ordered at a roadside inn to whet the traveller's thirst, but whatever the drink might be, there was little to tempt him in the way of food.   Perhaps the development of cycling in the last twenty years of the century encouraged the inns to improve as to cooking ; they needed it.   When safety bicycles came into fashion in the beginning of the nineties and women bicycled with or without men companions, they at last had the means of getting about freely and seeing their friends. They then demanded decent tea, lemonade and other temperance drinks at the inns they passed. Tea shops in town had a similar history. They did not exist till women took to going about freely, and once they were set going both sexes took full advantage of them and could not imagine how they ever did without them.

The furnishing of the cottage was always a little different from that of the corresponding cottage in England. In old days there was usually one or more shut-in ' box beds ' in the living-room and these box beds were used for many purposes besides sleeping in ; they were, for example, useful stores ! In the country it was a very general custom for the mother and father to sleep in the kitchen or living-room. In Scottish cottages there is usually no ' upstairs ' as in England, but another room than the kitchen for sleeping in and for ' best ' ; and very often a slip room between for either girls or boys. The ' but and ben ' mode of building[1] has survived many changes and it seems to belong to the country, but occasionally in addition to the ground floor there is some sort of attic in the roof. In the far-away Highlands one can still see children brought into a ' stair house ' descending as one might a ladder, never having seen the like before ! In the kitchen there was usually an ' aumry ' (armoire), an arm-chair for the

[1] A one-storied cottage with room at either end.

father and plain deal chairs for the rest ; also an open fire with a ' sweigh ' or hook and chain on which to hang the ' girdle ' or flat iron on which were baked the scones.   In old days there was also a salt bucket stand-ing by the fire, for salt was taxed and precious.   By the end of the century little ranges gradually appeared to the comfort of the housewife.   If she had an oven and hot water she was saved an infinitude of trouble, but these things in the country are of recent years ; before that cooking had to be of the simplest.   ' Recon-structed ' cottages which have actually got coppers for washing clothes and possibly a bath were not thought of in the last century.

Of old customs there were so many in Scotland that one cannot do more than mention some of the more general.   There were, for instance, the Beltane Fires which some connect with Baal worship and which are fires lighted on the mountain tops on the eve of May Day ;   the Well worship, now practically extinct, though the names and traditions remain ; the Curfew bell still in some places existent ; the lyke-wake of which we shall hear in dealing with the Highlands, and formerly a jovial rather than austere entertainment ; Riding the Marches, a useful custom in defining boundaries, and so on.   But Hallowe'en, ' the night when a' the witches are to be seen,' is still vigorously kept in villages, or was so in the nineteenth century, with its bonfires, guisers or guisards and burning nuts.   Then came the New Year's Eve amusements when there were battles between the flambeaux holders and when the guisers were all afoot visiting the houses and asking for handsels. Christmas, of course, was not observed. Besides these there were innumerable local customs, such as chalking (or 'calking' as it was called) the doors on certain days, usually those observed as market days.

Every sort of communication, of course, improved as the century advanced. Lord Cockburn relates as a marvellous fact that in 1834, at an important political dinner held in Edinburgh in honour of Earl Grey, at which Brougham was present, the *Times* staff sent reporters of their own, and that they left the room at midnight on Monday and at one o'clock on Friday the paper arrived with a full account of the proceedings. 'Post-horses, macadam roads, shorthand and steam printing never did more. . . . They posted up in thirty hours, which was considered a wonderful proceeding, as indeed it was for a journey of 400 miles by horse conveyance.' An interesting fact is that Charles Dickens was, Cockburn believed, one of the reporters who took this wildly exciting journey.

It seemed in those days as though the 'thirst to annihilate time' was to be far from beneficial. If distances were diminished to one-tenth or a twentieth part, in twenty years London might be within fifteen hours by land of Edinburgh—a forecast more than realized in the given time, though Cockburn thought it was the ideal of a mere commercial mind and that it would add to wealth but not necessarily to happiness. It has certainly, as Cockburn foresaw, taken from the relative importance of provincial capitals ; Edinburgh in relation to the greater London is no more than Geneva is to Paris, as he foretold.

One of the drawbacks to the easy communication with England was that the temptation for the clever Scot to make his way there could hardly be resisted. So we have Ramsay and Smollett making their homes in London as did the Adams and other Scotch architects who saw scope for their work in the great buildings being erected. Raeburn was a happy exception to the general rule. He may have earned less money, but his reputation has not suffered by his patriotism. Lawyers like Brougham naturally made their way south as they do to this day, since the highest prizes are to be found in the Supreme Courts of the State. It was fortunate that Walter Scott's aspirations did not go in the direction of this sort of legal advancement.

Occasionally the Scottish upper classes made a visit to Bath for treatment for the gout but those who found the journey too expensive were content with the Spas or Spaws (as they were called) in Scotland, of which there were several. Pitcaithly waters were famous and so were others. The effects of better communication on rural Scotland were all to the good, hitherto the variety in conditions and customs in different parts of the country had been immense. In some parishes poverty reigned and there seemed no escape from it ; the two statistical accounts written by parish ministers in 1792 and 1837 respectively, which are such a mine of information, show this very clearly. There

A MECHANICAL BELLOWS MADE LAST CENTURY FOR
COTTAGE USE

THE SALT BUCKET ALWAYS KEPT BY THE FIRESIDE EARLY
IN LAST CENTURY

was no fluidity in rural labour and unemployment was constant and had no redress. The only source of help was from the poor's box and that was too often nearly empty ; wages were very low (though probably there were perquisites) even in times early last century which were prosperous for landlords and industrialists. However wages never fell to so low an ebb as they did in the southern counties of England. Agricultural workers in Scotland were always on a somewhat higher plane than the southerners after the nineteenth century began, and their work was better partly in consequence of this, and yet more because of the greater intelligence they evinced. Scottish agricultural workers were seldom without a fair education, even though it had to be paid for, and they looked on education as a necessity.

An unfortunate matter in the vicinity of towns was that paths and walks of all sorts that were open and free early in the century were gradually closed by proprietors. Consequently much pleasure to pedestrians was removed, and though a Society was formed for protecting the public against further robbery of its walks by ' private cunning and perseverance,' it did not cure the evil. Prescriptive rights were taken away and though protests were made, legal action was expensive and public agitation discouraged ; the poor were laughed at, as Lord Cockburn tells us. The people should be *humanized*, he says, and if trusted, he believes they would preserve what they are allowed to enjoy. He, of course, was advanced in his views on such subjects and would like to have seen country life

D

of the kind that is found in England, where people could have their quiet inns and be sober but happy.

As it was, there was a good deal of roughness and the people were not humanized. Certainly the boys of all classes were rough and rather rude. In the villages they shouted and hurrahed as vehicles passed by and occasionally threw stones, and in the towns there were constant ' bickers ' [1] with the ' keelies,' an opprobrious term whose meaning is uncertain but which seems to indicate rough and unruly lads.

The dislike of England by old-fashioned Scots had naturally decreased, but it was still present early in the century and certainly in the end of the eighteenth, as is evidenced by Lady Balcarres' triumph when she found the sheets in an inn two or three stages from Scotland absolutely as dirty as any that Scotch inns could boast of. Her triumph was short-lived, for the hostess is said to have replied in broadest Scots, thereby proving her origin : ' Na, na, my leddy, they canna be dirty for I never seed in my life twa cleaner young gentlemen than sleepit in them last night ' ! This story is related by Lady Anne Lindsay in her later years. Another dictum in the same autobiographical manuscript says of the Scots that ' 'Twas the taste of the time to hate us, to envy us, but not to despise us. . . . An obscoor deevil from the North was supposed to be born so ready dressed that he had but to come to London to make his fortune at once—Lord Chancellor, Commander-in-

---

[1] George Borrow gives a vivid account of their bickers in *Lavengro*.

Chief or anything.' The proud and rather bragging
Scot was apt to boast then as he did much later on
when complimented by an English fellow-traveller on
the undoubted fact that the two Archbishops of the
time were Scots, even though at the head of a Church
not their own : 'Aye, and had they stoppit at hame
naebody wad ha thocht onything aboot them ' !

CHAPTER III

THE RISE OF THE MIDDLE CLASSES

IF one were asked what specially characterized the century we are considering in Scotland, more especially the central part of it, one might well say that it was that a new orientation of society had arisen and that with the industrialization of Scotland and its superior education those who formerly would (with certain remarkable exceptions) have remained in the lower grade, so far as influence and status were concerned, had the opportunity of rising to a higher, given health, diligence and a certain amount of good fortune.

Perhaps it would make this clearer were one shortly to mention two typical men, one born in the town with no advantages of surroundings, the other in the country when the country was still a bleak and unpromising place so far as the prospects of making more than a fair livelihood were concerned.

The first is Adam Black, the well-known politician who represented Edinburgh in Parliament in his later years, and recorded the events of his life very fully in an autobiography. He only died in 1874, though he was born in 1784 ; and he thus lived as a public man through the greater part of the nineteenth century, taking a keen part in all its social and political activities.

In his autobiography he tells the same weary tale of ill-usage at school as we find in the lives of other Scotsmen ; the same stories of ' bickers ' between poor boys and rich ; for the aristocrats of George Square, the sons of lairds and peers, all attended the High School along with those like himself of less distinguished parentage. All would be armed with ' clackans,' wooden bats suitable for playing shinty or 'hails,' or hitting other boys' heads. Black's father, as was the manner of the time, joined with three or four friends in subscribing to a newspaper, and as in his case it was a Liberal paper it influenced his son, who witnessed the anti-Dundas mobs on the King's Birthday (the usual occasion for such risings), in 1793, and the ' meal mobs ' of the hungry women. Those had made a deep impression upon him. Young Black was destined for the ministry, but being influenced by the extreme Evangelical movement inaugurated at that time, he became a bookseller's apprentice instead. In the beginning of the century there were but twenty booksellers in Edinburgh ; however, bookselling in these days was not only as now an important trade but also a serious one, for the booksellers dealt mainly in folios and quartos, though it was true that Allan Ramsay demeaned himself by selling both ballads and wigs before he started his circulating library, that was the first to be instituted. Black's apprenticeship being over, like so many young Scots who could not support themselves in their own country, he made for London where he had the usual struggle for employment and consequent discouragement. Once work was found he gave himself up to his occupation but varied it by his religious pursuits. Finally he returned to his native city (for the first time observing that it had a characteristic speech) and set up shop in 1807. The great drawback to his success as a bookseller was that he was a Liberal in politics and an Independent in Church connections. He would like to have taught in the Sabbath schools which were coming into vogue but which were frowned on by the Established Church as likely to sow the seeds of mischievous political doctrines amongst the young. Kay, the inimitable Scottish caricaturist of the day, shows how the Church regarded this dangerous innovation. Adam Black's efforts, however, were frustrated not by the frowns of the Church but by the very prosaic reason of the unruly nature of Edinburgh boys ! He had better success in the more peaceful village of Portobello where he managed to enlist a hundred children.

It was not long before he became embroiled in politics, for the *Scotsman* and *Blackwood's Magazine* had lately come to birth, the latter famous for its wit and its venom, the other perhaps for less wit but more persistence. Anyhow, feeling was very hot, and Black, though Reform was a dangerous word in those days, set himself to the work of ' Burgh Reform.' Then came the risings of the unfortunate weavers at Boroughmuir and the *beheading* of three of them after they had been hanged ; this was termed the ' Radical War,' and it was the first occasion on which the famous word Radical was used in Scotland, though by no means the last. For now arose that middle class liberalism of which Black was a prominent representative and which was to characterize Scotland for most of the century.

Black himself was finally elected as a Liberal to represent Edinburgh in Parliament; an event which could hardly have been conceived of early in the century.

These struggles for Reform were not confined to the towns, for they existed in the rural districts also, as the life of the famous farmer, George Hope of Fentonbarns in East Lothian, shows. He was born a little later, in 1811, and as a young man went to hear Cobbett, who came to Scotland in 1832 at the time of the intense struggle for the Franchise, and may have been influenced by him. But not only did he adopt advanced political views : he went so far as to repudiate Calvinism—that 'agonizing faith' as he calls it—and in spite of the distress of his mother and horror of his family and friends joined the Unitarians. This was a formidable step in those days when orthodoxy in religion held its sway over the nation. Whatever orthodoxy or politics might say, Hope was a man who developed farming in such a way that he reclaimed what had been a sandy soil covered with furze bushes : he used lime and manures with good effect in the cultivation of his land, and so built and planted, in the forty-five years that he occupied his farm, that it was entirely transformed. When his lease came to an end in 1872, however, it was not renewed by his landlords, for his views were too advanced for them to tolerate.

George Hope was one of the remarkable men of the new rural middle class that had now made its way into power in Scotland and was moulding its destinies. His father, also the tenant of the same farm before it was improved, had had a hard struggle to make ends meet when the high war prices for grain declined, and in the wet harvest of 1820 the family lived on bread almost uneatable, for round every loaf there was a thick black streak. George never forgot the sufferings of these days of Corn Laws or famine, nor did many others of his time; and he and his compeers were resolved to make the recurrence of famines of this kind impossible by raising the level of Scottish agriculture to a higher plane and showing what Scotland was capable of. Without such men rural Scotland would indeed have been a waste as it had been a century before. And yet the intense division between laird and tenant, who ought to have worked together, was never bridged; political and social influences intervened.

In the century before this a middle class hardly existed beyond members of the professions—the clergy, the doctors and the lawyers of the less important sort, and the smaller lairds. The Church was in a category by itself, and the other professions had no influence to speak of—none politically and hardly any socially. It was, of course, the rise of Commerce that brought about the new alignment of the community. Commerce gained political influence with the Reform 1832, which had no bearing on the working classes, but it was long

before it had real social significance. Those who have
lived the main part of their lives in the century that
has passed remember how small was the influence of
the well-to-do citizen who was not received by the
élite of the towns, and how very small was that of the
prosperous ' merchant ' who made his abode in the
country, and how little his chance of being recognized
by the ' county '—the county gentlemen and county
ladies who directed the affairs of social life. If, like
Adam Black and George Hope, his politics were unsound, the chances were still less ! The landslide that
followed changed these things, and the change began
with the bad times at the end of the seventies so far
as country life was concerned ; its full effect came
later.

Looking back one is tempted to wonder why any
relief that new blood might have given, as times became
better and trade brought wealth, was not welcomed
everywhere, more particularly in the country amongst
the lairds. The life of a young woman in town had
certain reliefs—that of a girl in the country who had
family but little wealth hardly any, unless her parents took
her to Edinburgh for the balls. Victorian girlhood has
been so much stressed of late that it is perhaps unnecessary to say more of it ; but it was in many ways
more distressing in Scotland than it was in England.
There were probably very limited means of getting
about, so far as young women were concerned ; the
horses were required by parents, and possibly on the
farm, as many family letters and diaries show ; walking

was a muddy business and mothers did not like their girls going about alone.   There was no pleasant local society such as we read of in novels like Trollope's, because properties were large, and villages and small towns were only inhabited by those who were not ' visited.' Education was mostly conducted by governesses, sometimes good, sometimes bad.   The young men departed for their business, the army, navy or law, and the only social gatherings were the occasional, perhaps annual, balls in the country towns.   Lawn tennis became fashionable only in the eighties and it was played mildly ; croquet held the field.   The unfortunate girls had few chances of marriage and none of other occupation, for even gardening had not come into vogue for women.   Then the duties owed to parents were immense. Even if there were a troop of daughters all had to be within call ; there might be a row of girls at table, but if one were missing she had to be retrieved and put in her place.   The parents grew old and finally died, the eldest son succeeded under the laws of primogeniture, and entails were serious things in those days and could not be broken.   As much as possible went with the estate, and the girls, now very likely elderly women, had to take up their abode in a small house as near their former glorious habitation as possible.   They never lost their status ; they were ' county ' still and recognized as such, and often this was their means of escape from a long servitude, for they became very useful members of society when they had the chance of doing something for other people.   But it was a dim life compared with what it might have been, for they were often by nature such competent, splendid women.

On the other hand in some of the county towns there was no doubt a type of social life which brings *Cranford* to one's mind. The ladies predominated as was likely, but there were a certain number of retired professional men, soldiers and the like to give zest to the proceedings, and a mild sort of entertainment prevailed in a small but select community. If some honoured guest arrived, each household entertained him or her in turn, varying their guests by possibly one couple but including each member of the circle in every invitation.

Schools, colleges, athletics and bicycles broke into the quiet middle-class life and opened the door for a very different sort of career for the young women of Scotland. But the century was growing old when these new developments took place and they hardly seem to belong to Victorian Scotland. We must, however, never forget that there was a noble body of Scottish iconoclasts such as Flora and Louisa Stevenson, Anne Dundas and Clementina Guthrie Wright who broke open the closely barred male defences and made their way into Universities, Hospital-Governorships, School Boards and so on, and in doing so helped in the breaking down of the old tradition of female servitude where it existed. It had never existed everywhere; the highest ranks had not suffered as much as the middle, and Religion had given scope to many for useful work though always of a subordinate character, for even Deaconesses were not then invented. And in the homes the influence of the mother was great if often not officially recognized.

By the close of the century certain professions were opened to women, and it was clear that the devastating tide was to rise further, and that the old type of womanhood was likely to disappear. There were, however, still men teachers at the head of girls' secondary schools, so that women had not got the plums even of the profession that was peculiarly their own; and nursing as a profession had not got the place it now holds, and it was not only hard but miserably paid. It was the Education Act of 1872 that gave women the power to serve on Public Boards, and in the early seventies one or two managed to acquire degrees which would entitle them to practise medicine, and thus one of the most formidable barriers in the way of women's work was broken down. The greater part of the battle was fought in Edinburgh where the powers of obscurantism appear to have been deeply entrenched. That barrier fallen, the rest of the professions were more easily attacked, and it at last appeared as if women would eventually obtain the power of becoming economically independent.

One of the most remarkable developments in the past century, and specially in middle-class Scotland, has been that of Societies and Organizations of every sort and for every kind of object. Some existed no doubt in the eighteenth century, but they were very few and very select. In the nineteenth century societies arose for developing Art, for promoting Education, for social reforms such as the Protection of Children. As to Charities pure and simple they were innumerable, as were Missions at home and abroad.

This meant much more than appears, for it signified that everyone, voters and non-voters, including women, were brought into the life of the nation as factors that counted in it. When the doors were opened they came in with a flood, and at last everyone who took part could feel that he or she counted and might rise to be a Secretary, Vice-President or even to the giddy eminence of Chairman. Conversation was no longer restricted, as it was so much before, to the private affairs of the family or friends ; there were other interesting topics to discuss.

On the other hand many troublesome problems that had never appeared in the last century began to arise. People were not, for instance, concerned before 1900 with the word 'international,' for though Jeremy Bentham had coined it, the problems it suggests to us had not arisen; anyhow the idea of what it might signify has only become pressing in the twentieth century, for Bentham's visions were disregarded when prosperity and complacency supervened. Then the money question was also not the difficult one that it has grown to be. The teaching of Adam Smith and of John Stuart Mill was accepted more or less absolutely, and the influence of money on society, or the highly difficult problem as to how nations are to deal with currency, had not come into the picture.

The result of strictly entailing estates had, as has been

said, serious results on the younger members of a family. A public meeting was held in 1847 in order to concert measures for relaxing the entail fetters, with the Lord Provost of Edinburgh in the chair. It was the first effort to kick against what had been regarded as the most valuable breakwater against democracy. Lord Cockburn goes so far as to say, ' The mind of the age is favourable to freedom in the commerce of land.' Many heirs of entail fretted for emancipation when degraded by debt, but the freedom was not to come yet. The ' yird hunger,' the passion for possessing land, was strong in the Scot, and in the middle of the century it was something worth while for a small tradesman to get some acres of land and attach ' esquire ' to his name, for in old days this first step was essential. It was thought, however, that to abolish entail would be to make it possible that a lord should be a ' landless beggar,' which seemed an unspeakable degradation to the great order of nobility.

In 1848 an Act was passed for regulating and for abolishing entails under certain conditions, and the consequence as far as the great families were concerned was a matter of dread, which proved to be not un-justified. Miss Catherine Sinclair, daughter of the well-known Member of Parliament, Sir John Sinclair, and the author of the children's story book *Holiday House*, which with *Ministering Children* was read by all well brought up Scottish girls, writes in a very interesting way on this subject in her book *Scotland and the Scotch*. She says, in 1840, that Scotch entails are indeed made of ' tough

material' but that much property manages to escape
them, and as this is written before the 1848 Act was
passed it is significant. But she has also a strong indictment of the lairds of her day which, as she was a
competent observer, throws rather a new light upon
their character and doings. ' If,' she says, ' a muster
roll was called . . . of every landlord's name, how few
in their own places could answer " Here ! " ' ' She con-
firms her statement by telling that one gentleman had
inspected about fifty estates whose owners had vanished
to the Continent and elsewhere leading useless lives,
attending opera houses instead of churches, and this she
considers a mournful exchange, for life without hard-
ship and difficulties was unsatisfying. One cannot but
hope that she was exaggerating, for we do not always
have so depressing an account of Scottish lairds.

'We have lost,' Lord Cockburn says, in writing
of the nineteenth century, ' necessarily and for ever
the old social aristocracy, but we have got much out of
which something as good, though not perhaps so curious,
may be enjoyed. . . . A wise man would like to have
seen the past age, but to live in this one.'

CHAPTER IV

HOW THE SOCIAL SERVICES DEVELOPED

IT is difficult to believe that there has ever been in this country so complete a change in the view taken of the relations of individuals to one another as that which took place during the last century. In one aspect it would appear to have been even more marked in Scotland than in England, for Scotland had a more individualistic and self-sufficient quality at the beginning or middle of the century than had England. It would have been difficult, for example, in Scotland to carry on many of the ' charities ' which were absolutely a part of English rural life half a century ago, when, so far as material needs were concerned, the squire was a sort of *Deus ex machina* to the village as the clergyman in another sense was to the parish.

First of all the lairds and clergy were poorer, but, far more important, no self-respecting working man or woman would have received the gifts they were bestowed in the South. Dr. Thomas Chalmers advocated a system of ecclesiastical administration of the funds collected for the poor, and elaborated a very successful organization in his parish for dealing with them. But although this might have met the objections of Scotsmen, since the funds were so to speak derived from

Modern Moderation Strikingly Displayed

Dismiss; I order every one of you, go home and desire your Parents to teach you I have a right to be heard I say go Home —

Sir some of them have no Parents

S. Kay 1799

OR

A Ministerial *Visitation of a* Sabbath Evening School

KAY'S CARTOON OF A " MODERATE " MINISTER
ENDEAVOURING TO BREAK UP A SUNDAY SCHOOL

public collection and not personal gifts, the task was too great for the Church to undertake. Even Chalmers allowed that there were public services that must be administered by public officers. The duty of caring for the poor was, of course, finally laid on Parish Councils popularly elected. There were, however, during the latter part of the century immense voluntary efforts made towards alleviating the condition of the poor and endeavouring to counteract the terrible effects of the Industrial Revolution. These efforts were made without definite co-ordination, as voluntary efforts so often are.

The form that these new charitable efforts took was for the most part that of helping to start experimental schemes in the hope and belief that if successful they might later on be taken over by the State. These efforts were no doubt valuable and they gave interest to the lives of many men and women, especially to those who, through this very development of industry that appeared to have caused much of the evil, had come to possess a considerable amount of wealth. Large sums were given to ameliorate conditions that ought never to have been allowed to arise. Societies were established for helping the sick, the blind and the maimed : then again for mothers' welfare, for preventing cruelty to children and to animals, for establishing homes for the destitute, while guilds of all sorts presaged some of the great movements of the next century—Boy Scouts, Girl Guides, Women's Institutes and so on.

Such efforts, small at first, were not smiled upon when they actually arose in the beginning of the

E

century. Mrs. Fletcher, a somewhat advanced and yet
religious Englishwoman who came to Edinburgh in
1798, managed to prevail on the ladies of her acquaint-
ance to join with her in the institution of a Female
Benefit Society for the relief of ' maid-servants and
other poor women ' in sickness. The ' innovation ' was
looked on with deep suspicion, inasmuch as the ladies
were suspected of democratic principles, and the Deputy
Sheriff and Magistrates (who had to be consulted)
actually opposed the scheme when asked to sanction the
rules. For many years after this it was considered
wrong for women to take part in any public scheme,
whether for educational or philanthropic objects, and
very wrong to speak in meetings even among their own
sex. Quite late in the sixties a lady who had done so
(and on religious topics too) was said to have died of
cancer of the tongue in consequence ! Working among
so-called ' fallen women ' was likewise thought shocking
even after women had made some effort to help their
oppressed sisters south of the Border. As to charitable
societies, Mrs. Grant of Laggan, who might as a
minister's widow have been supposed to think differently, says in a letter of 1815 : ' You know my dislike
to any conspicuous goodness among females which
makes me shrink a little from Female Societies formed
with the best intentions.'

As the century went on the floodgates opened and the
good work proceeded mostly in the form of different
schemes of district visiting ; but even this was not too
popular with the over-pious, unless indeed it was con-

ducted on purely religious lines. Sunday Schools only
made their way with difficulty. By degrees, however,
there was a real awakening to men's responsibilities to
one another as well as to animals, accompanied by what
in looking back we cannot but feel was a strange callous-
ness. The Poor Law was stern ; no able-bodied man or
woman was entitled to relief however destitute of work.
Here the logic of the Calvinist seemed to argue that if a
man could work he should work, and find that work for
himself. The poor-houses, when instituted in 1845,
were houses for the poor, not work-houses as in England, and though they were intended for and used only
by the aged and sickly and children, the regulations were
hard. The food (up to the eighties or nineties at least)
was barely sufficient and the discipline was stern.
Paupers were too often ' nursed ' by one another ; no
encouragement was given to regain independence, and
' going into the House ' was so much a matter of shame
that the inmate was cut adrift from relatives and friends.
Children were mercifully often boarded out, and on the
whole this plan worked well.

Hospitals for the sick did not fare much better,
especially in the view of country people. There was a
general distrust of them, emanating partly from the
tales of the Resurrectionists and their supposed col-
lusion with the doctors, and partly because people did
not trust themselves out of their homes. From the
middle of the century (1845) when the Church ceased
to have the responsibility on its hands, the poor were
looked after by the Parochial Boards (under a Board of

Supervision) which in 1894 evolved into Parish Councils under the Local Government Board. Out-relief was the traditional form of help in Scotland. Pauperism taken as a whole was, however, less in Scotland than in England.

Let us now, however, leave poor law administration and look at how the country was managed from a sanitary point of view. As to this we know that we have not much to expect. We learn of Edinburgh, for example, that in 1800 scavenging was supposed to be a public duty, but it was left to be performed by the Night Watchmen. The Night Watchmen, presumably, had their own work to do and only in 1815 was any sort of staff appointed to carry out the sanitary duties : it was, of course, a wholly insufficient one. Lord Cockburn tells us that the Cowgate had an open ditch called the ' Coogate Strand ' which when in flood became a great torrent, not filling the cellars merely but almost the whole canal of the street. Near Holyrood there was a regular net fishery to catch what the river brought down !

Even in the sixties and seventies the cesspool system existed in the New town of Edinburgh as the ordinary system of drainage ; these cesspools were cleaned out from time to time, perhaps annually. And in the best houses the privies were often sunk below the ground because even after a water system was introduced there was difficulty in getting water into the house by gravitation.

In the middle of the century, however, people were

forced to deal with the dangers which had been brought
about by the new industrialism. In Glasgow specially
this was so, for it was considered by reliable observers
that the conditions there were worse than those in any
other town of the United Kingdom. Typhus epidemics
began in 1818 and recurred in 1837, 1847 and 1851,
alternating with cholera epidemics, and meantime the
population had risen from 83,805 to 347,000. The
death-rate from these diseases was immense, and as if
that were not enough the city was also devastated by
smallpox which seized specially on the unfortunate
Highland immigrants. Underneath these human erup-
tions there was, it was said, a continuous state of ill-
health among the people. Indeed the conditions of life
in Glasgow as stated in the reports of medical men in
the thirties and forties baulk description. People were
crowded into filthy dark cellars and there were openings
for water from which there was no drain: dirt and disease
were everywhere; fourteen and fifteen people occupied
one room, some of them on the floor with fever. Doctors
certainly urged the removal of the dunghills and pools
of filth and suggested paving the ' closes,' but in vain.
Wynds were often so narrow that a cart could not pass
along them, and out of these opened ' closes ', or courts,
in the centre of which was a dunghill. Edinburgh was
bad, but nothing like so bad as Glasgow. Only the removal of these loathsome hovels could do any good,
but in the absence of a sense of mutual responsibility
this was not possible. In this poorer part of the town,
the Chief Constable said, ' there is everything that is

wretched, dissolute, loathsome and pestilential.'
There were no privies, and as a considerable part of the
rent of the houses was paid by the produce of the dunghills ' it would consequently be esteemed an invasion of
the rights of property to remove them ' ! In one report
we are told that the people were ' worse than wild animals, for they withdraw to a distance and conceal their
ordure, but the dwellers in these courts had converted
their shame into a kind of money by which their lodging
was to be paid.'[1] Mr. Chadwick in 1842 thought the
condition of the population of Glasgow the worst he
had seen anywhere in Great Britain. These terrible
and hardly readable reports went on till 1849, while
the rich were daily growing richer ; and up to that date it
is stated that a household supply of water in the poorer
houses was unknown. Large numbers of the population were certainly of Irish origin, for the famine in
Ireland brought them to Scotland in vast numbers, but
many must have come from the Highland glens.

The extraordinary thing is that despite the outbreaks
of cholera which caused some alarm, nothing was done
till the seventies beyond causing houses that were
falling to pieces to be repaired. Some philanthropic
people did indeed establish three ' model ' lodging
houses, but of sanitation in the modern sense there was
none in the poorer parts of any of the Scottish towns.
In populous tenements there were only what were called

---

[1] *Public Health Administration in Glasgow*. Being a Memorial
Volume of the writings of J. B. Russell, Medical Member of the
Local Government Board in Scotland, 1905.

public privies, and these were resorted to by the men in the families but not by the women and children. Police Acts were certainly passed in Glasgow giving directions about scavenging, but they were a dead letter, though in 1843 an Inspector of Cleaning was appointed ; his work was, however, but a sort of bye-play to police duties and was not taken seriously.

Every epidemic was a tragedy, though regarded as a Divine Visitation by the pious, which relieved their consciences. The Royal Infirmary of Glasgow, which opened in 1794, was for seventy years the centre of the provision that was made for isolation, but of course temporary arrangements had to be made somehow for the many surplus patients who were, if the worst came to the worst, to have ' safe and speedy ' interment. The Scotch Registration Act took effect in 1855, so that after that date we have unquestionable statistics, which was a forward step. Then, too, Glasgow, after the cholera epidemic of 1853-4, entered on some practical sanitation. In 1855 the Corporation Water Works Act authorized new works taking over the two private companies which had hitherto purveyed water to the community.

The history of Glasgow water supply is interesting as it shows how difficult it was to achieve reform in matters of sanitation. In 1801 while the population of Glasgow was 83,769 the only public source of water supply was thirty public wells erected on twenty-four of the principal streets ; the wells were hopelessly inadequate and objectionable. People took their turn in

order to obtain even a stoup of water, though an enterprising citizen set out to perambulate the city with barrels
of water which he sold at ½d. per stoup. Then when
water was got from the river by a private company much
of it was unfiltered, and it was provided from a river into
which 30 small towns and villages with a population of
160,000 were drained. Every sort of difficulty in making progress was encountered by the Lord Provost
(Stewart) and his colleagues. In 1852 a Bill was sent to
Parliament but the opposition was so great that it was
only in 1855 that at last it became an Act. The advent
of pure Loch Katrine water was not, however, unani-
mously welcomed, for an old lady who all her life had
been in the habit of fetching her water from a certain
well which had been closed as being polluted was most
indignant, saying to a neighbour who urged her to take
her new gravitation water and leave the well : ' I just
canna thole (stand) that new water ; it's got neither
taste nor smell ' !

The extraordinary thing was that, since of course the
necessary work of improving the sanitary condition of
the city could not be carried out without taxation,
when in this wealthy city an Improvement Tax was
imposed, there was an outburst of popular feeling that
wreaked its vengeance on Lord Provost Blackie. In the
ward which he represented and which embraced many
of the plague spots, his re-election was challenged and
he was defeated.

In Edinburgh also the public wells were the only
source of water supply, and the water came from a

cistern right up the Castle Hill at very uncertain intervals. Hence the inhabitants had to assemble in
queues with every conceivable manner of vessel to wait
for the welcome rush of water. ' Wha's last ? ' was the
cry of the latest arrival, Mr. George Croal tells us, and
on a response being given, the line was continued until
the flow of water ceased. However, those who were
able to pay a halfpenny per barrel had their wants supplied by old men who earned a pittance by carrying the
water barrels slung on their backs right up the long
stairs of the high Edinburgh ' lands '.

After this time, however, sanitation was gradually
carried out mainly by erecting hospitals, for the existing
hospitals were overcrowded when outbreaks of fever
took place, and not only was there a very high rate of
mortality of patients but also of nurses.

After the last great epidemic of typhus in Glasgow of
1869-70 steps were taken to deal with public baths and
wash-houses, dairies, drain tests and so on. The
Infectious Diseases Notification Act of 1890 and other
similar Acts made the work of improvement easier.
Before that came the efforts to get open spaces and playgrounds for adults and children. Power was obtained
in 1875 to lay out and throw open the graveyards which
had been closed : mercifully the fact of being burial
places had saved them from the builder. The so-called
' Utopian idea ' of providing recreation grounds for old
and young in the crowded districts gradually took shape,
though as far as this is concerned the nineteenth century left much to be done in the twentieth.

Even in 1843 the condition of the poor was so serious that a Royal Commission was instituted to inquire into their condition ; a commission which showed how unsatisfactory the conditions of parochial relief by the heritors and kirk sessions when badly administered might be. But the whole question of the unemployed—the question that has been troubling us ever since—came to a head in the ' hungry 'forties.' There were 10,000 men unemployed in Paisley alone who could not get work and could not be allowed to die. ' Is it not the case,' Lord Cockburn asks, ' that until machinery does away with the need of human limbs this condition must recur in a manufacturing community ? ' The question never has been answered !

It was not till 1863 that a Medical Officer of Health was appointed in Glasgow, and that overcrowding began to be seriously dealt with ; the first scheme was one of ' ticketing ' on the door the number of persons who might occupy one room or ' house.' Then came disinfection regulations and the Vaccination Act. Following on a report of a Sanitary Committee in 1862, a much-needed ' Sanitary Office ' was opened in 1864. This was really the result of a visit of a deputation from the members of the Town Council to the chief towns of the United Kingdom, for they found that the sanitary condition of the towns in England was much better than that of Glasgow and that, even discounting what they allowed were ' the more cleanly habits of the English working class,' this was undoubtedly due to the powers of the local authorities in sanitary matters.

Even after this date Glasgow's sanitary work was of the minutest, and typhus still abounded. In 1865, however, the first municipal fever hospital was opened—a small one, but useful—and in 1867 the Scottish Public Health Act became law and it was easier for progress to be made. The first Sanitary Inspector was appointed in 1870. Then women sanitary inspectors were appointed, and finally a junior Medical Officer in 1892.

These new steps were followed by a much-needed reform of the nursing system. Dr. Gairdner of Glasgow in a paper regarding the nursing in fever hospitals in 1870 says that the number of respectable women who will encounter the danger, which is not exaggerated, is small. ' As things are, nurses have no organization as a class and no *morals*. The popular idea, particularly of a hospital nurse, resembles that of washer-women—drinking is inseparable from both. . . . Good people are, I fancy, assured that I have not yet learned to believe that drink and dishonesty are essential properties of a nurse. . . . Nursing is the last resource of female adversity. Slatternly widows, runaway wives, servants out of places, women bankrupt of fame and fortune, fall back on hospital nursing. When on a rare occasion a respectable young woman takes to it from choice, her friends most likely repudiate her, her relatives resort to various ways of concealing her whereabouts.' This shows how difficult it must have been to recruit for such a profession.

The Edinburgh Royal Infirmary was perhaps the most celebrated of all the provincial General Hospitals and its history throws much light on the history of nursing in Scotland and indeed on all social conditions. The development of medicine in Edinburgh under famous men like the Gregorys, Alison and others, gave special distinction to this hospital and made its history particularly interesting.

The first Report of the Hospital, dated 1730, gives a sad account of what happened to the sick poor, ' naked, starving, in the outmost Distress from Pain and Trouble of Body and Anguish of Soul ' who were allowed to come occasionally to the Hall of the Royal College of Physicians until the hospital was founded. The hospital was superintended, under the physicians, by a Mistress ' free of the burden of children ' who saw to the ' Plenishing ' and had to oversee patients and servants, for nurses only appeared later on. As usual in Scotland money was scarce, but everyone helped, even the labourers who gave a day's work gratis to the new building. Indeed there were piteous appeals to those who expended their goods in ' vain superfluities or perhaps vicious debauches ' which reflects sadly on the life of the day. One of the attractions mentioned is that a churchyard is close by !

By the beginning of the nineteenth century things became more regulated. There are nurses as well as the matron, now so-called, who see to the ' vivres ' for the patients ; smallpox patients are to be in a separate room with plenty of fresh air corrected with ' vapours of warm vinegar.' By 1816 the regulations are ahead of most hospitals of the time, and by 1841 the ' Mistress '

is given control not only of the nurses but of the porters,
and, with the Superintendent, of the resident clerks.
The two were to ' keep a watchful eye over the distribution of wines and malt spirits '—a very necessary in-
junction judging from all one hears of the behaviour of
the nurses. Nurses were to have £12 a year and night
nurses who were of a lower grade £10, ' but they will be
made day nurses when their conduct is such as to de-
serve it.' As a matter of fact the night nurses were
somewhat like charwomen, and often the nurse in
charge had to sleep in a sort of gallery above the ward so
that she might from a little window supervise their
doings while enjoying an atmosphere uncorrupted by
fresh air.

In spite of the disrepute into which they fell, things
went on slowly improving in Scottish hospitals. There
was always a religious element present in them, for the
Scripture had to be read *and expounded* in the ward every
day; but there was no clerical element as regards the
staff, as was often the case in England. The methods
seem nowadays crude and almost barbarous, but they
have to be judged by the standards of living of the time.
There was, anyhow, a homely atmosphere in the hospitals, not distasteful to either patient or doctor ; and
there were in Scotland skilful physicians whose training
was got by experience gained at the bedside rather than
by regular courses of lectures. And just as many of the
doctors and surgeons became famous like Lord Lister
and so many others who began their careers in Edinburgh and Glasgow, so there were among the stout

homely nurses fine souls as well as Gamps and Prigs;
and good nurses had great respect accorded to them.
When, for instance, young Lister came to grief climbing
up the Salisbury Crags with another equally young and
daring doctor, and they were carried into the Edinburgh
Infirmary bruised and sore, they were met by a famous
nurse named Mrs. Porter : ' A kent weel hoo it wad be.
Ye Englishmen are aye sae fulish, gaeing aboot fustlin'
(whistling) upon the Sawbath.'

By the end of the century nurses in Scotland were
trained according to the system of Florence Nightingale,
had their separate ' Homes,' their three years standard
of teaching, and regular lectures from physicians and
surgeons.   True to the democratic basis of Scottish life
there were never, as was often the case in England,
paying ' lady probationers,' but all were on the same
grade and for a long time they did much of the roughest
work.

As regards housing, the conditions early in the century must have been beyond belief, though we are without statistics.   In 1884 John Bright made his historic
appeal to the students of Glasgow University—to the
young manhood of Glasgow.   He told them that in
Glasgow 41 families out of every 100 lived in ' houses ' of
only one room.   Bright was wrong, inasmuch as he had
taken the census return of 1871 instead of 1881, but
still the conditions were so bad as to strike the imagination not only of Glasgow but of the whole national community.   Indeed, this eloquent speech might be said to
have set alight the flame of interest in the housing of the

poor, which has spread over the land. It is an interesting example of how one eloquent speech of a silver-
tongued orator can do more than volumes of statistics
unaided by its means. Dr. Russell had pointed out in
1880 that of the children who died in Glasgow before
completing their fifth year of age 32 per cent died in
houses of one apartment and not 2 per cent in houses of
five apartments and over, and that the lives of these
poor children in small houses were one continuous
tragedy; many of them were illegitimate, and every year
60 or 70 per cent of those who died under five died by
accident or negligence. Dr. Russell's indictment of the
social conditions of the town was even more moving
than John Bright's though he had not his gifts of
speech, for he had full and accurate information and he
made it clear that the mortality usually rises with the
number of persons per inhabited room. The death-rate
in the one-roomed house was about three times as high
as that in homes of four or more apartments. In the
last century, of course, drunkenness too, was a factor
that weighed heavily in the balance.

There is, however, one thing that we must remember
in regard to the Industrial Revolution. Though we
condemn the apparent disregard of human life and
humane conditions of life in themselves, the new industries that arose brought many advantages. They
brought wealth to the country and enabled a large
number of people who had been living in great poverty
to earn good wages and enjoy greater comfort. The evil
was that the employers considered that once they had

created these industries their work was done ; they had made no provision for the influx of men, women and children that crowded into the cities, nor did they see that this was a duty. Public authorities also disclaimed responsibility, as ratepayers emphatically did, and thus the consequences were disastrous.

It seems as if it might in this instance be helpful to pass to reports made in later times since they throw a light on the conditions of the past as to which the records are less detailed.

The Report of the Housing Commission of 1917, for instance, gives an account of the deplorable condition of the housing of Glasgow as it was even long after 1880, so that there cannot have been the improvement that might have been expected as the century advanced, though general sanitation was better. There were still in Glasgow ' dark and damp sunk flats ' below the level of the street in a whole street of high tenements. The stairs down to them were almost invariably dark and dirty, ' the passages pitch dark on the brightest day, so that only by feeling along the walls can one discover the doors.' In the class spoken of ' the stairs are filthy and evil smelling, water closets constantly choked and foul water running down the stairs, sickly cats everywhere spreading disease.'

Then the ' Miners' Rows ' of inferior class in the mining districts were often dreary and featureless places with houses dismal in themselves, arranged in monotonous lines or squares. The open spaces were encumbered with wash-houses and privies—often out of repair—

THE BRIDE, 20 YEARS LATER
As the Mother of Fourteen Children

GRETNA GREEN MARRIAGE CERTIFICATE 1785

These are to Certify all Person or Persons or whome it may concern that Richard Ryland of Tower Hill London and Harriet Frances Croft of Thatcham in Berkshire who came before me declairing themselves to be both single Persons was lawfully Married by the way of the Church of England and agreeable to the Laws of the Kirk of Scotland given under my hand at gratney Green this twenty-third Day of January One thousand seven hundred and Eighty Five.

and in wet weather they got churned up into a morass of semi-liquid mud, with little in the way of solidly con-structed road or footpath—a fact which added very greatly to the burdens of the over-wrought housewife. The impossibility of domestic cleanliness and order where this was the case need not be dilated on; but if the workers were on different shifts, the task of the house-wife was complicated by irregular meals and sleeping hours. ' If the pit is a wet one, the miner's soaking clothes must be left at the kitchen fire ; and as the kitchen is a sleeping apartment, even when there are one or two other rooms, the steam and the gas which are given off as the pit clothes dry are highly injurious to the children, who may be in one of the two large beds near by.'[1] Before pit baths were introduced, and these were by no means very popular at first with the miners or miners' wives, the bath had to be taken in the kitchen or scullery. Under such conditions, and with the disgusting ' privy midden ' which retained its existence in mining villages, it is extraordinary that any degree of cleanliness was preserved.

In 1844 Lord Cockburn tells of the institution of Public Baths for the poor. He made the most gloomy prognostications as to their possible success, though he agrees that the habit of cleaning the skin is undoubtedly useful. ' They cannot be made cheap enough and Sawney has not tidiness to keep them in order.' ' The poor will not maintain them. Baths, whether cold or

[1] Report of Dr. Maxwell Williams, M.O.H. for Edinburgh, quoted in Report to the Carnegie United Kingdom Trust.

F

warm, are the luxuries of a hot climate.' This was the general view and by no means exceptional.

In the less distinguished houses it is clear that the overcrowding which was and is bad in England was and is worse in Scotland. In Glasgow as late as 1917, which is beyond our century, but in regard to which we have interesting figures, 13.8 of the population lived in ' houses ' of one room, and 62.2 per cent, or more than half the population, in houses of one or two rooms. In Dundee conditions were worse still. In addition to this more than half the population of Glasgow (55.7 per cent) lived more than two in a room, and more than a quarter (27.9 per cent) more than three in a room ; indeed 10.7 per cent lived more than four in a room.[1] These figures speak for themselves. It does not surprise us that the infant mortality, i.e. deaths of children under one year of age, was greatly larger in Glasgow, and particularly in Dundee (where married women work out a great deal, leaving their infants at home), than it was elsewhere.

Town houses of the better sort approximate more to the normal English plan than rural houses ; the best are well and substantially built of stone. Scotland started the ' common stair ' to flats, a plan derived from France, though no concierge was supplied but only an ingenious mechanism whereby the occupants of each flat could open the front door from above.

[1] Report of Dr. Maxwell Williams, M.O.H. for Edinburgh, quoted in Report to the Carnegie United Kingdom Trust.

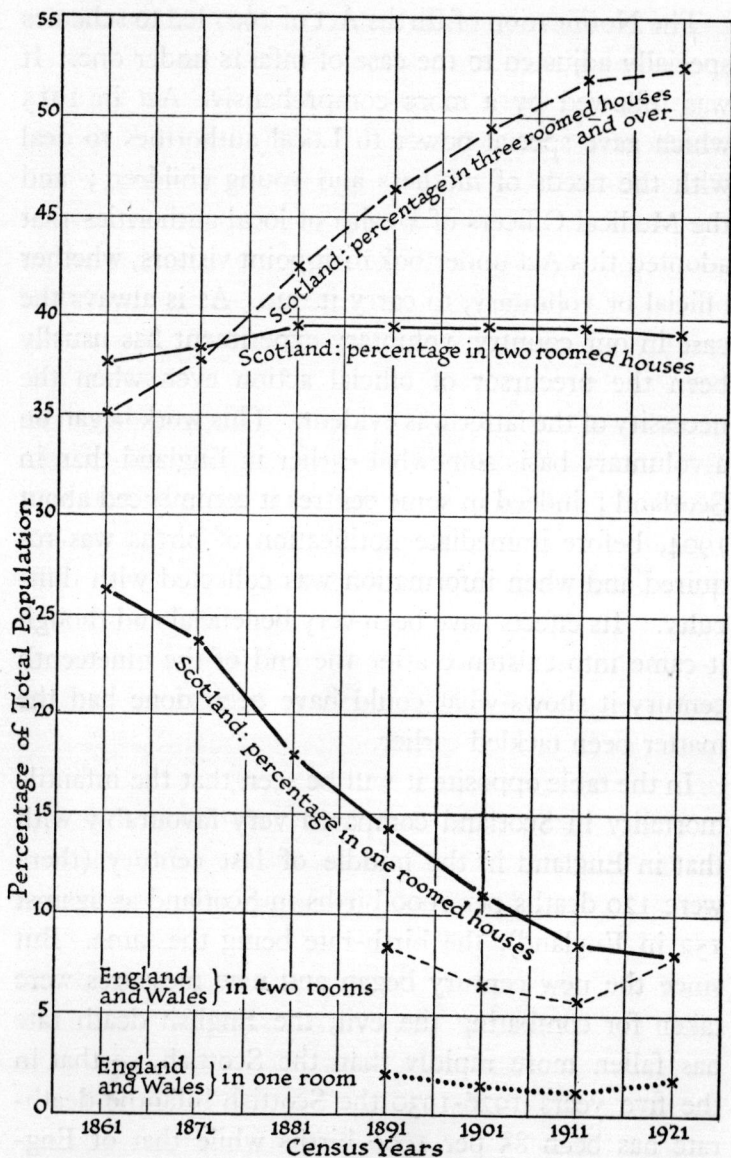

Table showing the respective Housing of Scotland and England and Wales from 1861 to 1922. As will be seen Scotland is much less well housed than England and Wales.

The Notification of Births Act of 1907 led to schemes specially adjusted to the case of infants under one. It was followed by a more comprehensive Act in 1915 which gave special power to Local authorities to deal with the needs of mothers and young children ; and the Medical Officers of Health of local authorities that adopted this Act undertook to appoint visitors, whether official or voluntary, to carry it out. As is always the case in our country, voluntary experiment has usually been the precursor of official action even when the necessity of the latter was evident. This work began on a voluntary basis somewhat earlier in England than in Scotland ; indeed in some centres it commenced about 1904, before immediate notification of births was required and when information was collected with difficulty. Its effects have been very beneficial and though it came into existence after the end of the nineteenth century it shows what could have been done had the matter been tackled earlier.

In the table opposite it will be seen that the infantile mortality in Scotland compared very favourably with that in England in the middle of last century (there were 120 deaths per 1000 births in Scotland as against 152 in England), the birth-rate being the same. But since the new century began and new measures were taken for combating the evil, the English death rate has fallen more rapidly than the Scottish, so that in the five years 1926-1930 the Scottish infantile death-rate has been 85 per 1000 births while that of England is only 68. It is the crowded areas in Scotland

Five year Periods

| 1856 | 1861 | 1866 | 1871 | 1876 | 1881 | 1886 | 1891 | 1896 | 1901 | 1906 | 1911 | 1916 | 1921 | 1926 |
| −60 | −65 | −70 | −75 | −80 | −85 | −90 | −95 | 1900 | −05 | −10 | −15 | −20 | −25 | −30 |

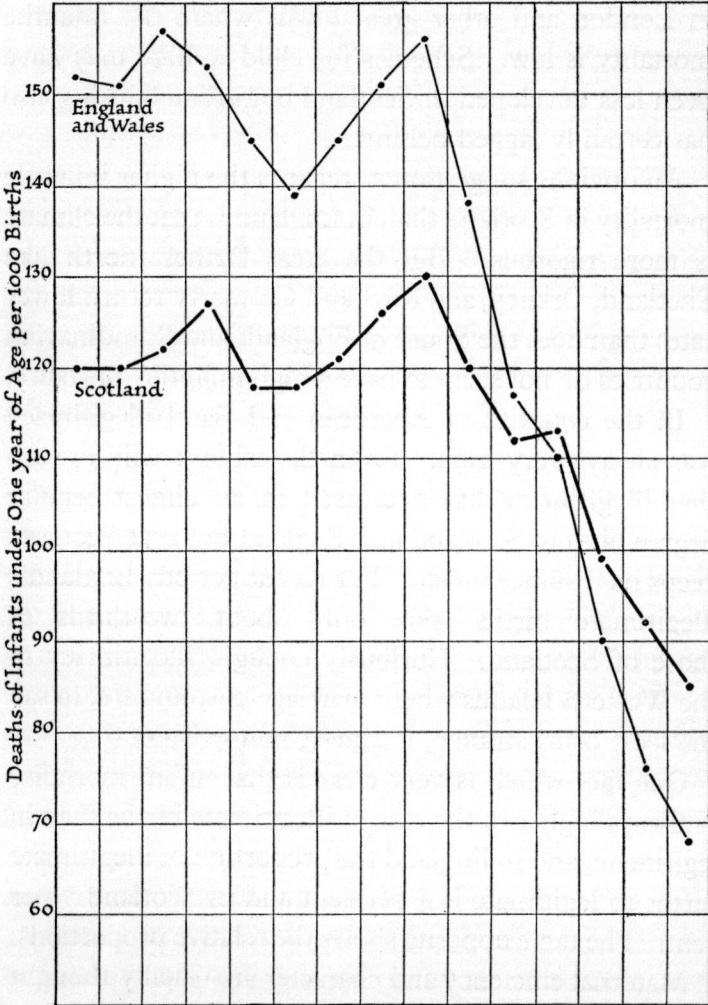

Deaths of Infants under One year of Age per 1000 Births

England and Wales

Scotland

Table showing Infantile Mortality for Scotland and England and Wales respectively from 1856 to 1926.

that have suffered most, and that there is no reason why urban areas should so suffer has been exemplified in London and other great towns where the infantile mortality is low. Schemes for child welfare may have been less developed in Scotland but urban housing also has certainly lagged behind.

An obvious suggestion as regards the higher infantile mortality in Scotland than in England is that the climate is more rigorous. But the areas farthest north like Shetland, Orkney, and Ross and Cromarty return lower rates than does the South of England, and Scandinavian countries do not seem to have a high infantile mortality.

In the counties of Aberdeen and Banff illegitimacy was always very high. From the table it will be seen that illegitimacy has decreased in an almost regular degree both in Scotland and England but that Scotland keeps its distance intact. For recent periods England's illegitimate births were only about two-thirds of those of Scotland. Curiously enough, illegitimacy in the Western Islands where marriage customs are, to say the least of it, strange, is almost non-existent.

One fact which is very clear is that infant mortality is always higher in the case of illegitimate births than in legitimate, and in England the proportion of illegitimate births to legitimate is 4 per cent and in Scotland 7 per cent. The table opposite shows the relative proportions.

Maternal efficiency and character are usually thought to be the most essential features in reducing infant deaths : more important even than housing or poverty, important factors as these are. Illegitimate children

are not well cared for as a rule, and illegitimacy has at all
times been more frequent in Scotland than England ;

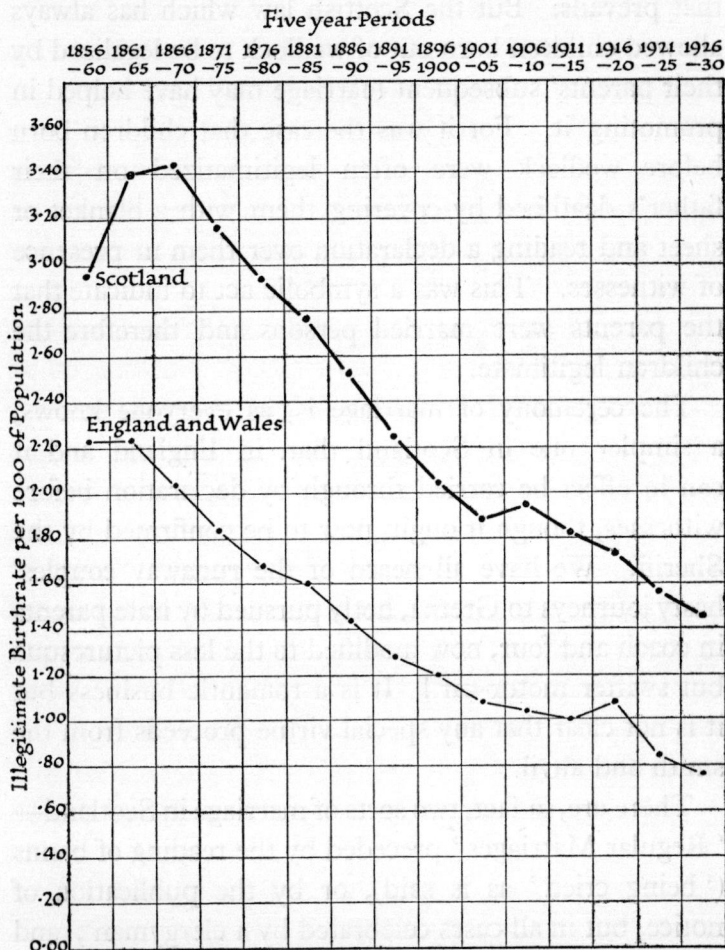

Five year Periods

| 1856 | 1861 | 1866 | 1871 | 1876 | 1881 | 1886 | 1891 | 1896 | 1901 | 1906 | 1911 | 1916 | 1921 | 1926 |
| −60 | −65 | −70 | −75 | −80 | −85 | −90 | −95 | 1900 | −05 | −10 | −15 | −20 | −25 | −30 |

Scotland

England and Wales

Illegitimate Birthrate per 1000 of Population

Table showing Illegitimacy Rates for Scotland and England and Wales
respectively from 1856 to 1926.

in both the social ban is often cruelly exercised. We
cannot, indeed, wonder at the illegitimacy in the rural

districts of Scotland where it is highest, when we re-member the nature of the houses and the bothy system that prevails.   But the Scottish law which has always allowed children born out of wedlock to be legalized by their parents' subsequent marriage may have helped in promoting it.   For it was the case that children born before wedlock were often legitimatized on their father's deathbed by covering them with a blanket or sheet and reading a declaration over them in presence of witnesses.   This was a symbolic act to indicate that the parents were married persons and therefore the children legitimate.

The ceremony of marriage is, as everyone knows, a simpler one in Scotland than in England and it can in effect be carried through by declaration before witnesses, though it ought now to be confirmed by the Sheriff.   We have all heard of the runaway couples' hasty journeys to Gretna, hotly pursued by irate parents in coach and four, now modified to the less picturesque but swifter motor-car !   It is a romantic business but it is not clear that any special virtue proceeds from the smith and anvil.

There are, in fact, two sorts of marriage in Scotland—' Regular Marriages ' preceded by the reading of banns (' being cried ' as is said), or by the publication of notice, but in all cases celebrated by a clergyman ; and ' Irregular Marriages,' not celebrated by a clergyman but simply registered on warrant of the Sheriff.   There are now indeed many ' Irregular ' marriages, for in 1930 they numbered 4065 as compared with 29,250 regular marriages. In 1926 there were 31,244 marriages altogether and of these 3,712 were ' Irregular.'

We do not possess figures for what happened in the last century, but it is interesting that Scotland now prefers to be married by the Presbyterian Church, when it does marry ' regularly.' In 1930 72 per cent of the regular marriages were performed by a Church of Scotland minister, 14 per cent were Roman Catholic, and 3 per cent were Episcopalian marriages.

Illiteracy, it is satisfactory to see, has practically disappeared from Scotland since the last century passed away, and many of those who lately signed by mark were Roman Catholics and presumably Irish born. Before the Education Act of 1872 (i.e. in 1869) 18,133 signed by mark, two-thirds of whom were women.

The Gretna Green marriages numbered 275 in 1928 so that these marriages did not by any means cease with the century that is gone. And of these 275 only 18 were registered. In 1929 there were 315 marriages at Gretna and 52 were registered. Without registration and ' marriage lines ' there is no documentary proof of marriage and the consequences are naturally economically and socially serious. Registration was directed to be made in 1855; before that time Gretna Green ' marriages ' had a higher status. An example is shown (p. 80) of the certificate given in the case of a runaway marriage. The attractive young bride of seventeen was still at school and an heiress. The husband was twenty years her senior and to point a moral the result should have been disastrous, instead of which it was a great

success ; for the lady not only bore her husband fourteen children, but lived a happy and adventurous life
afterwards ! It will be seen that grammar and spelling
on the so-called registration card were not of the best,
but the two parties concerned are said to have ' *de-
claired* ' themselves in the presence of witnesses to be
single persons and to be lawfully married ' by way of the
Church of England, agreeable to the Laws of the Kirk
of Scotland,' whatever that may signify.

Of course, lawyers did not like this sort of marriage,
and Lord Cockburn deplores the fact that the Assembly
of the Established Church in 1847 voted for the delay
of the Marriage Bill and consequently for the continua-
tion of the existing system, which in his view meant ' a
vote in favour of irregular and clandestine marriages.'

One imagines that the comparative ease with which
marriages were undertaken, and the greater facility in
breaking them (for divorce was procurable on the
ground of desertion as well as adultery), would have
made divorce more frequent in Scotland than in
England, at least before English law came more nearly
to resemble Scottish.

Apparently the divorce rate of the irregularly married
is much higher than that of the regularly married. It
is difficult to judge of this very accurately, but the
figures given by the Royal Commission on Divorce,
which reported in 1912, seem to indicate that this is so ;
for from 1898 to 1908 divorces averaged about 2 per
100,000 of the population in England and about 4 in
Scotland.

In 1898 there were 436 divorces in England and 145 in Scotland, and in 1905 there were 623 in England and 170 in Scotland. Divorce was, of course, very seldom resorted to in the middle of the century, for it was difficult and very expensive to be divorced; from 1855 to 1874 there were only 31 divorces or decrees of nullity of marriage. Since that date divorces have increased with fair regularity till in 1931 the number in Scotland has reached 569, the highest yet attained. It is possible that some of these might have taken place in England had the law allowed of it.

. . . .

We must now say something of Crime as it existed in Scotland during the last century.

In the beginning of the nineteenth century the preservation of the Peace in the Burghs, and the punishment of those committing minor offences, was in the hands of the local Magistrates. Each burgh had its own prison of some sort and to these prisons delinquents were sent, often in a very informal manner. These local prisons were not very secure as is shewn by a story which Lord Cockburn tells. An Alloa culprit was taken in a hired chaise to be lodged in the prison of Kinross. But while the horses were being fed he broke out, and wishing to see his friends in Alloa once more before finally decamping, he waited till the officers set out and without their knowing it returned to Alloa on the back of the chaise that took him to Kinross ! Cases of greater gravity than could be dealt with locally were tried by the

Procurator Fiscal, a county official who represented the Lord Advocate. If the cases were graver still they went to the High Court which went on Circuit to the principal places in Scotland. Sometimes the prisoners were taken, as now, to Edinburgh and tried before several Judges there.

Serious crime was small relatively to the population, but the sentences were severe. The death penalty could be inflicted for Robbery, Hamesucken (attacking people in their own homes), Arson and Theft, as well as for Treason and Murder. Transportation was a very favourite punishment up to 1853, since people became chary of capital punishment and yet wished to get permanently rid of their criminals if possible.

When Australia successfully objected to the transportation of certain of our criminals, places were built for the detention of convicts. The first convict prison in Scotland was at Peterhead. Corporal punishment and exposure in the pillory were usual punishments for smaller offences.

Police, as we know them, were only established in the middle of the nineteenth century, i.e. 1857, and the ' peelers ' of Sir Robert Peel, as one remembers them, were stout worthies who never changed their beat and became the friends of the locality. Before that nothing was done in rural parts ; but in towns paid watchmen were established as well as some volunteer constables, from all accounts often amusing people.

During and after the French Wars there was, of course, the usual agitation about real or supposed sedi-

tion which greatly concerned the governing classes.
The Penitentiary at Perth, an improved prison, was built
for the French prisoners of war and used later in the
ordinary way. Most prisons were thoroughly insanitary,
dark and filthy, but so were the houses of the people.
It was not till the movement for reform in the thirties
that there was an inquiry into the state of the prisons in
Scotland : before that no one knew anything about
them or even where they were, and each place was a law
to itself. After this inquiry Inspectors visited and reported, and the Lord Advocate was supposed to act on
their Reports. In 1860 a Prisons Act for Scotland
was passed, regulating the treatment of prisoners. It
provided for the transfer of sick prisoners to hospital
under given conditions, and made other humane provisions. Insane prisoners were henceforth removed to
asylums.

In 1877 a Prison Commission for Scotland was set up
and under it all prisons could be administered subject
to the authority of the Secretary for Scotland.

From the Report of the Prisons Commission at the
end of the century it appeared that the number of com-
mittals had immensely increased during the previous
fifty-five years ; quite out of proportion to the increase
in population. The population had increased from
2,742,000 in 1845 to 4,472,000 in 1901, and the com-
mittals from 18,000 to 67,000. The Irish appear to
have figured largely in these numbers, for on the last
day of the year 1901 there were in custody 1620 Scots,
167 English and 1092 Irish.

Drunkenness has been the bane of Scottish life ever since the Highland habit of whisky drinking came to the Lowlands.   There has been legislation on the subject from 1828 when the power of granting certificates to sell liquor was given to Justices of the Peace and Magistrates.   In 1858 certain restrictions as to hours and days were enacted.   Further legislation did not come till the twentieth century.   But it was much more the growing temperance movement, along with better education and a higher standard of living, that brought about improvement.   It cannot, however, be said that very much progress was made during the nineteenth century except in forming temperance societies.   The cure for drunkenness has come since the War, when the price of spirituous liquors has been raised, cinemas have been instituted, and sobriety has been found essential to drivers of mechanical vehicles.   To the end of the nineteenth century there were constantly to be found drunken cabmen and coachmen, drunken fellow-travellers by rail, and drunken holiday-makers.   In 1900, at the end of the century we are considering, Scotland drank 8,623,000 gallons of spirits, but in 1931 it was only 1,924,000 or a little less than one quarter. Those committed to prison in 1901 were 66,769, and in 1931 the numbers were only 15,683.

.   .   .   .

The lighting of towns is a very important social service and its progress is interesting.

During the eighteen thirties, we are told by James

Hedderwick that in Glasgow when darkness closed over the town and it became feebly illuminated with blinking oil lamps, the night watchmen or ' Charlies ' dozed in wooden boxes at certain street corners, sounded their clappers along their beats, and underneath the windows on the occasion of a fire or a row. They bawled out at intervals the hour and the state of the weather, such as ' Half-past-three, and a fine morning ! ' until the sun began to rise.

The lighting of the towns has been gradually transferred from private companies to public administration. Coal gas took the place of the old oil lamps, just as they took the place of the still older flambeaux which people carried about with them. The extinguishers for putting these out still exist on the doorways of the older houses. Before the days of gas when the streets were lighted by lamps they were few and far between. There were private lamps over the doorways but these were probably very seldom used. In Edinburgh the drawback to the animal or vegetable oil lamps then in use was that when they were freshly filled Russian sailors came up from Leith Harbour and drank the oil !

It was only in the middle of the century that mineral oil was substituted for vegetable oil in lamps ; and there was a long struggle between gas and kerosene for lighting smaller houses. Sperm candles, when used by richer people, were made from oil derived from the sperm whale, as their name indicates, and a licence was required to make both wax and spermaceti candles. Queen Victoria always insisted on having sperm candles used at her palaces; they were supposed to be better than the more modern paraffin candles which she regarded as inferior, and the original kind had latterly to be specially made for her.   In a country house there were sometimes sixteen wax candles in one bedroom; chandeliers filled with candles gave a delightful illumination.

It was in 1850 that James Young started distilling oil from a shale known as Bathgate mineral and thus set on foot the oil industry; and thereafter (from about 1853) mineral oils were used for illuminating purposes till the newer coal gas in some measure took their place.   Large country houses usually had their own gas supply and erected little gasometers in the grounds.   Early in the century cottagers of course made their own 'dip' candles by dipping the wick several times in prepared tallow fat;   failing these there were oil-cruisies.

Flambeaux were peculiarly Scottish, though, of course, they were a French importation, and they were made with great care for functional purposes.   There is still to be seen the account for flambeaux ordered by the Duke of Hamilton, Hereditary Keeper of Holyrood House, in 1752.   These were made of tallow and a mass of other ingredients by a very old firm of sealing-wax manufacturers and chandlers named Waterston, and each flambeau had a wick specially spun from lint for the purpose.   (The Waterstons also made and make wafers of flour which were and are constantly in demand).   The flambeaux cost 26s. a dozen, i.e. the cost of each flambeau was equal to about a man's daily

Old House in Saltmarket, Glasgow

G

wages at the time. But the Duke and his retinue marching down the High Street with flambeaux blazing ' at
his tail ' must have been a fine sight. The later Hogmanay flambeaux were much simpler affairs ; and
students used to use the same sort for their processions.

Illuminations were always most successful in Edinburgh where the natural formation of the land seemed
specially adapted for this purpose. A marvellous effect
was produced in 1932 by flood-lighting by electricity.
Those who saw it can never forget it. The great ' lands '
in the old town when every window or window-pane
had at least a tallow candle placed in it were, however,
most effective when looked at across the valley from the
new town ; and from the time when the House of Lords
practically acquitted Queen Caroline in 1820 and the
town was illuminated in consequence, there were quite
a series of royal celebrations which gave excuse for
illuminating the city.

When gas was introduced to Edinburgh about 1817
the illumination was of course more striking than in the
days of candles. But gas only gradually came into
common use, especially in private houses, and an
Italian Warehouse that ventured on the new departure
used to have quite a company assembled round its
windows to see it turned on ; the burners were formed
in the fashion of a star.

It is difficult to realize what it must have been on a
dark, cold morning before matches were invented, to
have with flint and steel to procure the desired spark ;
when this was obtained and the prepared tinder ignited,

a ' spunk ' about six inches long tipped with brimstone was applied and there issued the light of other days. The phosphorus friction match as now used was only invented in 1833.

In 1869 Glasgow established a municipal system of lighting and in 1888 Edinburgh did so. But a greater step still was that taken later on in 1890, when Glasgow Corporation obtained an Electric Lighting Act. Edinburgh followed suit next year. Electric light and power have made an enormous difference to the lives of the townspeople, and Glasgow was well ahead in the matter, for a private company lighted St. Enoch Station as early as 1879. The nineteenth century can take credit for this immense step forward, nearly as important as the utilization of steam early in the century. Its developments on the power side fall mainly in the next century, but in Glasgow it was decided to replace the horse tramways by electric tramways before the century ended.

CHAPTER V

THE DEVELOPMENT OF AGRICULTURE

The development of Agriculture testified to the progress which was made in Scotland after the political turmoils connected with the rising in 1745 subsided. From that time onward, but more particularly towards the end of the eighteenth and in the beginning of the nineteenth centuries, Scotsmen applied their minds to making the utmost out of their possessions whatever they might be. There were two things that helped them in this strenuous endeavour, firstly the fact that though they had little wealth and not many physical advantages, they had the essential in all endeavour, brains and the capacity from past education to use these brains; and secondly they were living in an era of progress. The Revolutionary period had mercifully affected Scotland with an impetus to construction rather than destruction, but it was a time of criticism, and a time when men knew that the result of failing to read a lesson might be fatal to themselves and others. Anyhow, it was now that Scotland came to realize what was being done elsewhere, and by good fortune she became possessed of a number of capable men who could not only think out schemes of reform but bring them into concrete form.

It is necessary, if we wish to understand the development of Agriculture in Scotland, to go back to its beginnings. If, for instance, we turn back to the seventeenth century we should find Scotland a backward nation rent by political feuds and unable to concentrate on her own improvement or welfare as a civilized nation. The beginning of the next century was not much better. The Union was brought about in the face of much opposition, and when accomplished the Scottish people felt it almost as a disgrace. The English had different ways from theirs ; they no doubt saw the financial advantages to be got from the ' Equivalent ' granted them, which delighted the shareholders of the Darien Company who never expected to see their money again ; but they had the sense of inferiority that a poor small country cannot but have in relation to a great and wealthy one which had just triumphed in warfare. It was hard for those who went to London to feel that the country on which they had set such store was treated as of no account ; it was even harder to see comparatively well-tilled land and prosperous-looking farms when the Scottish ones were so different. Certainly it was the business of the eighteenth century Scots to get alongside their rich neighbour in agricultural matters in any way possible.

When peace reigned, as it was more or less to reign in Scotland for so many years, indeed nearly until the twentieth century (for the French, and even the Peninsular and Crimean and Egyptian Wars, were fought by professional soldiers and made but little impression on the social history of the country, despite the fact that many of the fighting soldiers were Scots), the time for improvement came. Let us see what the conditions were on which this improvement was to be effected.

Corn was grown in the infield and outfield fashion and in rigs, i.e. cultivated strips near the house or hamlet with uncultivated ground beyond. That is to say it was grown in patches belonging to different people, perhaps twenty feet wide, with ' baulks ' between, and the baulks were covered with nettles and weeds. We can see traces of this extravagant and inefficient custom in the markings of the land to this day, especially when looked down upon from the air. There was no early ploughing, for little of the soil was drained effectively ; sometimes, indeed, it did not begin till February. There is no wonder that the reporter appointed to give his views on the Annexed Estates (those taken over by the Crown after the Rising) gave a grievous account of their condition. Many of the working people were living in a state of semi-starvation, hardly able to purchase the oatmeal that was their staple food, and having to fall back on ' bear ' or rough barley.

There is one thing certain, and that is that Scotland has never failed in forming societies for improving her conditions in agricultural as in other industries. The first of these societies was set on foot (as usual in high resounding phrases) in the year 1743 after a time of famine, and was supported by most of the lords and gentlemen of the country; they named their Society 'The Honourable the Society of Improvers in the Knowledge of Agriculture in Scotland.' These 'Honourable Persons moved by a generous and beneficent publick Spirit, resolved to put their Hands to Work, and their Pens to Paper, and so to employ their most strenuous Endeavours, both by Example and Direction, to promote the Improvement of their Country and raise the Spirit thereof to the greatest Height possible.' They really accomplished a great work by means of a sort of question and answer, what we now call by the disagreeable name of Questionnaire; but the real matter was that the more educated people in the land were anxiously searching for information; for they appreciated the fact that by England's better husbandry she had escaped the times of famine from which Scotland had suffered. Thus nearly every man of position and of landed property joined in trying to make a barren soil productive. The Improvers were followed by the 'Highland Society,' founded in 1784, with the object of improving the agriculture and manufacture of the Highlands.

The 'Improvers' did not confine themselves to agriculture, for they gave excellent recipes for keeping eggs by smearing them with mutton fat—quite sound recipes—for distilling spirits, and for making 'Drams' of cinnamon, sugar and spirits, which when 'jumbled up' are uncommonly like our well-shaken cocktails: again we can believe of Bohea that if infused in a pint of spirits 'it will have more Comfort in one Cup than in ten drawn of Water!'

We must remember that small stills were only made illegal in 1779 and that they were to be found existing in remote places for nearly a century longer. However, we cannot wonder that local ministers suggested that these ' improving ' societies were apt to lead to ' conviviality ' rather than pure ' improvement.'

Once set on foot, other Societies followed suit, but the Highland Society has had a specially interesting history, for not only did it operate by means of ' premiums ' for good agricultural and rural work, but it encouraged the study of the Gaelic language and the progress of forestry. Forestry, which had begun with vigour under its auspices, slackened in the earlier part of last century and only revived again towards the close under the influence of the Royal Scottish Arboricultural Society and the Board of Agriculture. Since the Great War it has, of course, developed further under the Forestry Commission, but that is a much later story.

The Annual Highland and Agricultural Show is one of the great features of Scottish agricultural life : its first meeting was in 1822 in a small enclosure in Edinburgh, and the drawings for entry money were only £51 10s. In 1919 the drawings were about £17,000 !

Agricultural education was also dealt with by the Society before it was taken over by the State. The Society helped to endow a Chair of Agriculture at Edinburgh in 1868, and it granted diplomas to young agriculturists who successfully passed its examinations.

SCOTTISH FARM, ABOUT 1800

SHOWING THE INFIELD AND OUTFIELD SYSTEM OF CULTIVATION

It also appointed a Board of Examiners in Forestry and altogether did the work which, of course, was later on taken over by the Agricultural Colleges and County Councils which provide teaching in agriculture in rural districts. Another good deed was its assistance in establishing the first Veterinary College in Scotland by giving a grant to Mr. Dick for teaching purposes in 1823. Dick had studied in the London Veterinary College which had been founded in 1793. The Dick Veterinary College was established in 1839 and it proved an invaluable institution, for little had been hitherto known about the diseases of animals.

Some of the smaller societies then formed proved abortive, like the 'British Society for Extending the Fisheries and Improving the Sea-Coasts of the Kingdom' founded by two public-spirited lairds, George Dempster and Sir Adam Ferguson, to check the ' alarming growth of emigration from the Highlands and Hebrides.' How shocked these good men would have been to have known that half a century later, in 1851, 2000 people would be 'cleared' in South Uist and sent to America by Lady Cathcart, the owner of the land.

If agriculture was backward in Scotland it was equally so in Germany and France. Both suffered even more acutely than Scotland from oppressive feudal exactions and bad leases. But undoubtedly the closer association with ' Southern Britain,' due primarily to the Union, did assist in the important work of introducing new methods of working the land ; and by the end of the eighteenth century progress had been made, for the instruction received fell on ground ready to receive it. It is rather interesting to know that in a country in which women's sphere was closely defined, women helped to bring in new ideas, and it is possible that the new blood brought from the South to a country in-bred in a really serious manner, as all Scottish family histories show, did more good than at first appeared. Lady Henrietta Mordaunt, married to the heir of the Dukedom of Gordon, introduced ploughs, fallowing and the making of hay—arts then unknown in Scotland —just as Mrs. Fletcher of Saltoun (a Scotswoman, however) introduced the making of holland cloth. The ' novel experiment ' of granting long leases also began as one century passed into the other, though it took long to materialize. The ' run-rig ' system gradually ceased to be popular and the soil was tilled to better advantage. Then the farm implements became altered and much improved. The first threshing machine was used in 1787 and after that a wonderful sight appeared, a plough which two horses could draw, instead of the old one which it took ten or twelve oxen to manage, with, of course, a man to guide them.

By the beginning of the nineteenth century leases had become longer so that tenant farmers had some encouragement in improving their farms ; and many of the small farms that then existed were thrown into larger ones ; land became enclosed, whereas it had been unenclosed before, and in some parts of the country hedges even appeared instead of the stone dykes of earlier days. But in most cases the dry stone dykes were preferred since they utilized the many stones on the fields, and were not expensive to maintain; hedges require trimming if they are to be of use, and birds collect in them.

It is undoubtedly necessary to remember the conditions as they were in the eighteenth century in order to understand the task that lay before the nineteenth, when gradually new methods of tillage arose, and new crops, such as cabbages and turnips grown in open fields, and hay grown from clover and grass seed, became common. The rural community changed but little all this time ; its members were conservative in all these matters and changes had almost to be forced upon them. As to their food, we must remember the immense value of the potato introduced to Britain from Virginia in the seventeenth century and partly popularized in England by the efforts of the Royal Society. In the latter part of the eighteenth century this hitherto despised vegetable became an article of common diet in lowland Scotland and ever since it has been a standby. We hear of it first in Scotland as grown in Kirkcudbright in 1725. Ireland adopted it earlier owing to the efforts of her own Raleigh, but France was even later than Scotland in accepting it as an article of ordinary food. Then the turnip, which was to animals as the potato was to men, was not properly grown in drills in Scotland for a long time to come. An Agricultural Society indeed grew them in this way in East Lothian in 1735, but we hear no more of turnips for nearly forty years after that, excepting as a delicacy for the rich.

In the *Life of the Fourth Earl of Aberdeen* an interesting account is given of how the young Earl found his estates when he attained his majority in 1805 and went to take possession of them. He discovered everything to be in the last degree backward as to agriculture, the people half savage and the gentry drunkards and coarse in their habits. But instead of selling his treeless, barren inheritance as he first thought of doing, he made up his mind to be an absentee laird no longer, but to plant and improve. The mosses were drained and the ' twelve owsen ' which ploughed the crooked furrows were replaced by horses and new-fashioned plough-shares were introduced. Roads and bridges were made to allow of carts being used, for pack horses had hither-to conveyed the grain to market. Liming, turnip grow-ing and sowing of the land with selected grass seeds were at first but slowly adopted by the tenantry, though the French wars and the rise of prices then brought about acted as a great stimulant in the work of progress. Schools and new farm buildings arose and Aberdeen-shire became one of the most productive cattle-raising counties in Scotland as well as one of the most intel-ligent.

In the nineteenth century the French wars helped agriculture most, for the British agriculturists then came to realize that they must literally put their hands to the plough. Flax was grown far on into the century as a crop because of its use for spinning. But it was then discovered to be uneconomic and tending to exhaust the soil. Whether used or not for the manufacture of linen on a large scale to meet the demands of the trade which had taken so firm a hold in parts of Scotland, it was constantly made use of for home consumption, and all down the lowland streams there were little lint mills where the lint was washed and prepared for the spinning wheel. There were also little mills for grinding corn, and these latter were causes of much contention, for, by the charters under which the land was held, people were forced to bring their corn to one particular mill to which they were ' thirled,' and which might be a great distance off, and bound to pay what were considered exorbitant charges. The many lawsuits that diversified rural life in Scotland were mostly concerned with feudal tenure and riparian rights and duties. It was in the latter part of the last century that there was an effective struggle for freedom from restrictions. Oppressive land tenure and leaseholds were gradually thrown off in the Lowlands while Acts were passed for the benefit of the crofters in the Highlands. All were given compensation for improvements made in their holdings and thus encouraged to make improvements. Gradually the face of the country altered and the introduction of a good class of sheep also helped to change it. For, unfortunately for the small holder, the large sheep farm was far more economic than the small crofters' holdings in the Highlands, and the crofts were ' cleared ' off the country to make room for these farms. In the Lowlands they also disappeared, though in a more gradual way. One sees many traces of the small holdings in the lowland hill country ; they may be traced not only where were the crofts but we may also see the little enclosures or ' Buchts ' where the ewes were milked.

Then the small black cattle of Scotland were no more. Instead of the painfully thin animals of the eighteenth century which, having no nutritive winter food such as turnips or clover hay, were kept indoors in a state of semi-starvation till what was called the ' lifting day ' came round and they were raised to their feet and set on the young grass, a good type of cattle was developed, partly by crossing with cattle from the improved breeds of the North of England, where Bakewell's methods had done wonders ; and partly by following these methods of selection and breeding from the best of the local breeds.

Originally the black cattle of the North had been too small to manage the journey on foot to England, while the heavier breeds of Fife and elsewhere were coarse and usually five to seven years old when slaughtered after working in the ploughs, and consequently uninviting meat. But this was altered with the increased use of horses for ploughing. Even the cattle that were in good condition on leaving Scotland were unsuited however for selling as beef by the time they reached the English market after travelling so far on foot. In Scotland itself it was difficult to get cattle sufficiently fat to salt satisfactorily for the provisioning of ships ; and frequently ships leaving Scottish ports had to call at English ports for their supplies.

Though the demand for beef increased during the

Napoleonic wars, it was only with the introduction of artificial feeding stuffs to add to the improved crops, and more especially with the making of railways and the conveyance of fat stock by rail, that Scotch beef became famous in the London markets. As a result of the fame derived from the Scottish cattle there arose great demand for good beasts from the fine herds of Scotland for breeding purposes in the Argentine and elsewhere.

Scotland relied particularly on its meat trade, and this development was in a way as important as the industrial development of the land. One could not exist without the other, so that both were necessary for the growth of the country before the days of modern methods of importing meat.

Sheep were originally supposed to be so delicate that they could not face the Scottish blasts and they were therefore cooped up in winter and only released in spring. It was by accident that the discovery was made that sheep are hardy animals and can face the weather as well as other creatures ; and it was lucky that it was so, for the high ground in Scotland would have been derelict without them. Formerly they died so frequently that braxy mutton, i.e. mutton hams made from the carcases of sheep that had died from disease, was common fare. New breeds were, however, introduced, Cheviots and Leicesters, but though Cheviots were the sheep of the Border country the black-faced were the favourites in the North, fortunately for the aspect of the country they adorned. The black-faced

rams with their great curling horns are always popular
with artists, and we know the tiny Shetland sheep from
their wonderfully soft wool that is so much used in
making shawls.

The breeds of cattle that made Scotland famous are
well known : the black polled Angus of Aberdeenshire,
the Galloways and Ayrshires in the south, and the
picturesque West Highlanders with their long horns
and shaggy coats. The Highland and Agricultural
Society and other local bodies did much to foster
stockbreeding during the century that is gone. They
also improved the breeding of horses such as the
famous Clydesdales, partly by giving premiums to the
owners of first-rate stallions and by paying for their
circulation through given districts for breeding purposes.

Scotland was not originally a milk-producing country,
but, with the growth of the industrial population round
Glasgow, Ayrshire became famous for its cheese and
butter-making last century, and with the establishment
of Agricultural Colleges and classes, methods changed
for the better. Scottish farmers or farmers' wives had a
good deal to learn as to the virtue of absolute cleanliness in cow byres and milkers : the latter virtue should
have been more easy to inculcate in Scotland than elsewhere since the milkers in Scotland are ordinarily
women ; but by the end of the century this lesson was
hardly learned.

Once the Scot learned how to cultivate the land, use
the recently discovered artificial manures, and also to

raise good stock (and new methods were hard of adoption by a very conservative race) farming went ahead, and in the nineteenth century farms in the Lothians and Ayrshire became models for England and elsewhere. Potato growing was taken up with zeal, and Scottish potatoes became famous and the growing of them lucrative : the country then took on a very different aspect from that which it had before the century began.

All this development took place at a time at which men all over Europe seemed to waken up to the need for practical things. It was influenced, no doubt, by the French Revolution, and yet it affected a world most adverse to revolutionary principles ; and it synchronized with an outburst of intellectual life and useful inventions. The results at first had their disastrous side no doubt ; there was machine-wrecking, as well as riots and misery caused by the new industrialism, which made a rural population a town population, and gave no facilities for making that town population happy and contented.

During the nineteenth century there was, of course, a constant effort made to introduce machinery in agricultural operations just as in industrial pursuits. It was a minister (the Rev. Patrick Bell) who first invented a fairly practical and workable reaper in 1827, and thereby gained the premium offered by the Highland and Agricultural Society. The fate of this really striking invention made by this farmer's son with the view of lightening the labours of his father's workers,

H

was the same as that of many such original inventions. It got little support at home, for probably
mechanism in agriculture was even less popular than in
other industries. The device was suggested by a pair
of garden shears which Bell happened to see and from
which he made a model machine of practical use.
Four of his machines went to America and they probably had some connection with the manual delivery
machine which preceded the self-delivery, and finally
the reaper and binder which became universally used.
It is thus to America that we owe this very useful
invention; but that is natural, since mechanical implements are almost essential when great tracts of land
have to be dealt with, and manual labour is scarce and
wages high. The impetus towards labour-saving
methods is much greater in America than in Great
Britain. There were many efforts made to produce
a satisfactory steam plough from 1837 onwards, but
the motor tractor and plough, driven by oil, have made
most progress; that, however, happened in the present
century. It is curious, however, that the horse swing-
plough invented in 1760 still holds its ground for
ploughing.

In old days most Scottish farmers had a 'dam' to
provide water power to drive the great wheel of the
threshing mill, or failing that, a mill driven more slowly
by horses circling round a 'horse-gang', as it is still
called. Later on the highly efficient, portable threshing
machine drawn and driven by traction engine came into
vogue for farms which had no threshing mill of their

own, the whole crop often being threshed in one day. The present century will probably see electrical power used everywhere, but that does not come within our province. It is not easy to move the farming world (whose knowledge is based on experience and greatly varying conditions which the onlooker is apt not to appreciate at its full value) to adopt new methods and new implements. The old ways have been tested by generations and are known and tried friends. But it is to the credit of Scottish lairds and farmers that they tackled the question of improving farming methods with vigour, despite special difficulties, and to a certain degree have conquered them.

Wheat, which was never the main 'corn' crop in Scotland, rose enormously in price during the French Wars, and though this was a temporary rise which ended in 1815 with the conclusion of the war, the twenty years of plenty not only encouraged the building of mansions and farm steadings, but also hastened the introduction of methods of tillage of land hitherto counted as derelict. Men could hardly be expected to realize that there would be a period of depression after the war in spite of corn laws, or that when that passed over it would be followed by the great depression of the later seventies or following the opening up of the rich prairie land of North America. The time of prosperity had caused rents to be nearly doubled, and the débacle was calamitous. The acreage cultivated had increased immensely, but in 1879 things were so bad that the Government appointed a Royal Commission to enquire into the causes of the agricultural distress, and as a result of the report of this Commission many benefits were granted to the tenants, such as compensation for improvements made by them on their farms. Indeed, from this time, a series of enactments was passed in the interests of the occupier. But all this did not stem the decrease in growth of corn and green crops which began after the bad years. The acreage of grass land alone increased, and stock raising took the place of arable farming to a great extent. Of course, as we know, corn growing and other cultivation was encouraged during the Great War, but the increase has not been permanent and consequently the labour required to be done on the land has decreased.

We may just mention certain of the subsidiary pursuits of the farming population, some of which, like poultry keeping, took a lowly place before they were properly understood or practised.

As to poultry, says a writer a hundred years ago, ' these unthrifty creatures should not be kept.' They no doubt furnish a delicacy which ' causes the judgment to be guided by the palate ' but they consume three times as much food as they produce. This is strange teaching for the present day when poultry-keeping has risen from its humble beginnings with the wandering mongrel hen to its culmination in the highly developed lady who so often helps to make up for the delinquencies of her prouder and larger neighbours in the farmyard. Even in the end of last century the virtues of poultry-keeping and the value of good trading were known and recognized. But in former times the farmer had to keep his 'kain hens' for his landlord, and the poor cottagers had to keep them for the farmer—a strange, illogical system for so profitless a crop. But of hens, often old favourites of the mistress, there must have been a certain supply: else how could Caleb Balderstone have bespoken the 'auld brood hen' that Mysie grudged so much when the Master of Ravenswood appeared with his guest!

On the other hand 'lords and lairds' had been directed to make deer parks, cunningaries (rabbit warrens) and dovecots (doocots or pigeon houses), but in King James VI's time no one was to build a dovecot who had not land around it of a certain value. The end of dovecot building was, Robert Somerville says, that 'if a poor man with a starving family found himself forced to take some of your thieving pigeons to preserve his life you may get him hanged,' or 'if he refuse to surrender you may shoot him.' The writer of this diatribe against the pigeons which in flocks destroyed people's property and might not be touched explains that he has no part in the ' cant of the modern philanthropists ' who think that theft should not be capitally punished : ' There would be no living in a country like this where trade exposes so much property continually to the covetous, if the gallows did not protect it.' But one feels from his bitterness that he had personally suffered, and hence he could evidently feel for the starving man who took the law into his own hands and also suffered for it. Pigeons, he says, came in flocks of over a thousand at a time upon a field of wheat ready for the sickle, and there is no wonder that he felt bitterly towards them or, respectable citizen that he was, almost distrusted the well-established laws of his country as they were in 1813 which prevented his having his desired revenge. Rabbits do not appear to have been the pest they later became until the ' Hares and Rabbits ' or Ground Game Act of 1880 was passed, giving the tenants the right to destroy them. But the writer just quoted advises that they should be kept absolutely out of any access to ' growing corn.' On the other hand, he thought that the improved tillage caused the number of bees kept to diminish and possibly to yield less honey. Possibly this was owing to the destruction of the wild flowers and weeds which gave them the source of their honey. Bee-keeping was usually popular when heather was near.

There is one thing that greatly improved the country a century ago, and this was that the land was drained to quite a large extent, and sodden soil useless or almost useless for agriculture was made fertile. The old, large drains were filled with common land stones (covered with straw, turf or something of the sort to keep the earth, until it settled, from falling in and stopping the drain) : sometimes thorns were used instead of stones. The clay drain pipes, such as we now know so well, were then introduced, and made an enormous difference to the state of the land. Early in the century when labour could be got for one and sixpence or two shillings a day a great deal of work was done in this direction. But what were known as the Government drains were too small and usually inserted too deeply in the ground, so that they often did not prove as effective as the old stone drains which are still to be found.

We must say something of the farm servants in rural Scotland. In the early part of last century those who lodged in the house received wages of about £10 to £14 sterling per annum, but the greater part of the work was done by married men living in cottages, and in the south, as in Northumberland, called hinds. The hinds were paid largely in kind but their yearly wages were about £25 in value. According to the writer quoted above these people held a high place proportionately to their fellows in other parts of the country. Nearly all could read and most write a little, and all got some education for their children.

As has often been done before and since, the same writer recommends payment to farm servants in kind, not money, in order to prevent extravagance or furnish temptations to dissipation. The 'lower classes' were apparently to be dealt with in a different way from their 'superiors,' and were supposed to have had temptations unknown to these latter ! By the new cottage system of giving land to the cottager and wages in kind it was stated that his labour was not interrupted, he had no rent to pay and so on ; the cottagers 'acquire such habits of saving that they lay up a few pounds for old age.' One would like to have heard the other side of the question ! Female servants in 1823 received £2 or £2 5s. in the half year, day labourers sixteen to twenty pence per diem. Probably such wages were considered good at the time and compared favourably with those of other workers of the same sort.

The regular working staff of a good-sized farm consisted of a grieve, a foreman ploughman, an ordinary ploughman for each pair of horses, a cattleman, a shepherd, and occasional men, women and boy labourers. The engagements were made at the six-monthly feeing markets, often the scene of much drunkenness; the married men 'feed' for twelve months and the unmarried for six months. There was a curious love of migration from farm to farm, even for married men, and as this involved a 'flitting,' often in shocking November weather, the damage to health and furniture was considerable. On the other hand expense was not involved since the carts were always supplied by the employers and the move gave a certain sense of adventure. At one time everything in the cottage was removed, even window frames and fireplaces, but this extraordinary and uneconomic custom died out.

Besides much paying in kind there was in the Border country nearly up to the seventies of last century a curious system of 'bondagers,' i.e. a householder on a farm without an 'outworker' in his own family undertook to have living with him a girl or boy who would work on the farm.[1] These bondagers were paid as 'outworkers,' and 'outworkers' were understood to be members of the household willing to do work on the farm; they might be male or female and were always

[1] *A Farmer's Fifty Years in Lauderdale*, by R. Sherra Gibb.

valued assets and were to be found all over southern agricultural Scotland. About 1880, when machinery was beginning to come into vogue on the farm, a farm servant's wages were about £20 a year in money, but he got free house, possibly coals, potatoes, oatmeal and various other ' gains ' so that the wage might be equivalent to £50 a year at least. A grieve or steward, of course, got more. Wages for ploughmen and cattle-men have risen to over thirty shillings a week with perquisites, but most things are dearer. Unlike the present time, wages in old days were paid six-monthly and there were no definite holidays excepting certain days established by custom, but just before the war wages rose and were paid monthly, perquisites became less and holidays became more definitely arranged. During the war, of course, a complete change was effected. There are now half-holidays nearly every Saturday.

In many parts of Scotland, though not in all, young ploughmen if unmarried live in ' bothies,' i.e. in a room or rooms set aside for them in the steading and not in the farmhouse itself. There they cook, etc., for themselves, but there is an arrangement with the plough-man's wife to wash for them, and they are supplied by the farmer with bedding, kitchen utensils, etc. The effect of this life has not been of the best. The cooking is bad and the mode of living is rough.

Nor, perhaps, has the effect of the advent of Irish workers, whose labour in harvesting grain and potatoes was so much valued, been to the good. These workers

were of a class content with the barest accommodation—
a barn to lie in sufficed—and before machinery came to
relieve labour the extra help was very useful. But
though decent people, their very satisfaction with
shockingly bad conditions tended to lower those
amongst whom they settled; for many of them did
settle, and took up their abode in the country of their
employment.

The agricultural worker had a natural desire to have
more control of his own life and to be a partner in the
industry which he often definitely loved, rather than
a wage-earner merely. His work, unlike the mechanical
work that industrial conditions often supply, was capable
of giving the feeling of fellowship in labour which he
desired, and under the best conditions he had it. His
womenkind are now finding something of what they
need through the Women's Rural Institutes that are
doing so splendid a work in giving value to women's
lives and showing how they count. There was little
done for the farm labourer during last century and his
life was a restricted and rather sordid one until he
married and had home interests to engross his attention.

The Highlands have always presented problems of
their own quite different from those of lowland regions.
In the lowlands there were certain Acts of Parliament
which aimed at enabling small holdings to be created,
so that a farm labourer might have the chance of becoming a tenant. But in the Highlands, though the
old clan system had in the eighteenth century passed
over peacefully enough to the landowner system, less

sympathy was shown. The landowners when sheep rearing became lucrative, considered that the small crofts on which a precarious livelihood was gained should be ousted in order to make room for sheep farms, and 'clearances' took place which caused a deep feeling of resentment. This will be dealt with later on.

CHAPTER VI

THE CHURCH OF THE PEOPLE

IF to the influence of Luther we may ascribe the general
Reformation, with its doctrine of Justification by Faith
and the break between the Romish and the Protestant
Churches, it is to Calvin that the Scottish Reformation is
due. There was in the Scottish break with Romanism
no effort after the compromise which was characteristic
of the Church of England as finally established. Calvin's
doctrine was like Luther's, that man's salvation was an
individual matter between man and God and that no
external authority could come between these two.
But it was also a doctrine of life in the world : Calvin
decreed the control and direction of the social life of
men and women : they were to live in the world the
sanctified life that only those first justified by Faith
could live. The Sanctification by the Spirit was the
necessary result of Justification by Faith, and this
meant a life of strenuous endeavour undertaken with
the help of God, and thus advancing His Kingdom ;
but works without Faith were valueless. Calvin's
doctrine was stern in spirit and heroic in action. There
was no alternative between being eternally saved and
eternally damned. We were predestinated and fore-
ordained by God, but that did not hinder us from

taking advantage of the mercy held out to us, and thus in a sense possessing Free Will.   That is to say Free-Will and Predestination were complementary to one another; one could not exist without the other, and the inspired Bible was an absolute guide in all difficulties. This seems a hard creed, but as far as the denial of Free Will is concerned it is difficult to controvert it as even materialistic philosophers have found, for no one can deny that every effect has its cause.   And if Calvinism is indeed the hard and unreasonable creed that some assert it to be, how, we ask with Froude, has it possessed such singular attractions in past times for some of the greatest men that ever lived ?

The Church had been the source of European culture throughout the Middle Ages, but the weakening of its power and the impulse to all sorts of activities in art and letters brought about by the Renaissance gave a challenge to a body hitherto supreme.   Calvin's system was a new and added challenge and it proved itself to be the influence which was to mould Scotland's life for centuries.

It is necessary to explain the nature of the creed in order to understand the hold that Calvinistic Presbyterianism, when finally established, had on the life and conduct of the people of Scotland.   Calvin had been trained in law and his doctrine was above all things legal and logical; and thus it appealed to the Scottish people and gave immense power to the clergy and other office-bearers who were appointed to carry out its teaching and discipline.   A logical, systematic view of life permeated the whole social outlook ; its influence on religion was profound, and the very language of religion became technically legal. The conviction that all the less important parts of human life were of little account as compared with those concerning the relationship of man to God, and to man's being justified in God's sight and redeemed through His Son, meant that the whole of life was to be lived in the constant realization of this fact. The human side, art and beauty, were only to be valued as holding a secondary place, and were never to be allowed to come between us and our God. Hence Churches should be plain, services simple and personal : adornment was to be set aside and singing, unless straight from the heart and in the words of the inspired Book, to be deprecated.

This makes it comprehensible how subsequent generations—even those who were forced to disclaim some of its extreme doctrines—were influenced by the teaching. If they broke from it they all did it with pain, for the religious tradition was born in their very bones. There was of course little room for scientific or political questioning of this belief. Every child learned it in the Catechism taught it from infancy along with its Biblical 'proofs.'

As the nineteenth century went on there were indeed various breaks with the old doctrine. The first 'Awakening,' it is true, was towards a closer adherence to the orthodox doctrines, and arose from dissatisfaction with the latitudinarian and 'moderate' doctrines then being preached. But in the middle of the century a new Evangelicism arose which derived its origin from England and later on from America. This concentrated on Salvation by Faith and was expounded as a Free Gospel which set aside old shibboleths. This, again, was succeeded by what is known as ' Modernism,' which, vigorously repelled as it was by the orthodox in the last quarter of the nineteenth century, has now a strong influence in the Presbyterian Church. Despite all these movements, however, real as they were, the old traditions hold a place, recognized or unrecognized, in the hearts of most patriotic Scotsmen.

.   .   .   .

Shortly before the nineteenth century dawned there were new fears and dreads in religious circles. After the Revolution had firmly established Protestantism, and the chances of a Stewart King who might have thrown the country into the arms of a Catholic France were blighted, there was perfect liberty to follow the Presbyterian religion which had been so unhesitatingly adopted. But not only were the ' Moderates,' so-called, preaching a doctrine far removed from the pure word of truth, but atheistical bodies and individuals were threatening from without, and the only safety for the church seemed to be strict adherence to the doctrines of the past. The eighteenth century was full of struggles against unorthodoxy, and secessions were made on various grounds, several concerning the taking of the civil oath. Meeting houses abounded, and the

Established Church lost much of the high position it had held, even though its buildings were still well filled and new galleries were being built in them. For all respectable people ' went to church.'

But the French Revolution, and the end of the Dundas administration brought with them many changes : men arose who said that the Church must be awakened out of her slumbers. Even Sunday schools began to be formed and missions to foreign lands discussed and carried out, though it was long before these advances took a real hold of the people. Then came the time when the great Whigs, Sydney Smith, Jeffrey, Brougham and Francis Horner, began to attack the citadel of Toryism. Patronage, i.e. the claims of 'patrons' of livings and great landlords to appoint the ministers without regarding the wishes of the parishioners, was attacked, and a battle began which was to rage for half a century. The ministers appointed were usually those who had been tutors in the families of their patrons, and the higher-minded ministers, like Dr. Carlyle of Inveresk, objected to this system which to them savoured of Erastianism. Lay preaching, such as that of the brothers Haldane (who gave up their naval careers and prospects to do this when their efforts to send a mission to India were frustrated), came into vogue in order to arouse the country from what they called its ' spiritual death ' and from ' damnable heresy.' The Established Church, however, followed its orthodox, unimaginative way till forced into life by those who seceded from it. Everything not of a conventionally religious sort was still condemned. The kirk session still exercised its disciplinary powers, and going to church was still considered a sign of grace which no respectable citizen could disregard, but the real religious life was outside in the various dissenting churches and meeting houses. Thus there were in the nineteenth century in Scotland two tendencies running alongside of one another—one of genuine religious feeling, participators in which truly valued the means of grace and endeavoured to live a life consistent with their profession, and another which regarded the ordinances of religion merely with a traditional respect. The Church had held a place of vantage in Scotland for so many years that it possessed a power which could not be displaced; but it was fortunately able to learn from its dissentients to face its difficulties and finally rise above them. It had, in old days, suffered persecution for its tenets, and they had become part of the very being of a man or woman of Scottish birth.

For long, indeed, there had been little else than religion to occupy the ordinary man's attention, when he concerned himself with matters beyond the present, or to act upon him as a civilizing power. Ordinary politics hardly affected him, and the British Parliament was so far away that its doings seemed remote ; but, of course, the tide of agitation for Reform soon took hold of at least a section of the population. Robert Burns proved the poetic interpreter of human experience and love of freedom as known to every Scot not entirely dominated by religious fervour ; and he showed how a

I

man without education, beyond that of the good literature which was open to every Scottish lad by the constant reading of the Bible, could express what existed
below the surface of smug morality and subjection to
ecclesiastical supervision. It was Burns who expressed
for men what they felt about their loves, their quarrels,
their backslidings of all sorts when dissociated from the
veneer that had been cast over them. He made the
life real which had been artificial; for of course the age
was one of artificiality in social life. It is rather interesting that despite his frequent coarseness of expression
and mockery of unreal religious forms, the Church has
had the understanding never to reject him. It would
have been dangerous to do so, but there was more in
the matter than that, and the Churchmen knew it.

There were customs in the Church that seem to us
strange and indeed archaic, but they held their place
because they had a meaning or a memory that the
people of Scotland loved to preserve and would have
been loth to part with. That is to say, they were to
them part and parcel of that clear and logical faith that
they adopted when they declared in their Confession
that there was no other end for being in the world but
the glorification of God and the joy of living in His
presence for ever. That was their philosophy as well
as their religion; and both were necessary to them.

Many of the old forms did in time pass away as they
had to do; the cutty stool for penitents, for instance,
did not survive long after the beginning of the century,
and public rebukes passed into the culprits being

'dealt with by the Kirk Session' in comparative privacy. The metal 'tokens' admitting to the Lord's Supper were by the end of the century seldom seen, and 'Fencing the Tables,' i.e. warning those who think of presenting themselves for Communion unworthily, became less formal, just as the observance of the Fast Days that played so large a part in the life of the early nineteenth century gradually dwindled when secular interests took the place of religious. The Fast Day, indeed, finally reduced itself into the prosaic but officially recognized Spring Holiday so far as the towns were concerned, though it can be seen as of yore in the remoter north and west as a day when business absolutely stops and the people really go to church not once but several times in the day.

One of the notable facts in church history is the beneficence of the people despite their poverty, and contrary to the character they usually receive. All those who have looked through the old records of Kirk Sessions or Presbytery are struck by the entries of small gifts to poor people outside the bounds of the area dealt with. Perhaps it may be a 'poor man from Morocco,' a 'slave escaped from the Turks,' or an 'object,' i.e. deformed person of some sort, and the sums given are minute because the coffers are minutely stocked. The will to help was there. When improvements had to be carried out in manses or other church buildings in remoter parts of the country and clerks of works could not be afforded, a simple mode of getting satisfactory work was to make the contractor take a solemn oath that it

Divisions and Re-unions in

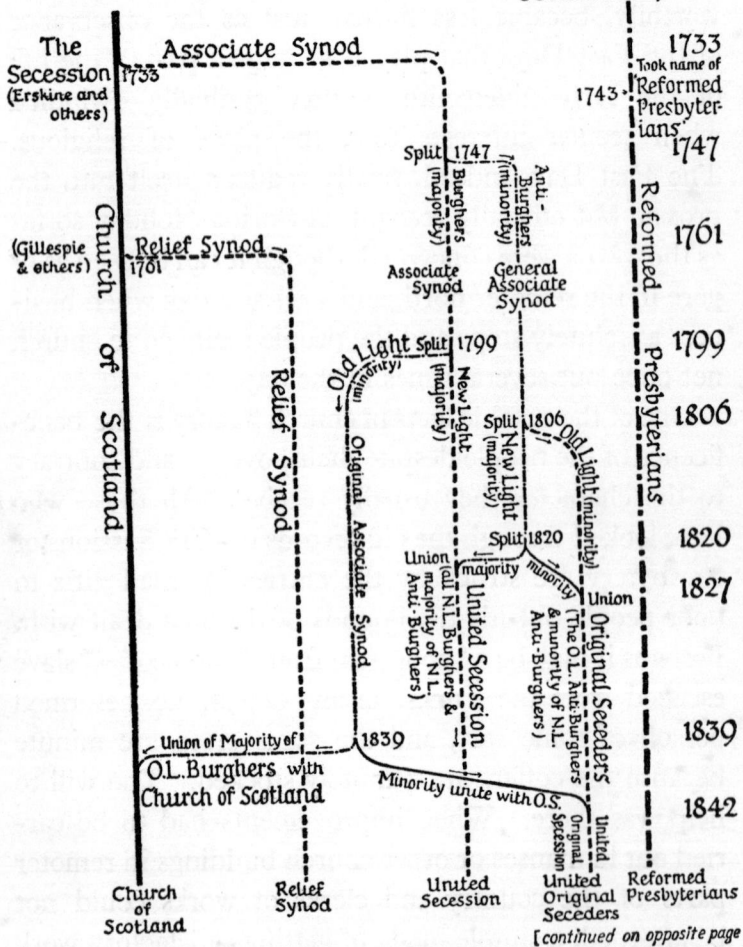

Church of Scotland
as established at the
"Revolution Settlement."

"Cameronians"
(who would not
accept the 1690
settlement.)

1690

The Secession 1733
(Erskine and others)

Associate Synod

1733

1743 · Took name of
Reformed
Presbyterians

1747

Split 1747

Burghers
(majority)

Anti-Burghers
(minority)

(Gillespie & others)

Relief Synod
1761

1761

Associate Synod

General Associate Synod

Church of Scotland

Relief Synod

Old Light Split
(minority)

1799

New Light
(majority)

1799

Reformed Presbyterians

Original Associate Synod

Split 1806

New Light
(majority)

Old Light (minority)

1806

Split 1820

majority

minority

1820

Union
(all N.L.Burghers &
majority of N.L.
Anti-Burghers)

United Secession

Union
(The O.L.Anti-Burghers
& minority of N.L.
Anti-Burghers)

Original Seceders

Union

1827

Union of Majority of
O.L.Burghers with
Church of Scotland

1839

Minority unite with O.S.

United
Original
Secession

1839

1842

Church of Scotland

Relief Synod

United Secession

United Original Seceders

Reformed Presbyterians

[continued on opposite page

This intricate Plan shows clearly the various Secessions

SCOTTISH PRESBYTERIANISM

continued from opposite page]

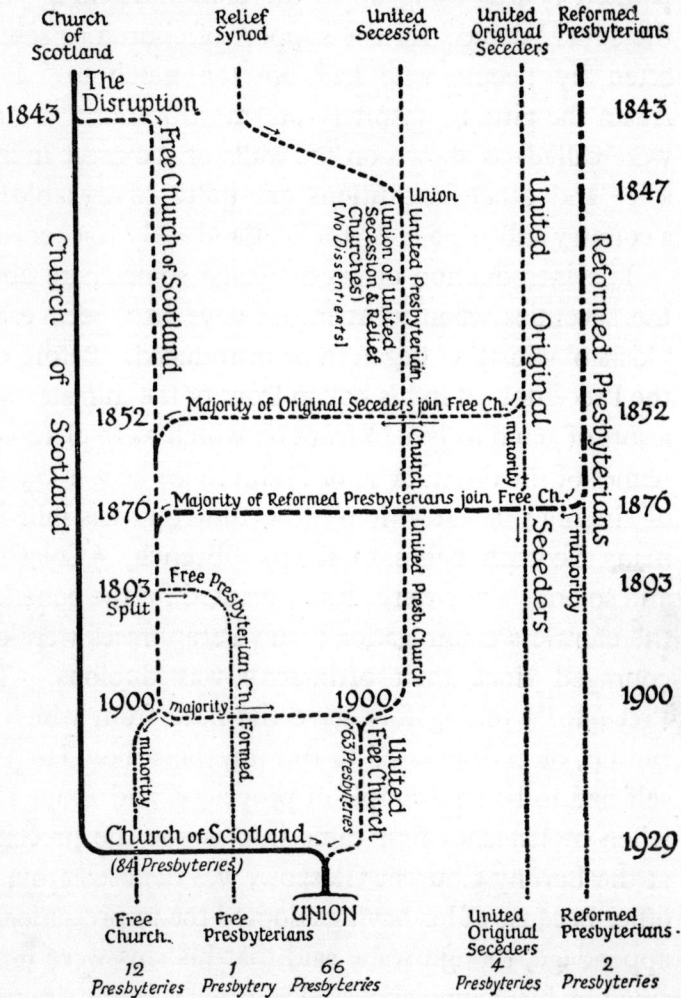

and Reunions of the Church of Scotland.

would be well and honestly done : this was apparently quite successful. All these things betoken an honourable spirit of helpfulness and consideration as do the painted boards hung up in the churches telling of all the sums ' doted ' for the support of church or school, often by people who had not too much to ' dote.' Again the gifts to hospitals (or ' mortifications ' as they were called) as shown on the walls of the great infirmaries and other institutions are quite remarkable for a country still as poor as was Scotland early last century.

The introduction of organs came somewhere about the seventies when what in old days had been called ' kists o' whistles ' began to be introduced. Before that the Precentor sat in his box in front of the minister with a sort of stand or lyre in front on which were placed the names of the dozen or so of Psalm tunes he was capable of singing ; ' Martyrdom ' (the tune that has lulled so many Scottish babes to sleep), ' French,' ' Coleshill ' and so on. They were clearly printed for the benefit of the choirless congregation ; and Paraphrases were discouraged since their orthodoxy was dubious. The Precentor's tuning fork gave the note from which he ran up, or endeavoured to run up, the scale. He himself had to be an example of propriety, and about 1838 when moustaches first came into vogue the precentor at the Barony Church, Glasgow, was deposed from his office because of his having adopted the unprecentorlike appendage, though some said that his sins were intensified by his having appeared as Francis in the drama of *Rob Roy* ! The holder of the office had also, of course, to observe an attentive demeanour, and it has been known that when the discourse was lengthy (as it usually was) and the church hot, he had to resort to having a piece of holly placed conveniently under his chin in order to keep him awake !

Reading the lines before singing them went out of fashion early in the century, though carried on in the remoter districts very much later. It seemed an unnecessary matter when all adults could read, but it had a curious impressiveness of its own when the reading was in a monotone. The prayers were long and tiring as the congregation stood to pray and sat to sing ; these customs survived to the end of the century only, and then mainly in the rural districts.

One of the first organs to be met with in a Scottish Presbyterian Church was placed in St. Andrew's, Glasgow, by Dr. William Ritchie in 1807. A small instrument was played for a Sunday or two in the church and then such a tumult arose that the whole city of Glasgow was in a ferment. The Presbytery and the citizens generally objected to the ' terrible innovation,' and the little ' chamber ' organ (reputed to have been built by James Watt) was cast out from the church. Treatises were written on the subject in which it was pointed out that musical instruments were not employed by the Christian Church under the new Dispensation, that they began to be used in times of Popish darkness and superstition, and that in proportion as ignorance and idolatry prevailed, the use of them increased. To use them would be ' contrary to the

Directory for the public worship of God which pro-
hibits all devising, using and anywise approving any
religious worship not instituted by God Himself.'[1] The
Lord Provost intimated that Dr. Ritchie would be
' responsible for the consequences of a breach of the
peace ' in case he used his organ. The Presbytery took
the matter up with heat and a committee appointed
by them reported that ' to avert so direful a calamity
from our Church—to crush in the bud so scandalous
a prostitution of sacred things, the Magistrates and
City Council and the Presbytery of Glasgow have
in this instance done their duty with integrity and
honour.'[2]

The unfortunate Dr. Ritchie had travelled in Germany and Holland, as tutor to Lord Kintore's son, and
had evidently imbibed advanced ideas, for there is a
rumour of an eagle as a reading-desk as well as the hated
organ which roused such commotion and which (it still
exists) is such a little one. He was glad to be ' trans-
lated ' to Edinburgh High Church and shortly afterwards he became a Professor of Theology there. A
picture shows him and his organ on the way to the
capital city blithely playing and whistling the old
song ' I'll gang nae mair to yon toon ' as he looks back
on the town of St. Mungo !

It was said that no one had realized ' to what a length
enthusiasm for music will carry its votaries,' and
Dr. Andrew Thomson realized this and deliberately

---

[1] *Treatise on the use of Organs*, by Rev. James Begg, 1808.
[2] *A Statement of the Proceedings of the Presbytery of Glasgow*, 1808.

CARTOON OF THE REV. DR. RITCHIE ESCAPING FROM
GLASGOW WITH HIS ORGAN ON HIS BACK

fled from Edinburgh on the occasion of a Musical Festival, knowing well that if in town he could not resist the temptation of going, and if he went it would give great offence even to his fashionable congregation of St. George's !

Lord Cockburn tells us that in 1845 an extraordinary occurrence had taken place in that an Independent Congregation in Edinburgh had given £200 for an organ which was to be set up in their Meeting House. Yet in 1860 many of the clergy ventured to attend an Oratorio without censure—so far had feeling changed by that time.

It seems strange on looking back that what appears to be so small a point as the manner in which a minister was to be appointed should cause a turmoil throughout the whole land. But the Church of Scotland has a democratic order which gives a living and personal interest in Church politics to every communicant and adherent, thereby distinguishing itself from most of the other great churches of Christendom. This interest settled largely on the choice of a minister whose place it was to express the views of the people in Assembly as well as act as their pastor at home. The people cared for their minister as a jealous parent cares for a child, criticized him, but defended him against outside attack. The minister, on the other hand, was on the whole attentive to his duties, visiting his flock assiduously and taking a real interest in their welfare. In early days there was even an annual examination of the parishioners, but this was given up in the middle of the nineteenth century though every pastoral visit concluded with a prayer. And the people responded in a remarkable degree to efforts made on their behalf. They used, for instance, at 'preaching' times to make spontaneous gifts of good things to replenish the minister's larder, and took a genuine pride in seeing that he lacked for nothing, thus keeping up the dignity of the parish which was regarded as a matter of great importance.

Now to have a minister 'intruded' on them by the patron of the living was quite contrary to their principles of liberty of worship, and after a dispute that had been simmering for a century things came to a head in 1843 when the so-called 'Disruption' took place and the great Dr. Chalmers left the Assembly at the head of a large body of ministers and elders, thus rending the church in twain and forming a new church named the Free Church of Scotland. The breach was not filled up until another century was reached and when the grievances had been removed.

The scene when the Disruption actually occurred must have been a remarkable one and it is graphically described by Lord Cockburn. He tells how the Moderator in his robes read his protest against the action of the civil court which constrained him and his brethren to abandon the Establishment, and then proceeded to walk away followed by 193 members, ministers and elders. They marched through a mass of cheering people to another Hall : ' No spectacle since the Revolution reminded one so forcibly of the Coven-

anters,' says Cockburn.   Every class had joined the
Free Church; it had been said that Presbyterianism
was not a religion for a gentleman, but in this case the
gentry had not been ashamed of Presbytery, 'not
ashamed of it even with the additional vulgarity of un-
endowed dissent.'   'Peers, baronets and knights joined
the Free Church.'   Some of these ministers (about 470
withdrew) sacrificed valuable livings (some of about
£1,000 a year) by their action.   'No one appears to
have been capable of witnessing their proceedings
without being softened and awed.'   At one stroke these
ministers lost the manses they had lived in, the high
position they held in the parish, the prospects of their
children : 'It is the most honourable fact for Scotland
that its whole history supplies.'

It was indeed a remarkable phenomenon and it
coloured Scottish life for a great part of the century.
It was, for one thing, an exemplification of how much
people cared about the Church and its polity, for there
was practically no one, rich or poor, who was not concerned in it one way or the other.   Curiously enough it
also opened the way for a new type of interest for a vast
number of people, women as well as men.   A new
Church, beginning without a penny (though it ended by
possessing millions) which had to set on foot not only
church buildings and ministers' stipends, but also day
schools and Sunday schools and every sort of mission,
and organize the ' schemes ' of the Church in duplicate,
meant a state of affairs quite unparalleled in Scotland.
Every human being set to work ; women's work at last

was valued and even children contributed their mites, and in one year half a million was collected. The result was that Scotland was over-churched as far as buildings were concerned (for there was no union meantime with other Secessions), but that was a small matter as compared with the zeal that was evolved. The zeal indeed was evolved all round, for the Establishment, which had early in the century fallen into easy ways, was incited to try to fill up the serious gaps made in its resources, since the richer people had mostly deserted it.

But the other side can not altogether be overlooked. There was a spirit of rivalry, and sometimes ill-feeling, that made Scottish life less wholesome where ecclesiastical matters counted. Unfortunately sites for churches had been refused by lairds, and schoolmasters had been deposed, thus causing bitterness of feeling. The two great Assemblies met simultaneously; there was no unpleasantness; all were outwardly friendly—but there was a difference.

Some of the old functions, too, were shorn of their glory now that the people were divided. In the Royal Burghs the magistrates used to go to church officially once a year in all their pomp, and now being many of them dissenters they did not care to do so. The same was the case with the Judges of the Court of Session and Exchequer who used to attend the High Church in all their splendour. Fox Maule could not be installed as Rector of Glasgow University because he was a Free Churchman.

The Established Church was in a curious pass, be-

cause it had been decided by Parliament that the congregation's dislike of a presentee was to be disregarded
unless it was justified by what the Presbytery might
regard as good reasons. Hence the congregation, if
they did not desire to have the official presentee as their
minister, charged him with extraordinary defects such
as ' occasional exuberance of animal spirits,' being
' destitute of a musical ear,' ' an unnatural conformation of one of his feet ' and, of course, bad doctrine,
deadness of prayer and general odiousness. Some of
the ladies said in their remonstrance (for women members had equal status with men) : ' We weep in secret
at the prospect of being forced to leave this sacred edifice in which we and our fathers have worshipped . . .
yea her very dust to us is dear.' And they were probably
right. ' The club feet and unmusical ears,' as Lord
Cockburn says, ' were only resorted to in aid of the
great and true objection, that after trying the presentee
they found him evangelically dead.' His services were
' wersh '—distasteful to all who liked salt.

On the other hand it did not seem as if the Free
Church, which had just obtained its emancipation, was
disposed to give complete liberty to others. As regards
Tests, for example, the Free Assembly of 1845 would
only recommend their abolition so far as those holding
their own evangelical Christian faith were concerned,
thereby excluding Unitarians, Jews and Catholics ;
of course they were against the Maynooth grant. The
dawn of liberality in the House of Commons alarmed
both the Scottish Churches and undoubtedly the spirit

of the Church as a whole was intolerant, more intolerant than was Parliament. Thus tests were finally abolished by Parliament in 1853 against the desire of the Commission of the General Assembly. But the munificence of the new Church was immense. It not only supplied its own needs but gave £15,000 to help the Highlands in the time of famine. The Church had also much to do with the establishment of most useful Ragged Schools (started by a minister named Dr. Guthrie) for the very poor.

The difference in doctrine between Free Church and Established appeared to the outsider hardly worth the sacrifices made for it. But the new Free Church seemed to attract the ablest of the theological students who in their turn became able ministers and professors like Campbell Fraser, Robertson Smith, George Adam Smith and many more.

In the Highlands the question of Patronage was also keenly disputed, for it is recorded that there was an unpopular presentation by the Duke of Sutherland to a living at Assynt and when the Presbytery met to ' settle ' the presentee (a worthy man), the highlanders, who wished to have their own candidate appointed, descended upon them armed with clubs and cudgels and forced them all to return. However, the rioters were recognized, summoned before the Justiciary courts at Inverness, and duly sentenced to imprisonment.

As the century wore on secular interests arose, the electorate extended, and politics, which had been repressed and could only reveal itself in demonstrations such as those of the Radical War of 1818 or the agitation before the Reform Bill of 1832, could now express itself as it wished and advocate the secular reforms it demanded.   And in one sense the Church was less prominent for that reason. But the effect of religious teaching remained even after its forms altered.   Those who no longer could support the old faith in its original form differed with sorrow in their hearts, and such was its influence that they never ceased to feel its existence in their lives and conversation.   Truly the Scottish religion with all its faults proved itself a religion worthy of its founders.   The pity is that while it was so deeply engaged with its own tenets it left the secular side of organized life to follow its own course and thus brought upon itself its own retribution.   It was not the religion that was at fault, but the manner in which it was presented.

Those who separated from the Church from time to time were men such as Campbell of Row, whose heresy in 1831 was to support the Universal Love of God and the possibility of Salvation for all men.   The question of eternal punishment was again a problem which caused a United Presbyterian minister to be excluded. Later on, in 1881, Robertson Smith was deprived of his professorial chair on account of his studies on the Old Testament history.   This narrow outlook did infinite harm to the Church.

Early in the century the parish ministers certainly were not always what they ought to have been.   Their characters improved in spirituality as ' Moderatism ' passed. There were, of course, drinking parsons, especially in the Highlands where everyone drank. Mr. Sage, a Highland minister, tells of a neighbouring parson who volunteered a trial of skill with an English gentleman who had ventured to taunt the Scottish lairds for their slender attainments in the ' manly science of drinking.' The Englishman called for tumblers but Parson Rory called for a bottle of port wine which at a single draught he emptied into his stomach and was never the worse for it !

Things altered for the better as the more evangelical section of the Church came into power. But the parish minister, on the other hand, sometimes had a difficult time with his heritors or landowners. The stipend was often given with a grudge and there were many delays for which ill-grounded excuses were supplied, and vexatious disputes occurred in order to obtain the money which would allow lawful debts to be paid. Those who joined the Free Church in 1843 gave up much but gained in kindliness of treatment, though every penny given came from voluntary contributions.

The other strong body in Scotland called the ' United Presbyterians ' (usually known as the U.P.'s) was composed of a union of two early secessions from the Church of Scotland. In 1900 they united with the Free Church which thus assumed the name of the United Free Church of Scotland. This prepared the way for the great re-union of 1929 when the U.F. Church united with the Established Church, thus bringing into one the three great branches of the Church in Scotland. There are a few irreconcilables, i.e. the so-called ' Wee Frees '

EARLY CURLING STONES

OLD STREET OIL-LAMP
FORMERLY USED IN STIRLING

TIRLING-PIN
THE EARLY SCOTTISH FORM
OF DOOR-KNOCKER

HOUR-GLASS
USED IN GLASGOW CATHEDRAL
TO TIME SERMONS

OLD KIRK-LADLE FOR COLLECTING OFFERTORIES

who had disapproved of the 1900 Union and the 'Continuing Church' who objected to the 1929 Union, but they represent a small and decreasing body of opinion.

The original Secessionists were strict and very conventional for, in 1849, a resolution was passed prohibiting the probationers or ministers from *reading* their discourses in the pulpit unless the Presbytery had granted them permission to do so. The idea was that the words must come spontaneously and from the heart and not from deliberate forethought, and it was considered a sign of lukewarm-ness to 'use paper' so that the ministers who did so were careful to disguise the fact. This proved, however, a terrible trial to some of the young ministers who struggled vainly to 'commit' their sermons. Some concealed their notes in the Bible and surreptitiously looked at them. Others spent days on the hills repeating them. The difficulty was enhanced by the number of heads required in the long discourse and the fact that for evangelical preachers the 'Plan' (i.e. the Plan of Salvation) must always be included in the sermon.

It was seldom that any of the seceding ministers' stipends were grudged them, even though the congregations might be poor. The minute emoluments that are often found in England would not have been tolerated. All denominations, however, expected their minister to maintain his position in dress even when taking rural walks. A seceding minister has been severely reproved for taking off his coat in walking on the hills and again for playing on the violin. All this

K

was altered as the century went on and in the eighties even a grey 'pepper and salt' was permitted on occasion; and sometimes even Seceding ministers were also permitted to play on musical instruments on week-days. No charges were made for burials or marriages as in England, but presents of one kind or another, even if but a pair of gloves, were often offered by those who could afford to do so.

In the Highlands the older Secessions had not taken effect in the eighteenth century and the Established Church in 1843 was in full possession till the Free Church largely supplanted it. It was dominated by the 'Moderate' section. Mr. Sage says that when he was inducted to Resolis in 1824 there was no roll of communicants; and thus, of course, the roll had not been 'purged,' which is the expression used in Scotland for its verification. Though there was indeed an annual Sacrament, few attended and those who did were given the 'tokens' without enquiry; there were no elders and no list of the poor.

In the Highlands in old days no assessments were made for the poor, but for their benefit 'ladles' were handed round by the elders and a charge was made for the use of the 'mort-cloth' or pall at funerals. Small donations were also given to every kirk session in the county by the successful candidate at a Parliamentary election, which made a welcome addition to the funds. In addition to all this there were fines imposed on account of immorality on those delinquents who could pay instead of standing public rebuke, and this was a

common matter in the eighteenth century. The whole
receipts might amount only to £40 and had to cover the
expenses of coffins for the poor, communion tables for
out-of-door services, etc., as well as actual gifts to the
poor. The records show how pitifully small the grants
given were.

The cases tried by the kirk session were not only for
immorality so-called ; they included those of defama-
tion of character, though this hardly came within
ecclesiastical jurisdiction except as it pertained to communicants who might have to be struck off the roll
were the accusations proved. Then in Scotland, as all
readers of Scott know, poor people may be put on the
roll of pauper litigants and carry on their cases free of
charge. But first of all the kirk session of his parish must
certify (1) that the litigant is poor and unable to pay law
expenses, (2) that his moral character was irreproach-
able, and (3) that he was not known to be a litigious
person. These assurances must have been difficult to
supply in the case of Peter Peebles !

Then the Church had to see to the school and schoolmaster. Mr. Sage found a school in disrepair and a
schoolmaster verging on decrepitude who would not
retire. A new school had to be built with a garden for
the schoolmaster. This took three years to carry out,
with the help of an Education Society, and it cost
£48 13s. 1½d.

The journey to the annual Assembly of the Church in
Edinburgh was a long and difficult one for Highland
ministers to face and they seldom undertook it. But

the great gathering then held in St. Giles' Cathedral, with the throne on one side on which sat the Lord High Commissioner in his robes, surrounded by his pages, made a deep impression on country ministers. After all it stood to them for the Parliament of the nation as well as of the Church, for the English Parliament was foreign and remote and the Scottish Parliament of a century and a half ago was comparatively insignificant. About 1820 the Lord High Commissioner held a levée in the Merchants' Hall and from there walked with his two handsome pages and some dignitaries of the city to St. Giles' Church where he was received by the Lord Provost and Magistrates in their official robes. The streets were lined with detachments of cavalry and infantry. Hospitality was always dispensed at Holyrood House and there was great interest in seeing the Commissioner's Dinner Table, for which a small charge (twopence) was made. About 122 were entertained. The first of the season's green peas then appeared and early chickens were sent in from the country. Later, though the public dinner was abolished, the Commissioner drove with his coach and six horses to St. Giles' to the great admiration of the populace.

As regards the observance of the Sunday, there were several things absolutely forbidden by the Church, such as bathing or swimming, watering a garden, riding (unless to Church) and all games and travelling. For a long time the Highlanders were not as strict in their Sabbatarianism as the Lowlanders, owing, perhaps, to the fact that Episcopalianism and Roman Catholicism held their ground in many parts of the country. But when the new movement made its way north, none were stricter than they. Even in the south it was a common practice to pull down the window blinds on Sunday, and certainly all walking was forbidden, above all in church hours. A curious point was that if work had to be done the usual implements must not be used, however much they facilitated the operation. Thus potatoes, if they had to be got out of the ground, must be scraped up with the fingers, no wheelbarrow could be made use of to bring the turnips to the cattle, no water carried in on Sunday, and the writer has found a button which had come off a glove to be worn at church fastened on intricately with wire to obviate having to use a needle! Letter writing must be delayed till twelve o'clock struck, as of course must shaving! The result was a restfulness that many busy housewives say they envy.

A story is told of Dr. Buckland, the scientist, who when he went out one Sunday with his slim hammer in hand was accosted by a woman who asked him what he was doing. 'Only breaking a stone,' he said. 'Na, na,' she replied, 'you're doin' waur than that, you're breakin' the Sawbath.'

Until the seventies there was a half-yearly celebration of the Sacrament, and this included a Fast Day, services on two or three week-days and a long 'diet' on Sunday; the period was appropriately known as 'The Preachings.' Travellers still remember their dismay on arriving at a city on a Fast Day to find it a city

of the dead, no shops open and no business or amusements possible.

There were, of course, some social distractions in
the Church. A favourite entertainment in religious
circles was the fruit soirée, pronounced serrēe, which
was held at a missionary or other church function and
at which bags of buns were distributed, followed by a
'service of fruit.' The speeches were of the amusing
kind and there were gifted ministers who could tell
stories well and make these entertainments enjoyable if
not specially edifying. But these and similar functions
were of late development and incidental. The main
matter in all Scottish churches was the sermon, and a
minister who was 'on his trial' was always judged by
his preaching. His sermon had to be logically built up
and divided into suitable heads leading to a conclusion.
The length was never under half-an-hour but usually
much longer, and in winter the two 'diets of worship'
were run into one so that there was a second sermon
preached after a psalm had been sung to betoken the
end of the first, and perhaps an interval in which to
take a 'piece' or bannock. The snuff mull, handed
round, was useful in keeping the male members of the
congregation awake on a hot summer's day.

By the end of the century great changes had been
made. The old doctrines were seldom preached in their
original form; modern views had been introduced and
modern ways adopted. But these seem to belong more
to the twentieth century than to the nineteenth though
they arose long before the last century ended.

CHAPTER VII

THE EDUCATION OF THE PEOPLE

EDUCATION has taken a place in Scotland hardly inferior to that in any of the countries of Europe, though some of the northern nations run it very close. It may be that it was not specially distinguished on the technical side ; it was lacking in technical efficiency in the old days because of the lamentable poverty of the people, and when this poverty in a measure disappeared, it took a line which was one-sided and somewhat academic. But there was always a real passion in it—a passion which came very near the passion for religion, and which had much in common with religion.

As has almost invariably been the case, at least until the Soviet Government arose, religion and education were associated from the beginning, and at first were scarcely distinguishable. If we go back to the days of Knox and the Resolutions passed between the years 1633 and 1696 to have a school in every parish—knowing well that this was impossible of realization—we are aware that those who promulgated this decision meant not alone a parish seat of learning, but a centre from which should emanate the teaching of a good church-man in the sound doctrines of the faith, for these were considered essential to good education. It seems hard that Knox and his colleagues never saw the realization of their dreams and that the nobles who never played any but a poor part in Scottish history were not impressed by them or moved to action.

The scheme of John Knox and the reformers was admirable in theory. Their idea was to have an elementary course for children up to the age of eight ; next a grammar school taking pupils to the age of twelve ; a college or higher grammar school to the age of sixteen ; and finally a University course to be completed about the age of twenty-four when the learner had to be removed to ' serve the Church or Commonwealth.' All classes were to be compelled to attend school, rich and poor, the former at their own expense, the latter at the charges of the Church. The whole organization sounds marvellously modern, for no father was to be permitted to ' use his children at his awin fantasie ' and the masters were to have ' honest stipendes ' and even stupid children were not to be let off too easily but were charged to continue their work so that the ' Commonwealth may have some comfort by them.'

Naturally this scheme was not original ; it was partly borrowed from foreign sources, but clearly it was impracticable in the state of the country at the time. It was also ecclesiastical and mediaeval ; but though it was only a vision of what might be, it influenced the educational ideals of the Scottish nation for the centuries to come. That is to say it remained an idea firmly imbedded in its nature that Scotland ought to have a national system of graded education with free teaching for poor and clever pupils, and above all that there should be no distinction of class, the only aristocracy being that of intellect. This was a momentous decision to make.

Throughout the troublous seventeenth century Church supervision of schools of one sort or other continued until the Presbyterian Church of Scotland became paramount in 1690. It was not till a century afterwards that there came to be an effort to get the control of the schools transferred from the Church to the State. In a measure, however, the Church retained its hold until the Education Act of 1872 when the superintendence of schools was committed to popularly elected school boards which might teach religion or not, but if they did so, the teaching was subject to a conscience clause.

It was not that secular education was considered inferior to religious ; but the two were so bound up that it was impossible to separate them ; hence education from the first had a theological bias such as curiously enough it has never lost. Not that there is, for instance, more religious teaching in the elementary schools of Scotland than in England, but the teaching that is given is more thorough : the catechism is a profound theological treatise, and though the instruction in it is now not always given in day schools and that in the Bible is not compulsory, the latter at least is infrequently objected to and the catechism is taught elsewhere. There are, of course Catholic rate-supported schools for the education of Catholic children, but none where there is no opportunity of having religious instruction if desired. There is another way in which religion has impressed itself upon education and has added to the national bias. For many generations the great aspiration of a Scottish parent of the working-classes—of a mother in particular—was to have bestowed upon her one clever son who might hope to enter the ministry. No sacrifice was too great to accomplish this great task. The result has been that education in the nineteenth century took on its academic tendency—both because the individual parents had the desire for it, and because the feeling of the country and those in authority went that way. There was always the sense that a less academic form of education was of a lower grade so that to give it would be to place the boy in a different social standard, and hence only the stupid boys were as a rule passed into the ' Modern Side.' Latin for a boy of parts was regarded in the last century as an essential if he was to take his place in the world as equal with, or better than, his competitors of a different rank or country ; it had been absolutely essential for the wandering scholar of former ages who found himself, with Latin, at home in a foreign University and able to converse with his teachers and fellow students, and hence in those days it was spoken as a matter of course. Then Philosophy was the study which was to give him a wide outlook on life ; it was the study most Scotsmen yearned after in one form or another. The scope was so large that it was divided into Metaphysics and Logic, Moral Philosophy and Natural Philosophy, the last being the least essential and ranking with Mathematics. In addition to these there was not much else for the ordinary man to learn. It is true that later on the Literature of his country was found to be a worthy subject of study, and doubtless such matters as modern languages and Geology and Botany came to be optional subjects of study in Universities. Mathematics, too, was of course studied, but if a young man had no disposition for this form of learning he was allowed to escape easily from the clutches of the examiner.

It will perhaps be best to say something of what the ordinary village school was like before passing on to the higher education of Scottish lads. The parish school was after all the basis on which all else was built, and it gave the poorest peasant the chance of a high career and was able to carry him on into the Universities which in early days demanded no entrance examination. The result was that the number of students who reached their portals was nearly six times what it was in England. Characteristically, there was always an objection to receive Government grants which applied to ' schools for the poor.' Such grants would, it was said, be against the tradition of Scottish education and reduce it ' to the uniformity of English elementary schools.' They would also tend to make a distinction of class wholly opposed to Scottish tradition.

But, important as was the school, it was usually housed in what we should call a hovel, low-roofed and ill-ventilated and miserably poor. In the eighteenth and nineteenth centuries trade was expanding along with the rapidly increasing population; but as the purchasing power of money decreased the unfortunate schoolmaster was given no increase of stipend. The General Assembly brought the matter before the Lord High Commissioner, but the landed proprietors, always an obstacle in those days, were adverse, and the Ministry paid no attention. Consequently the schoolmaster received but a pittance, eked out by odd perquisites from the children, such as peats for the fire and cockfight dues. There was also the Candlemas offering on February 2nd, when every boy was expected to bring a gift ranging from sixpence to a crown, and when he expected a holiday in return. This went on to the middle of last century. Hugh Miller in *My Schools and Schoolmasters* gives a vivid account of his schooldays in Cromarty, of the yearly cockfights which left the floor stained with blood, and of the way the boys claimed their school due of twenty peats from every boat that crossed the Firth, armed with pebbles and other missiles. The teacher was a ' stickit minister ' and the school a straw-thatched cottage with a floor of mud.

The marvellous thing is that through all these discouraging conditions the schools were valued and respected, and people struggled to get their children educated. When the nineteenth century came in, an Act was passed which increased the schoolmaster's salary and required a two-roomed house for him to live in; and Lord Cockburn in his *Memoirs* relates that most of the lairds and Scottish members were indignant at being obliged ' to erect palaces for dominies'! Unfortunate dominies! their lives were hard, though not perhaps really unhappy.

The poor little village school had, however, its use as an educational centre for all classes of the people. The feudal tradition brought with it a certain Scottish respect for birth and family that seems to the Southron absurd, and which yet was devoid of the subservience that so often obtains between one class and another; there was in any case no snobbery of wealth. It is interesting to read in the accounts of family life among the Grants of Rothiemurchus how they deplored the results of sending their boys to Eton and ' losing them to the family'; and again how the Mackenzies of Gairloch rejoiced in escaping the fate of being sent to a Public School and thought they were better men in consequence. What both valued was the freedom of speech derived from common meeting in learning or games. Lairds' sons and workers' sons met on equal ground; for if the laird's son did not actually attend the school, he met the other boys in games and very likely had the dominie as his instructor.

It is extraordinary that in Scotland, just as in England, the school buildings were so long in a condition of squalor. Even in the latter part of last century there were in the towns and bigger villages a number of schools; for besides the parish school there were still numerous ' venture ' schools living on the children's fees, aided perhaps by small endowments. There was often but a single room in which several classes were held; the floors were dirty, the sanitary arrangements almost non-existent, air was vitiated, as a Report made in the eighties on the air in schools clearly shows. There were a few old maps on the wall, a blackboard, and many slates used (in primitive fashion) by the children for their sums. The tawse (a leather strap cut into tails) was always on the master's and mistress's desks, even when the age of the children did not exceed six or seven; it was the one 'equipment' that never was forgotten, and was faithfully made use of for boys and girls alike. There were no organized games and there was constant truancy, well punished when discovered. There was nothing attractive in the externals, and children suffered from many ailments which were undiscovered. Yet they were not necessarily unhappy, though they endured many things they ought not to have done.

By the passing of the Education Act of 1872 the pall of examinations fell upon the schools. In those days little children were individually examined and 'passed' or rejected for promotion; and the inspector was a dread ogre descending on the school, against whose appearances pupils and teachers alike quailed, praying for good temper and good weather. How the teacher must have longed for the good old days of freedom! Ever since, the authorities have been trying to remove the pall and make the inspector the helpful visitor and adviser he now is. Individual examination of pupils and payment by results were mercifully removed in 1890. But the system more or less remained as long as external examinations were demanded by the powers that be, even though 'record' came to be taken into account. Efforts were certainly being made to allow of more freedom, but the old idea of education that made it of the grammar school type continued to reign. That is to say, the traditional kind of education still continued to find favour for many pupils whose needs and capacities would have been better suited by alternative courses of a non-academic type.

In Scotland secondary education did not develop in the same ways as it did in England, and there was no sharp division between it and elementary education. There were, of course, High Schools or Burgh Schools in the larger towns, but many lads who could not go to these schools, which were practically restricted to those actually residing in the burgh bounds, managed, through enterprising schoolmasters, to prepare themselves for College. After all, the College (for the word University was not much used) had standards hardly higher than those of a secondary school. In early days it certainly was so, and the professors had hard work to impart the elements of classics to many of their students, for parish schoolmasters were by no means all efficient teachers ; and even until the end of last century the first-year students were doing the work of boys, and boys indeed they were. Later on the junior class was given up, since secondary schools undertook the work. A century ago (1833) lads went to College as young as fourteen, and even sixty years ago sixteen was still an ordinary age to commence University studies. These young boys took four years to complete their courses in Arts; but if a previous examination had been passed, this period might be shortened to three years. This went on till about 1888, when the system of connecting schools with Universities came into vogue, and a School Leaving Certificate was instituted which led naturally from school to college. Those outside the school had to pass a corresponding University examination.

The Burgh or Grammar Schools were under the management of the Town Councils, and once a year the keys of the school were formally handed over to the Town Council by the schoolmaster, as a symbol of their rights. The children of all burgesses attended the school, to whatever social scale they might belong. Lord Brougham said that of his classmates one was a nobleman and others the sons of shopkeepers in the lowest parts of the town, and all sat together without any idea of difference. Greek was not usually taught, but in the beginning of the nineteenth century Dr. Adams introduced its teaching to the High School of Edinburgh after it had dropped out for a century or more. This, however, was considered to be an encroachment on the work of the University. Of course Latin was the main subject of study (except in the smaller burghs, where English was taught), and in most cases girls were taught along with boys. As the nineteenth century advanced the 'inferior' branches began to make their way, and gradually English literature, history and geography, and then mathematics, came into the

Valentine

EDINBURGH UNIVERSITY, THE OLD QUADRANGLE

curriculum, and special masters were appointed to teach them.

By the side of the Burgh Schools, proprietary schools arose with a more liberal curriculum ; they usually included science in their teaching, and possibly commercial subjects of a kind ; they were called Academies. The Town Council sometimes helped to establish these institutions. Perth Academy was the first to introduce science into its curriculum, and it did this in the eighteenth century ; its example was soon followed by others.   There were also great Hospitals for boarding and educating poorer children, such as that endowed by Heriot, the ' Jingling Geordie ' of *The Fortunes of Nigel*. These were in the latter part of the century altered in character, and made available for secondary education generally.

The Disruption of 1843 led to Free Church schools being established, and a great increase in school accommodation resulted, which, as the supply of buildings was far too small, was useful. But even with 626 newly-established schools (as well as special Training Colleges for the teachers in the lately formed Church) matters were not satisfactory. The schools were many of them very poor, and despite all efforts about 90,000 children, mainly in the populous districts, attended no school at all, as the Commission of 1867 reported. The remedy was found in the Act of 1872, which mapped out the country into 984 districts with School Boards, and made education compulsory up to thirteen years of age ; and in 1891 elementary education was made free for all

L

children between five and fourteen years of age. The later Act of 1918 made other changes nearly as great, but this goes beyond our period.

We must remember that it was only after 1839 that education in Scotland was helped by the Government at all, and though the Act of 1872 put matters on a new footing it was not until 1885 that the Scotch Education Department came to have an independent existence. Control had long seemed to the Scots to proceed from London, and this feeling existed to the end of the century, despite the changes that were made. Rightly or wrongly the people of Scotland felt that they had not the power of developing their education on their own historic lines.

There has always been a good tradition of ability among the Scottish teachers. Parochial teachers before the Act of 1872 had a reputation for scholarship, and most of them had received a University education. This was true of the old parish schoolmasters; but it was hardly true of those employed to teach the children in the numerous congested centres of population in the time of industrial activity. The sad condition of these poorer children caused Sunday Schools, once discouraged by the Church, to be established. Then came further development on voluntary lines for improving methods of instruction and for giving training during the week, until an organization arose called the 'Glasgow Education Society' which formed in 1834 a 'Normal Seminary' for the training of teachers. This proved the beginning of the system of Training Colleges in Scotland. Out of it grew the pupil teacher system whereby promising boys and girls were apprenticed for five years for learning their work and receiving instructions; after which they competed for scholarships to a 'Normal School' as Queen's Scholars. This system, though it seemed a dubious one, was liked by many teachers; it was finally abolished, and after 1873 Normal students were allowed to attend the University classes. Of late years the system has been wholly changed and all men teachers have to be graduates, and many women teachers are graduates also.

The Universities (Scotland) Act of 1858 made many important changes in their administration. After this time the system of graduation in three years for those who had passed a preliminary examination was established, and an all-round educational scheme was devised in which Classics, Philosophy, Mathematics and Natural Science were the essential parts. Honours could be obtained in any of these subjects. A further Act of 1889 remodelled the constitution of the Universities and made provision for the instruction of women. Women were admitted to graduation courses in 1897, and now they form nearly a third of the student body. All the Faculties were opened to them. The financial side of Scottish Universities has been a difficulty, since they do not enjoy the endowments possessed by the old English Universities, and two million pounds given by Mr. Carnegie in 1901 was not an endowment but a Trust for paying the fees of qualified students who made application for them, and for improving the means of advanced study and research.

The remarkable thing about Scottish Universities was the large part they played in national life. They were cheap and numerously attended, but there was little individual instruction, and students could take their degrees simply by attending lectures and giving satisfaction in examinations; for the lack of endowments, like those of Oxford and Cambridge, makes it impossible to support a satisfactory tutorial system. The social side was also lacking, though in the twentieth century efforts are being made to provide for this, through residential halls, gymnasia and playing fields. Last century there were few students who played outside games, fewer still who thought they had time to play them.

The Universities have certainly dominated education generally from the primary school upwards. The young people of Scotland have always been urged by their teachers to turn their attention to professional careers, and the consequence was that the Universities were crowded with students aiming at and succeeding in taking a degree, many of whom might possibly have done better work had their energies been directed elsewhere. The Universities have no doubt benefited pecuniarily from their many students, but while students increased enormously, the teaching staff did not increase in the same degree. Glasgow has not one half the number of teachers that Cambridge has, yet she has 5000 students—that is, more students than Oxford, and

only a few hundred less than Cambridge. Edinburgh
has nearly 4000 students. The Scottish University
classes are enormous, especially the classes known as
cultural.

One is forced to consider the present position of
things since it is the outcome of the ideals and methods
of the past, which had certain faults, despite many
virtues. After all, University life had little to offer if
it confined itself to attendance at lectures and did not
concern itself with bringing the student into personal
relation with men of wider knowledge and outlook, and
if it did not allow of young men and women meeting
in Societies and Unions to learn the lessons that can
only be learned of one another. If students come to a
University town from another town or a far-off suburb,
attend their lectures and return as speedily as may be,
there is little education in the process. Such a life is
inferior to the old traditions of University life, simple
as they were. The problem is one which must be met
if the country is to keep up the high standard which it
has had in the past, and which is and has been of such
importance to it. A century ago the two great English
Universities were very different from what they now
are ; the standard of learning and discipline amongst
the undergraduates was not high, and the teaching was
at a low ebb ; while the young Scots were all serious
students, since their future depended on their work.
It would be disastrous were the Scottish students to
lose the high place that they then held.

The drawback to the old University education which

aimed at concentrating on ' the Humanities,' as its studies were truly enough called, was that account was not taken of the fact that the individual is a living being whose life brings him into touch with every kind and sort of person and circumstance; and hence it tended to become abstract and pedantic. This point of view also served to prevent proper recognition of the education of the adult if such education were conducted on non-academic lines. It seemed as if adult education which neither came under a ' Code ' nor belonged to a University was of no account. During the present century there has been an advance in regard to extramural lectures and education for workers, but such teaching has to be done almost entirely on a voluntary basis since the Government grants are eaten up by what have been recognized as Government schemes. There is no room for what many regard as ' frills,' but what might make life so much fuller for many men and women.

There is a consolation, however, in the fact that, despite its deficiencies, interest in education remains. Travellers have often been amused by hearing conversations in public vehicles respecting the thrilling question of who is taking his ' Leaving ' or going to the ' Normal ' or even aspiring to his B.Sc., when the corresponding class in England would be discussing the prospects of the heroes of football teams or cricket elevens. Scotsmen have always cared about education, and the very fact that they have disputed as they did in the eighteenth century over the momentous question of whether school or College should teach Latin or Greek was evidence of this.

The only people who did not appear to sympathize with learning were the heritors who paid the school-masters so miserably, while the fees got from scholars had to be so small. Students at College could be boarded for £10 per annum; but they usually got round the difficulty of maintenance by arming them-selves with a sack of meal which served them till the next ' meal holiday,' as it was called, came round. Despite all these difficulties the Medical School managed to have 660 students in the first year of last century. If the student chose medicine as his profession the examination for entrance to the University was the same as for the Church or the Law.

Scottish Universities were fortunately well supplied with ' Bursaries,'—the ' Bourses ' of the French—many of them left by those who valued education but were none too well endowed themselves. These bursaries were small open scholarships which just sufficed to carry the student through the four years necessary to pass through the Faculty of Arts, and were mostly awarded on a test consisting mainly of Latin prose composition. They were competed for by lads of seventeen or eighteen years of age: if successful the young men tried to earn a small subsistence to eke out their finances by coaching backward schoolboys, or by doing manual work in vacation time.

Sometimes it is thought that the struggle for learning —for ' getting to the College '—has been exaggerated, and that the tales of the boys who went off with their sacks of meal at the beginning of the session were at least tales of very far away days. But the ' economies ' that these lads had to practise right through the nineteenth century were very real. In the middle of last century we are told of Aberdeen University that ' the work of the winter session was often interrupted by the call to mourn for a class-fellow who had succumbed to the threefold pressure of privation, over-work, and the rigorous climate,' and that to read the prize list of thirty years before was like listening to the roll-call of a regiment at the close of a severe campaign.[1] Sir James Barrie bears this out, and almost all who know rural life in Scotland remember the frequency with which young men, brilliant students, fell by the way, owing to their unhealthy mode of life, cooped up in crowded lodgings, after having been used to encountering the free breezes of the heavens. What was true of Aberdeen was true of the other three Universities.

The Rev. Norman MacLeod gives an interesting account of how the normal Highland boy went to College, and he describes the Glasgow College as it appeared early in the century when one entered its great courts. He also tells of the bustle of the High Street ' with its filthy crowds of squalid men and women, its ragged children and besotted drunken creatures, and whatever else combines to give to it a look of vice and poverty unsurpassed by any street in Europe.' He entered with

---

[1] *Life of Alexander Whyte*, by G. F. Barbour ; also *Life of William Robertson Smith*.

awe the rooms where Adam Smith and Reid taught, and James Watt studied. The students lived in the more respectable but far from aristocratic streets in the vicinity ; a small room could be obtained with free cooking and attendance for a few shillings, and this room was usually shared with another student. The young lads had been sent off with few, but well-made, clothes, a ' crook ' of butter, a mutton ham, kippered salmon and other provisions from the paternal manse and they made it last out their term.

William Chambers was a typical Scottish student who struggled with difficulties, though he did not with all his endeavours reach the University. He used to rise at five in the morning to read aloud to the workers in a baker's cellar for two and a half hours, for which noble work he was paid only by a hot roll ; then he went to work hard in a shop for the rest of the day. There were few means of self-culture in Edinburgh for those who were not University students. The School of Art, the precursor of Mechanics' Institutions, was not set on foot till 1821. Shop hours were from 7.30 a.m. till nine at night, with no relief on Saturdays. Notions of amusement Chambers did not dare to entertain; and as his wages were but four shillings a week he managed to spend on food only threepence halfpenny a day—porridge and buttermilk for breakfast and supper alike, costing one penny each, and kail broth and bread at three-halfpence for dinner. This small expenditure was arrived at by buying in quantity and dividing the purchases between the various lodgers in the rooms where he lived.

The difficulty young Chambers had was to find a place where he could do his scientific experiments, and this he found in the house of an old Highland porter, distinguished, as porters were, by a pewter badge. This man occupied himself in clasping broken china and similar occupations; but he had another more lugubrious trade, that of walking as a *saulie* before the higher class of funeral. Mutes bearing tall poles, shrouded in black drapery, and called gumflers (from *gonfalon*, a standard) also walked, but he was not one of these superior people. This strange being also acted as grave-digger, and from pieces of wood, which were thrown to the surface in the process of excavation, he made common fiddles and clock cases, so that he was a man of many occupations.

Chambers' father worked as commercial manager at the salt pans at Joppa, then a smoky, ill-smelling place. The salt makers had been serfs and sold along with the property on which they dwelt till 1799, when the last remnant of slavery was abolished in Great Britain. The salt was sent as contraband goods across the Border to England, where the duties on salt were higher than in Scotland. The goods were got across the fells during the night in carts.

Chambers' father lost his situation and health, and he and his brother were left in a parlous condition. The younger one was bent on going to College with the view of qualifying for the ministry; but no bursary was available, and his efforts to study without warmth or proper food were pitiful. He had, for example, surreptitiously to use a Latin dictionary which lay in a bookstall, and to study his Latin verse in miserable lodgings in the West Port, close to the scenes of Burke's murders, where the Chambers brothers lived. It was then that the two thought of setting up a bookstall from the collection of books that remained in the family from better days, though they were not worth more than two pounds in all. A miserable chaff bed and a rug, in the queer little shop or stall in Leith Walk, which connects Edinburgh with Leith, proved the beginning of a great publishing business.

Not only the Chambers, but several of the other printing and publishing firms for which Edinburgh is famous, grew up in the same way from stalls and shops on the smallest scale. They had their chances at the trade-sales and their attendant dinners, which were then part of the process of trade book-buying. Books on those occasions were handed round for inspection, the seller acting as host. Cheap editions of books out of copyright were at this time being printed, though hitherto no one had dared to disregard the recognized etiquette of the profession, which left these books to their original publishers. All new enterprises were helpful to the struggling lads, who began to bind, and even to print with their own hands, when there was, owing to wet weather, nothing else to be done; in fine weather things went better, especially when stationery, and even flutes, were added to their stock. Inside the shop there was but poor accommodation for the salesmen ; even the water they used had to be purchased at a halfpenny a pitcher from a cart laden with a barrel, which every morning passed by, announcing its advent by the blowing of a horn. Despite all difficulties the brothers managed to start a circulating library, helped by the popular Waverley Novels, always in demand by readers.

Something further should be said of libraries, since they were the only source of education to so many young Scots. Scotland, of course, had its public libraries in early days, but of a simple and very inadequate kind. In the beginning of the eighteenth century the Church awoke to the need of books for the ' poor and ignorant people,' and recommended to the Presbyteries to institute libraries in Highland parishes for their use. As usual, funds were lacking, but there were some small endowed libraries which the ecclesiastics rather unsuccessfully tried to get hold of. The Society for the Propagation of Christian Knowledge had funds, however, and arranged to place libraries in different parts of the country ; and with this object it sent abroad boxes of books, each containing about thirty-eight volumes, and placed them under the charge of the ministers of the Presbyteries, who were fined if any books went astray. This was the beginning of the system of rural libraries which was set on foot in the present century. However, the character of the books was not the same, for the older books were often Latin folios, and probably the ministers themselves were the main readers, as well as the curators of the collection.

Later on things did not improve ; the country was unsettled, the Church was not energetic, and travellers expressed surprise that there were so few public libraries in Scotland, while private houses like Braham Castle had magnificent collections. Lord Cockburn, in criticizing the work of a Dr. Dibdin in his *Northern Tour*, speaks of libraries (which Dibdin did not try to see), such as those of Darskimming, Aberdeen, Arniston and Minto, which he regarded as far better than many Scotch ones which Dibdin praised. The beginning of the century with which we are dealing brought a great change. Not only were there attempts at founding Subscription Libraries in the cities (like the Chambers'), but a certain Provost Brown got a good circulating scheme set on foot in Haddington in 1817. There were excellent and serious collections connected with the Mechanics' Institutes that sprung up in all the towns. Libraries were also established in connection with the Co-operative movement associated with Robert Owen ; there were likewise quite a number of libraries founded by groups of people on small endowments. The difficulty always was to find money for maintenance, and for buying new books.

The Public Libraries Act of 1850 was extended to Scotland in 1853, and after that time burghs might provide library buildings and impose a halfpenny rate, hoping that private beneficiaries would give a helping hand, and meet any deficiencies in providing books.

There were various Amending Acts later on, and the possible rate was raised to a penny in 1854, but not till 1920 to the more satisfactory sum of threepence. Airdrie had the honour of founding the first Public Library in 1856. Glasgow did not follow suit till 1877. But the immense development in public libraries in the nineteenth and twentieth centuries is largely due to Mr. Andrew Carnegie's munificent gifts and to the Trust he founded for the benefit of libraries as well as for other objects. This ' United Kingdom Trust ' was able, not only to help to set on foot the scheme for establishing rural libraries all over the country, but also to found a National Central Library as a lending reserve for them so far as serious books are concerned. It was aided in its work by the passing of the Education Act of 1918, which gave powers to the County Education Authority to establish rural libraries for adults as well as for children without imposing any limit to the amount to be spent in doing so. Thus it was not trammelled by a low rate as the burgh libraries had been ; and though this is outside our purview, it should lead to great developments in the present century.

The National Library of Scotland only came into existence when the ancient and famous Library of the Faculty of Advocates was transferred to the State for this purpose but the Advocates' Library itself had been founded by the Scottish Bar as early as 1682, primarily as a Law Library. General literature was not, however, disregarded, and in 1709, after the Union, Queen Anne conferred upon the Library the right to claim a copy of every book entered at Stationers' Hall—a privilege continued by all subsequent Copyright Acts. It became impossible for the Faculty to carry on the Library on so great a scale as was required out of its own unaided resources, especially as facilities to the public were given, and hence an Endowment Trust was set up, generous contributions were announced, and the National Library of Scotland Act received the Royal Assent in August 1925. The Library is, like the British Museum Library, one for research and reference.

Before leaving this subject we should mention some of the many men and women of education and distinction who made Scotland famous during the century, and who owed much to the education they received. Professor Whitehead says [1] that Adam Smith and Hume are the last of the great Scotchmen who mark the traditional affiliation of Scotland with France which had survived from the earlier centuries of joint antagonism to England. The intellectual life of Scotland, he thinks, was not then to be associated with that of England, which at the same date was negligible. This was, of course, not so in the nineteenth century; but Scotland continued to distinguish herself in letters equally with her neighbour, though perhaps not in the French tradition. Voltaire says that ' to-day rules of taste in all the Arts, from epic poems to gardening, come from Scotland.' She had, to begin with, Walter Scott and Burns (though he belongs rather to the earlier century),

[1] *Adventures of Ideas*, 1933, Cambridge Univ. Press.

Carlyle, Louis Stevenson, Alan Ramsay, Hogg, Galt, Christopher North and Hill Burton the historian. She may also claim Byron as a Scot. In Art she can boast of Raeburn, Watson Gordon, David Roberts, Francis Grant, Graham Gilbert, Daniel Macnee, David Wilkie, and later Sir George Harvey, David Scott, Noël Paton, Robert Herdman, Fettes Douglas; and in landscape painting Alexander Nasmyth, the Rev. John Thomson, Horatio McCulloch and Sam Bough. And if we pass to the later part of the century there is the rise of the Glasgow School, influenced by the French impressionists: there were Orchardson, Pettie, Chalmers, McTaggart, D. Y. Cameron, MacWhirter, Sir George Reid, James Guthrie, John Lavery, Alex. Roche and W. Y. McGregor, only to mention some of its members.

In architecture Scotland was also distinguished, for even after the days of the Adams she had such men as James Gibb who built St. Martin's Church in London and Mylne who built Blackfriars Bridge, Kemp of the Scott Monument, Lorimer and so on.

This is a creditable list for a small country, but Scotland has also done much for culture in other directions. Even in handicrafts she has kept up her reputation, so far as fine gold and silver work and excellent furniture are concerned.

Scotland's women have not distinguished themselves in literature or art as greatly as did those of England in this century. Susan Ferrier was a good novelist and so was Mrs. Oliphant, Mary Somerville was a scientist, and Lady Nairne was a wonderful writer of songs. Lady Anne Lindsay, the author of *Auld Robin Gray*, who died in 1825, hid her light successfully under a bushel, as others may have done; for she tells how, when in France a French lady at a party spoke of her as being a writer, 'I stole away as soon as I could, well knowing that if my countrywomen were to hear me so named it would have been the death warrant to all chance of my gaining the honest heart of an anti-bluestocking Englishman for the rest of my life'! *Auld Robin Gray* was said to have been sung most beautifully by Adelaide Kemble about 1840, when an operatic company came to Edinburgh from Dublin, and when a concert was given in the Assembly Rooms. There were other writers of song, like Mrs. Cockburn and Jean Elliot. These women writers aimed at providing something better than the coarse ballads of the day.

The Scottish Academy was a small affair at first, but in 1838 we find Cockburn struggling to get it given a Charter and £300 a year under the Queen's patronage, so that it might become a ' Royal ' Academy. There was an institution called the ' Association ' to which by the payment of one guinea the subscribers had a chance of gaining a picture, and the artists had a certainty of a sale, and that appears to have been successful in Edinburgh, for 2000 persons subscribed.

There were many ' Literary Clubs ' in Edinburgh and Glasgow, favoured by distinguished men, and characteristic of the time. Cockburn, in his *Journal*,

M

speaks of the Bannatyne Club, which began about 1820 and had in 1832 one hundred members, each paying five guineas yearly. It in turn produced the Maitland Club of Glasgow, the Abbotsford Club and the Iona Club, and there was said to be as much canvassing for admission to the mother club as for a return to Parliament! 'The Maitland' and 'the Bannatyne' are, Cockburn says, 'the best examples of bibliomania that Scotland has as yet exhibited.' Of minor clubs Geikie mentions the 'Spendthrift,' the 'Oyster' and the 'Dirty' Club.

As to the theatre, there is not much to tell, for the passion for acting came later on. In old days the theatre was dubbed the 'Nursery for Sin,' and was taboo to the respectable. Mrs. Siddons helped to give it another character and managed to fill the house with clergy and magistrates. Indeed, she somehow raised the theatre to a higher level in Scotland. It was in the old Theatre Royal in Edinburgh (which was taken down in 1859 in order to make way for the Post Office) that Mrs. Siddons had her triumphs. Porters and servants had to browse for a night on the streets on mats and palliasses in order that early admission might next day be obtained to the box office! Theatres, however, had a precarious life, for those in Edinburgh and Glasgow were both burned to the ground—many thought as a judgment upon them. The Glasgow theatre was one of the finest then existing, and at it Edmund and Charles Kean used to play; while the drop-scene was painted by Nasmyth the artist.

In Science and Philosophy Scotland was hardly less distinguished than in Literature and Art during the nineteenth century. We have only to think of the professors in Edinburgh and Glasgow to realize the truth of this statement. There were Hutton and Geikie as geologists, Sir John Leslie, Brewster, Waterston, Thomas Graham, Clark, Maxwell, Tait and Kelvin as physicists, Lister as a surgeon, Simpson as a physician; while in Philosophy there were many celebrated men such as Ferrier, Hamilton, Campbell Fraser, Pringle Pattison and the two Cairds. The great University traditions were thus carried on from the time of Principal William Carstares in the beginning of the eighteenth century, and the nineteenth century had every reason to be proud of her Scottish sons.

CHAPTER VIII

THE INDUSTRIES OF THE PEOPLE

WE have seen how the Union opened up many new opportunities for trade with England, owing to the removal of tariff barriers. It also did so with the colonies, and particularly with the West Indies, and the American plantations. It has often been a puzzle to understand why Scotland, a poor country, was able to import enormous quantities of tobacco, the main freight of the Clyde ships, but as a matter of fact Glasgow was only a clearing house, since most of the tobacco went to France.

This was but the beginning of Scotland's commercial prosperity, and the connection of its great commercial families with America. Agriculture was really the keystone of all her future fame in the movement known as the Industrial Revolution, though perhaps the word Industrial Evolution, used by Mr. Henry Hamilton, who is the latest authority on this period, is more suitable to describe the movement. Without the wonderful advance in agricultural methods made in the end of the eighteenth and early part of the nineteenth century it would have been impossible for the other trades to develop, or for factories to be carried on. The immensely increased population had to be fed, and agriculture itself became a commercial undertaking. On its basis the various trades we shall speak of depended, though the capital required no doubt came from the original tobacco trade with the plantations. Trade such as the woollen industry and the linen industry were directly dependent on agriculture; but the cotton industry, which prospered greatly after the destruction of the tobacco trade by the American War of Independence, was only indirectly dependent, since it drew its supplies of raw material from abroad. The founding of the Carron Iron Works and the development of the mineral resources of the country had, again, no direct connection with agriculture, but they had very real indirect dependence on it.

Gradually manufacture and agriculture became separated. For long, as we have seen, the making of cloth was carried on by weavers and village people in close touch with the land. The weavers were, however, not entirely their own masters. They were working for capitalists who supplied the material and sold the goods, and the wages they earned decreased as factories arose. The work was hard and, as we shall see, the apprentices were none too well treated, and children's labour existed without supervision. These low wages hindered the quick development of power-loom factories and handwork continued till the sixties or even the seventies of last century.

Many of the evils of the factory system existed under the old régime, where sweating was often carried on, but the new system was less friendly and the workers were less masters of their own lives. Hence the system seemed alien and hateful, though it should really have brought about better conditions had it been operated in a more friendly spirit, and had the human side been thought of as such, and not merely, along with capital, as a counter in the game.

There was another element in the Industrial Revolution which must not be forgotten, and that is the great development of communication by road and rail. Wade's military roads had no influence on economic development; but the many roads built in the early nineteenth century affected it greatly, especially the work of the Highland Commission for Roads and Bridges, with Telford as engineer. Nor must we forget the Forth and Clyde and other canals, which brought the rich arable counties of the Lothians into touch with the industrial West.

It must always be remembered that at length a country troubled not only by war but also by factions was at rest. For long she had never had the opportunity to develop her resources or even to realize that they existed.

On the political side the new movement transformed society from being an aristocratic community governed by a few to a democratic community governed by many. It also gave power to the many, not only by their votes, but through the work they were called upon to do—skilled work as well as unskilled—and the many demanded (and did not at first get) not only a share in the wealth that their hands produced, but also educational and other opportunities to fit themselves for playing their part in the work of the world. We are apt to think of this period as a limited one, and for convenience' sake it is here treated as such, but really it was the opening of the flood-gates that have never since been closed, and so far as we know never will, unless a new system of government is adopted.

We must now consider some of the principal trades and occupations that opened themselves to men and women in the first half of the nineteenth century.

Let us begin with a notable Scottish industry, that of the manufacture of linen. We must not forget that this was no new thing in Scotland, for Christian Shaw, the daughter of the Laird of Balgarran, began about 1725 to manufacture fine thread from the directions of a friend who had seen the process in Holland, and who founded an industry which has brought great wealth to Paisley. It was a little later—in 1735—that Harvey of Glasgow got the secret of making tape also from the enterprising Holland. It was fortunate that there were always Scottish travellers ready to pick up fresh ideas when they met with them.

Scotland had indeed for centuries been a cloth-making country, using her own flax and wool when those alone were available, just as we see it done in the Highlands to this day. There were little water-mills for fulling the cloth mechanically, of which we find traces still on our rivers and burns : these little mills carried on the work hitherto done by hands, or rather feet. There was much hand-spinning and weaving, both of linen from the flax grown at home and wool from the sheep's backs. The careful housewife would even collect the wool left by the careless sheep in briars and thorns, and tease it out. We know from the prowess of the third Mrs. Balwidder in *The Annals of the Parish* how she kept her maids hard at work spinning the ' wearisome pound of tow '; and other mistresses did the same all over Scotland, for all were proud of their home-spun napery. Yet this was at the beginning of the nineteenth century when, as we know, power-looms and factories were developing, though the process of dis-placing handwork was slow.

The linen trade had grown rapidly during the eigh-teenth century, and in the beginning of the nineteenth century it was carried on for the most part in Fife and Forfar (Angus); Aberdeen and Perth followed suit, and Dunfermline excelled in the beauty of its damask. Scottish housewives loved to have some of its double damask beautifully designed tablecloths. Dundee was famous for its spinning-mills, which early in the century were driven by steam-power. Flax, hemp and tow were imported into Dundee for manufacture, and finally Indian jute took the first place. Later the manufacture was largely carried on in India by Scottish firms, owing to the cheapness of the Indian labour. Bleaching, dye-ing, calendering and cognate industries are mainly to be found in the eastern counties and towns. Floor cloth, made from flax, jute and linseed oil, is a special product of Kirkcaldy, where it was invented in 1847 by a Mr. Michael Nairn and at first named ' Nairn's Folly,' so little did people believe in the development of linoleum and wax-cloth. This was an industry which spread later to England and abroad, and became an important one.

It is to be noted that cotton at the end of last century seemed to take the place of linen. It was the industry of the famous mills in New Lanark carried on about 1785 by Owen, the philanthropist captain of industry. Cotton was at that time Scotland's greatest textile industry, and prior to 1792 the work was all done by water-power. It had shared in the boom which occurred in England owing to the war with the American colonies, which caused the raw stuff to be imported from the West Indies. The humid atmosphere of the West of Scotland was supposed to favour the industry, but the only direction in which it survives is that of thread-spinning, which holds the leading position at Paisley under the direction of the firms of the Coats and Clarks. Suitably enough there is near Paisley the great sewing-machine factory of the Singers, which naturally has an influence on the industry.

As regards the weaving and spinning of wool, the Border burghs have, since 1820, been the home of the tweed manufacture which is celebrated in Scotland. The wool of the native Cheviot sheep was suitable for the purpose, and in the Border country there was a plentiful supply of water before steam was used, and land was cheap. Most of the weavers round Gala-shiels and Hawick were famous fishermen as well as weavers, as the streams around may bear testimony !

As time went on, Scottish wool was insufficient for the work, and wool had to be imported and treated as was required. Much skill was needed in arranging and mixing the colours so as to provide a varied cloth. The same industry is still carried on in some of the eastern counties further north, while shirtings belong to Glasgow and the West.

Kilbarchan weavers were famous for their well-known prayer : ' Oh Lord, give us a good conceit of ourselves ' —a prayer that, in their neighbours' opinion, was answered to the full ! The weavers originally made Paisley shawls and scarfs. When weaving failed, printing of the shawls was resorted to, and the printing was so good that it required an expert to detect the difference between printed and woven goods.

In the Highlands, and more especially in the Outer Islands, the production of the old hand-spun and hand-woven and hand-dyed tweeds is still carried on and is encouraged by Highland Industries' Association : it is a native industry which cannot be rivalled and which is likely always to have a certain luxury market.

There are many other forms of textile industry in Scotland, such as the making of blankets, shawls, hosiery and underwear. Carpets have been manu-factured in Kilmarnock for generations; but Glasgow and Aberdeen have more lately taken up the industry with vigour. Paisley in the beginning of last century was, of course, famous for her shawls made by hand-loom weavers, and in the eighteenth century French weavers were brought from Spitalfields to help them.

Though hand-loom weaving continued in a degree until the nineties, it had been fighting a losing game ever since the end of the French wars and the depression which followed.   The clickety-click of the loom was, however, heard in the village streets and the country towns for many a long year : only when one weaver fell out he was not replaced by his son, who had made his way to the mills or perhaps to foundry work.

The lapse of hand-loom weaving, whether of linen or wool or the popular admixture named wincey (though wincey is now made with cotton, not linen), was in some ways a loss to Scotland, for the weavers were a fine intelligent set of men who took an interest in politics.   They used to hold what they often called their ' parliament '—a meeting at one of the outside stairs which were so common in Scottish villages—to discuss the news in the one newspaper, which was supplied by a fortunate possessor.   They were, how- ever, dependent on the ' merchant ' who took their wares and made a stiff bargain, and the work was hard.   The weavers often worked several looms, having perhaps a boy to help them, a boy who also had hard work, standing on the damp earth with bare feet in the cold, or else on his bonnet; and their earnings fell while their hours of work increased. Wages latterly varied from 15s. to £1 a week.   Also the weavers' ' shops ' were usually damp, since the dampness was beneficial to their work, and hence they became martyrs to rheumatism.   Women and children helped to fill the pirns, and occasionally women also wove.

The trade would have ceased earlier but that the power-looms were slow in being established owing to difficulty in getting skilled mechanics to deal with the machinery. The greatest expansion of the power-loom took place in the sixties, and after that the hand-loom weavers died out, excepting that they were occasionally used as pattern makers in factories.

But, above all, Scotland discovered that literally she had a mine of wealth in her coal and iron. As early as 1760 were started the Carron Iron Works, which were to make her famous; and Pennant, in his *Tours in Scotland*, describes them as being, even in 1769, 'the greatest of the kind in Europe.'

It was at Carron that coal came to be used for furnaces. In earlier days charcoal was the medium made use of, and hence ironworks were established about 1727 at places like Invergarry in the Highlands, where timber was plentiful; but the timber was coming to an end and it was fortunate that other smelting methods were discovered, and that it was found that coal could be used for this purpose.

The Bairds were amongst the most prominent and successful industrialists who contributed to the success of the industry and amassed great fortunes thereby. The production of pig-iron increased rapidly during the nineteenth century, from 20,000 tons to much more than 1,000,000 tons a year; and, of course, the invention of the 'hot-blast' contributed greatly to the increase. Blast-furnaces used to be a familiar object in the landscape in the industrial belt of Scotland, especially at night, when the flames rose up from 60 to 100 feet. The Scottish deposits of ironstone are now mainly exhausted but large quantities are imported.

Carron ceased to make warlike ' carronades ' or any sort of guns, but Carron and the adjoining Falkirk became famous for the production of more peaceful malleable goods of iron. The foundry at Falkirk was for a time the second largest in the country, and at these works stoves, grates and other domestic articles were made, as well as the castings of iron bridges, etc. In Coatbridge and the district near it, malleable iron is also produced. It was to meet the necessity for a more serviceable instrument in carrying out large forgings that James Nasmyth invented the steam-hammer in 1839.

After various attempts at organization, in 1871 the Steel Company of Scotland was formed for the manufacture of steel ; and the output of steel far exceeded that of malleable iron. Some of the steel companies combined its production with shipbuilding, and were thus able to build large warships from their own resources. There were, of course, in addition a large number of firms engaged in mechanical engineering such as locomotive-building. The locomotives were used at home and abroad.

Work in the coal mines in the beginning of last century was depressing enough. The mines were shallow, the coal was often carried along the pit bottom to the pit mouth by women and even children, and the hours were long. Mechanical hoisting, worked first by horse-power and then by steam-winding engines, ultimately took the place of the coal buckets carried with so much pain and labour. When human beings were made use of they received for this terribly hard labour but eight-pence a day, and it was not till 1842 that the employment of boys under ten years of age was prohibited, along with the employment underground of women. Gradually men and ponies, and then small railways, were used to transport the coal, and coal-cutting machines worked by compressed air were often utilized. The extension of underground machines for cutting and conveying coal grew far more rapidly in Scotland than in England.

The main coalfields in Scotland are those in Lanark and Ayr, the Lothians and Fife; and during last century there were constant endeavours to find new sources for coal in view of the great industrial demands, all dependent on coal supply. Coal was, of course, not only essential for the production of iron and steel, but also for the ever-increasing generation of propulsive power on land or sea, as also for the manufacture of gas. In 1908 the output of coal was thirty-nine million tons, and of this Lanarkshire produced over one half. The Fife and East Coast ports, on the other hand, shipped a large quantity abroad. Up to 1899, when she was surpassed by the United States, Britain was the largest producer of coal in the world.

Oil shale was found in Mid and West Lothian, but unfortunately there was not much natural oil to be got from it, so that the crude oil had to be distilled from shale mined for the purpose; and the trade was therefore carried on under difficulties, and against

competition from the Caspian, Burma, etc. After a
boom, following Mr. Young's successful experiments,
the number of oilworks declined with the prices.

Shipbuilding was the mainstay of the heavy industries of the West. It was always reckoned that if shipbuilding were prosperous, all the industries in the West
would be so also. The Clyde valley had for years been
pre-eminent in shipbuilding, and the development of
this work took place in connection with the development of the coal, iron and steel industries, though of
course it existed before the days of coal, and while
wood was still used in building ships. The deepening
of the River Clyde made access easy for large vessels
from the sea, and the Clyde became known as ' the
premier shipbuilding river.'

In point of equipment the shipbuilding yards were
the finest in the world until the post-war debacle of the
present century. During the nineteenth century all
sorts of inventions were brought into being and many
changes made.

The first Clyde steamer was constructed in 1812 by
the engineer Symington, and later on the same firm
produced the *Cupid*, a Clyde steamer which went
aground so often that it was called the ' Stupid '!
Great progress was made from the early days, when
Symington and Taylor, with the help of Mr. Miller of
Dalswinton, made a momentous experiment in steam
propulsion on Dalswinton Loch; and soon various craft
plied amongst the scattered watering-places on the
Firth of Clyde.

Then the screw was substituted for the paddle, steel for iron, two cylinders were used instead of one, also triple and quadruple expansion engines, and finally there came the turbine rotary engine. Amongst the great ships built on the Clyde early in the present century may be mentioned the unfortunate *Lusitania*. By degrees the use of oil (internal combustion) engines developed, and types of motor vessels arose beyond calculation. Many battleships were Clyde-built during the nineteenth century and employment was thus given to large numbers of men in the Clydebank area.

It is amusing to find how Edinburgh prided herself on being uncommercial, and how people like Dr. Carlyle looked down on the rapid commercialization of Glasgow. Lord Cockburn in his *Journal* is horrified by the idea of introducing manufactures into Edinburgh in 1835 : he thought that to have weavers' power-looms and steam-engines would ' increase our population and our pauperism, our wealth and our bankruptcies ; but they would leave it Edinburgh no more ! ' He allows, however, that even when he wrote this, the town was in a state of insolvency ; trade had left Leith, docks were bankrupt, the College had not a shilling. Even the great libraries and charities were dying of hunger. This was the rebound after the prosperity of the war, when 'everything was glittering and gay,' and useless offices were multiplied ' under a gallant contempt of every feeling except the expediency of having a place for every man worth being bought . . . nobody thinking that a true balance-sheet must one day be struck, and few men

THE CLYDE BETWEEN THE BROOMIELAW AND THE POINT-HOUSE, 1835
FROM LITHOGRAPH BY DAVID ALLAN

indeed so silly as to risk themselves by suggesting so dull a truth.' We seem to know it all too well. But Cockburn was wholly averse, in spite of all this, to letting steam redress the evils, at least as far as Edinburgh was concerned. He had to submit to the inevitable to a certain extent, but he may be thanked for saving much of the beauty of a beautiful and romantic town; his name is still one to conjure with for that reason.

Of other industries, chemical works on a large scale were for the most part established in the West, and many discoveries were made in regard to the utilization of chemical products, especially the bye-products of other industries. Edinburgh manufactured fine chemicals such as medical chemicals, surgical dressings, etc., while the dyeing industry had its home in Perth, where in the dyeworks of the Messrs. Pullar Mr. W. H. Perkin carried out his famous experiments.

Greenock was the centre of the industry of sugar refining, but foreign competition pressed hardly on the trade; sweets and jam-making held their own in Glasgow, Paisley, Dundee and elsewhere. The fruit-growing industry in Perthshire has been influenced by this trade, but its development belongs mainly to the twentieth century.

Paper-making was another nineteenth century Scottish industry, and so were milling, baking and brewing in different parts of the country. Small breweries, so characteristic of Scottish towns in former days after home brewing ceased, could no longer compete with

N

the larger ones and gradually died out. Distilling of whisky has, of course, been a characteristically Scottish industry since the days of the illicit stills of the Highlands. After great opposition, smuggling was in a measure put down by the prosecution of offenders (there were 1400 prosecutions for such contravention of the law in 1825), and by the end of the century the large distilleries held the field unchallenged.

Whisky took an extraordinary hold on Scotland after the Union, or, rather, after the malt tax was imposed in 1725 ; the last was a small tax but extremely unpopular. Smuggled spirits were brought into Scotland from Holland and France, and in every remote portion of the coast this trade was carried on without any feeling that this infringement of the law was wrong. There was also a belief, which gave great satisfaction, that by smuggling the English were being deprived of the proceeds of their unpopular imposition ! Town Councils and the Church no doubt condemned the ' prevalence of smuggling and tea drinking,' for much of the tea imported had never passed a custom-house any more than the whisky. But all was in vain, and the worst was that whisky drinking became as common in the Lowlands as it had been in the Highlands ; indeed the illicit trade was only partially crushed in the early part of the nineteenth century ; for in a small way stills were carried on till late in the century, especially in lonely glens and far away straths. The great matter was to ' juik the gauger,' who, poor man, had adopted an unpopular profession.

Slate quarries and granite works are other forms of Scottish industries. Slate came into vogue after thatch went out of fashion, and Scotland was well supplied with it in the Highlands. Granite, despite its hardness, was used for building in Aberdeen as early as 1741, and its use was extended later on when it was utilized for paving, tombstones and other such things. Most of the new industries, indeed, simply supplanted the old, just as glass- and bottle-blowing arose as pewter ceased to be used. 'Fleshers,' as butchers were called, became common in every small town after the killing of 'The Mart' became no more required, and carpets in 1760 when people were no longer contented with bare floors. This is how the latter industry took the place of the making of 'blue bonnets' at Kilmarnock.

In Scotland the publishing of books and the retailing of them have usually gone together so far as the eighteenth and early nineteenth centuries were concerned. In the early part of the nineteenth century the famous 'Ballantyne Press' and 'Constable's' came to grief, as we know so well from Walter Scott's unfortunate connection with them; and hence the Blackwood firm was left supreme. But popular publishing, which was usually combined with printing, soon came in with the Nelsons, who started as booksellers in 1798, and became publishers and printers in the next century. Some of the trade migrated to London, but printing remained a Scottish industry and the improvement in the necessary mechanism of printing was largely due to Scottish inventors.

As one reads the lives of men who made their way in Scotland one is struck by nothing more than the immense difficulty they had in laying their hands on books. They had, indeed, at home, Boston's *Fourfold State*, *The Marrow of Divinity*, *The Pilgrim's Progress*, and possibly some 'Collection' of extracts, but little beyond that. Telford, while still a journeyman mason, wrote in a local paper an address to Burns in which these words occur :

> 'Nor pass the gentle curious lad
> Who o'er the ingle hangs his head
> And begs of neighbours books to read ;
>   For hence arise
> Thy country's sons, who far are spread,
>   Baith bold and wise.'

It was the case that the only literature poor boys could purchase were cheap and often scurrilous prints, till in the year 1820 a statute was passed imposing a stamp upon such cheap publications with the view of stopping seditious propaganda. This made periodicals, other than those that were purely literary, difficult of issue. It was felt, however, that something must be done in order to allow popular knowledge to be diffused. The School of Art was started in Edinburgh in 1821, and two years later Dr. Birkbeck founded Mechanics' Institutes in London and Glasgow respectively ; and then in 1825 a 'Society for the Diffusion of Useful Knowledge' was set on foot. This Society issued series of cheap treatises in science and indeed on every branch of knowledge ; and it seemed to open the floodgates for a profusion of more or less instructive literature, which was found to pay. One sees traces of the type of literature that appeared amongst old books, for little libraries for mechanics and country people and others began to arise. There were again serials like the *Cornucopia*, full of all sorts of oddments, extracts from books and poor jokes. William Chambers was the first seriously to take the matter up, and in January 1832 he issued at ' three halfpence ' *Chambers' Edinburgh Journal*, which has kept its place in, and influence on, Scottish life to this day. Even the price never varied. The success of this magazine was instantaneous, and it held its own over all competitors because it was not too abstruse, and understood working people's needs and capacities, as the Society for the Diffusion of Useful Knowledge did not do. The fact of one man, or one firm, undertaking the editing, printing, and publishing, along with actually writing much of the matter published, was characteristic of Scotland in those days, where there existed no sharp distinction between the different activities of writing, printing and publishing. Nelson's school-books, for instance, were actually written by members of the firm. When there were brothers in partnership the division of labour was simpler. In the case of the Chambers, one brother was an essayist of a direct and simple nature, who could avoid the sins of essayists of the day, in being, for a wonder, neither pompous nor dull.

About 1840 there followed *Chambers' Miscellany*, and in 1868, though begun in 1859, the famous *Chambers'*

Encyclopaedia which became known throughout the world. It was preceded in 1844 by the more original *Cyclopaedia of English Literature*, the first of its kind.

As regards Scottish newspapers and magazines, one cannot imagine any but a Tory newspaper existing under the rule of Henry Dundas. But after his day passed there was a reaction, and the younger spirits, Jeffrey, Horner and Brougham, established the *Edinburgh Review* on completely different lines. This was in 1829. It challenged both the Tory *Quarterly Review* and *Blackwood's Magazine*, the popular magazine on the other side.

As to newspapers, there were the *Edinburgh Advertiser*, owned by Donaldson, who established Donaldson's Hospital; the *Edinburgh Weekly Journal*, in which Scott and Ballantyne took a part; and the *Edinburgh Evening Courant*, which became a daily and only died in 1886. But the great event on the side of reform was the starting of the *Scotsman* in 1817. It began as a bi-weekly, but in 1855 became a penny daily paper of the most influential sort.

Glasgow also had a liberal paper in the *Glasgow Herald*, founded in 1783 as the *Glasgow Advertiser*, which became a daily paper in 1859. The *Dundee Advertiser*, which was founded in 1801 as an advanced Liberal paper, catered for the north-eastern counties.

It is likely that the quality of thrift should appeal to Scots, and as banking and insurance are simply the application of thrift to public and private life, it is not surprising that Scotland, and Edinburgh in particular as the metropolis, should be famous for their banking system. This dated back for a couple of hundred years, but the insurance of life and property, so important in a civilized community, developed in the nineteenth century.

If we go back far enough we find that some banking had been carried on by the goldsmiths, always notable figures in Scottish history, as is exemplified by George Heriot, the ' Jingling Geordie ' of the time of King James I, who was a money-broker as well as a rich and prosperous goldsmith. Before the rebellion of 1745 the old chartered banks came into existence, then the establishment of local joint stock or private banks arose, and finally came the founding of the Commercial Bank in 1810, a period which ' is marked by amalgamation and consolidation, and by the building up of the great national banks of Scotland.'

The Bank of Scotland was founded in 1695, and it was the great scarcity of coin in Scotland that led it to issue one pound notes in 1704. One pound notes were for a very long time characteristic of Scotland, and their frequently greasy condition made the Englishman smile, until he, too, had to use ' Treasury notes,' though he claims that they never reach the same depressing condition as did the Scottish pound ! The Bank of Scotland was accused of Jacobite leanings, and the Royal Bank of Scotland was set up in 1727. It is impossible here to follow out the complicated history of banking in Scotland, but the founding of the British Linen Bank in 1746 is of interest, for it was designed to promote linen manufacture in all its branches ; it did this with wonderful zeal, having a warehouse in Edinburgh and agents in various places for giving out flax and receiving back the yarn or cloth for which it paid in notes. Gradually it withdrew from mercantile affairs and finally became a banking corporation in 1849.

The ' Royal ' was naturally the favourite with the Government, and once the troubles of the rebellion of the '45 were over (during that time the notes and specie of both banks were lodged in Edinburgh Castle) most State banking business was done through it. The army was paid in Royal Bank notes, and the carrying on of Wade's roads was paid for by means of tellers sent from Edinburgh on horseback into the fastnesses of the Highlands, carrying notes with them to pay the soldiers employed on these important undertakings. The notes also went to the great agricultural ' Trysts,' or markets for cattle, held at Crieff or Falkirk, and were paid out in return for specie.

The Coutts family rose into prominence about this date. John Coutts, like most bankers, began as a merchant (this time in wine and cloth), who also lent money. He and his family for generations lived and worked in the President's Close, Edinburgh, and he took into partnership Sir William Forbes, who belonged to an old and penniless family and was originally apprenticed to him. Sir William Forbes & Co. merged in the Union Bank of Scotland, and a younger

WEST INDIA MERCHANT
Eighteenth Century

POLICE
Nineteenth Century

OLD GLASGOW COSTUMES

brother of the second John Coutts, who died in 1822, founded the firm of Coutts & Co. of London.

Gradually, during the nineteenth century, banks established branches in the small towns; but for a long time there were no local banks, and as there were always lawyers, or ' writers ' as they were called, they lent out money on mortgage, which was a less satisfactory system than banking proper.

During last century there have been various monetary crises, which may perhaps encourage us somewhat in later days. In 1823-26, after the French wars, there was a very serious time of depression owing to the mania for forming joint-stock companies, many of which were unsound. The crisis of 1847 was due to the railway mania and rash speculations, aggravated by a bad season. Then there was prosperity till 1857, when there were serious failures; and in 1878 the City of Glasgow Bank suspended payment, and the unfortunate shareholders had to make up the deficiency in the assets. The Scottish Banks and Insurance Offices have on the whole had an honourable history; and Edinburgh has been a world-known centre for the latter, as might be expected of a thrifty and honest city. Insurance has enabled private people to provide for their descendants and has allowed business to be carried on with comparative security.

If we pass from land to sea, fishing was originally prosecuted for the most part on the West Coast, but by 1826 the lead passed to the East, from whence the fish were sent to the Baltic ports. Later on steam-power was used for trawling. The herring fishing gave employment to all sorts of outside people like gutters, carpenters, sailmakers, etc., and the curing and smoking of herrings and haddocks was an industry in itself. Towards the end of the century the inshore industry had diminished in importance : the trawling industry cramped the former trade. Those who know the Outer Islands have seen the bands of Highland girls who come yearly to Peterhead, Yarmouth, and other centres of herring fishing, to gut the fish ; and the girls who thus had to cross the sea were often condemned to sleep in the open, let the weather be what it might. As usual they resorted to song, and Gaelic songs—pathetic, but fairly cheerful at first—would merge into solemn psalms as the waves rose and things looked like preparation for another world !

Fishing villages always had characteristics of their own, and the fisher people had little intercourse with the rest of the community, even if they lived close by. The picturesque garb of the fishwives, and their sturdy appearance as they carried their heavy creels of fish on their shoulders, has always been admired.

John Jack, writing in 1844, gives an interesting account of a typical fishing village in Fife, that of St. Monance. There were then salt wells by the sea. These were cut in solid rock and so retained a full supply of water when the tide receded. A factory for salt production was later established, and in the factory the sea water was boiled and clarified with lime till all superfluous matter was thrown off by evaporation : the saline particles remaining in the pan were collected into a receptacle, and when this was drained out and cooled it was stored in the Girnal at Pittenweem for exportation. 'Sunday salt' was specially valued as having had a specially long time to crystallize in the receptacle. 'Sunday salt' was also used with the dry potatoes eaten on Sunday, when the minimum of cooking was permitted. Duty on salt was very high, being about four-fifths of the price of the article itself, so that smuggling was assiduously carried on, and it was not difficult to abstract the salt for private use. With the abolition of the salt tax the factory disappeared.

The fisher people were usually very religious but also full of superstition. Jack, for instance, tells of certain animals, such as pigs, being held in great antipathy as boding ill, and, if mentioned at all, being termed the 'brutes' or 'beasts.' When a boat left the harbour the question of 'Where are you going ?' could never be asked. The spider had a good reputation, as, indeed, it has always had in Scotland owing to the old story of how it saved Scotland in her time of need, when Robert Bruce was encouraged by its efforts to form a web, not to lose hope but try again. No well brought up Scottish child fails to know that story.

.   .   .   .

It is necessary to speak of another side of industry, for during the nineteenth century there has been one long battle for the rights of the workmen as against the masters. Great fortunes were made by those who had, in the eyes of the work-people, profited unduly from the results of the work done by their employees. Then there were the terrible periodic trade depressions which brought great suffering to the workers; and in the towns there ensued a misery which was met in a wholly insufficient way by unorganized charity. It was believed by many that had the capitalist employers considered more the necessity for caring for the interests of their work-people, and less for the profits to be made, there would not have been the unrest that there was, or the political agitation. It is unfortunately true that little care was bestowed on the food, health and housing of the people, until they obtained certain rights for themselves by agitation. There were serious riots about 1816-1824, when combinations of workmen were prohibited and when all efforts on the part of the weavers to get a decent wage were frustrated; a strike was put down by law, and the leaders were imprisoned. With great difficulty the right of collective bargaining was, however, obtained in 1825, and trade unions were established in the various trades with the view of guarding their respective rights. The Reform Bill of 1832 did not do much for the workers, and a demand for universal suffrage followed. Then came the Chartists, but the agitation for the People's Charter was not supported by the trade unions, who worked for constitutional methods of redressing grievances, for securing increase of wages and diminution of hours of work.

In the nineteenth century the unions concentrated their energy on organizing a Labour Party to further the interests of the working class, and opposed reform by way of revolution. It is well known how far they have accomplished their ends, but the work became merged into that of England, although not all the Scottish unions identified themselves with those of the southern country.

Co-operation has also played a great part in urban working-class life in Scotland; and it even made its way to the villages, so far as the distributive side is concerned. The movement began through the efforts of the weavers—always a progressive body of people—in the eighteenth century. Groups of weavers began to meet in the 'village parliament' where political questions were discussed. And at the end of that century (in 1799) Robert Owen became the manager of the New Lanark Twist Company, started by Dale. This was a very interesting communistic society of villages, each containing about a thousand people. The children employed had to be dressed in peculiar garb, as Romans or Highlanders. Owen was a real philanthropist who cared for the unfortunate pauper children who were sent to work in the mills, educated them on most modern principles, and taught them to dance and sing. This last, combined with his unorthodox religious views, proved his undoing with his Quaker partners, and probably with the Presbyterian population; but though he failed in realizing his ideas he helped to found the Co-operative movement, though his idea of Co-operation was no doubt Socialistic. In a measure he also helped in the movement towards Trade Unionism, besides pressing to get a Factory Act passed dealing with the employment of children. His connection with New Lanark ceased somewhat disastrously in 1828.

It was only in 1852 that the Industrial and Provident Societies' Act, which gave the sanction of Parliament to the Co-operative system, was passed. The Scottish Wholesale Society was started in 1868 for the supply of the retail Co-operative trade all through the country, and thus Co-operative production, which was to take a considerable hold on Scotland, was set on foot.

CHAPTER IX

IMPRESSIONS OF SCOTTISH LIFE

WILLIAM COBBETT made a tour of Scotland about the same time as that of which Mr. George Robertson writes in dealing with the Lothians, and he travelled through some of the same country. But Cobbett was, of course, full of political matters, and especially of the passing of the Reform Bill, for which he believed that the working people of the country, and they alone, were responsible ; and in the course of his travels he was always looking out for cases of oppression from their employers and superiors. The consequence was that what struck the Ministers who compiled their Statistical Accounts as admirable and praiseworthy, was to him repulsive and reprehensible ; so much is there in a point of view. The threshing machines, for instance, that were so much admired by them, were to him simply labour destroying ; they were even beginning to be turned into *steam engines*, to him anathema. Indeed, before he reached Scotland, he writes that ' the labourers live in a sort of *barracks*—that is to say, long sheds with stone walls and covered with what are called pantiles. They have neither gardens nor privies nor back doors, and seem altogether to be kept in the same way as if they were under military discipline.

207

208 THE SCOTLAND OF OUR FATHERS

There are no villages ; no scattered cottages ; no up-stairs ; one little window and one door-way to each dwelling in the shed or barrack.' One fancies that the writer might have waited till he had seen all this for himself. He calls the farm a sort of manufactory of corn and of meat, the proceeds of which, with very little deduction, go into the pocket of the big landlord. The men, he declares, are compelled to feed upon those things which ' we in the South give to horses and dogs.' In those far away days the same process of what we now call rationalization was going on: the people were, he considered, being swept from the land by the introduction of new methods. The Poor Law, or absence of Poor Law, in Scotland shocked Cobbett greatly, especially as ' Scotch and Irish renegadoes ' got into England and ' robbed the working people of the compensation for their patrimony,' though they were apparently soon sent back and ' tossed upon their own soil ' ! He allowed, however, that through the Churches much was done to alleviate the sufferings of the destitute ; but claimed that even where there was a certain compulsory assessment it was inadequate. He admired the marvellous fertility of the soil (without giving credit to the plans for making it fertile), the great crops of corn and turnips in the Lothians through which he passed (40 tons of turnips on an English acre), but when the southern ' chop-sticks ' [1] acclaim ' how delightful this land must be with lovely cottages and prancing pigs ' he goes on to disillusion them, and tells them of the large farms, large

---

[1] As he calls his correspondents in England.

farmers' houses and buildings ' as big as a little town,' of a threshing machine worked by horses, water, wind or steam—for steam was introduced about this time to farms near the coal-pits. But for the men there was what he calls a ' boothie,' where they live and sleep, instead of living in a friendly way with the master and mistress as in the South. They hire for the year and cannot quit service under severe punishment. The ' boothies ' of the married men were as described before. To make the most of the room they have to make berths, and are squeezed up, man, woman and children with their meal and working tackle. The food, oatmeal porridge, barley-meal and pea-meal, seems to him beyond contempt ; no wheaten bread, beef or mutton. The family has NO HOME, and the bailiffs are grinding ruffians who are often recommended to England because of the work they enforce from their men. The good labourers of Suffolk are advised to keep clear of farms managed by such cruel men, who might put them in ' boothies ' and feed them on food usually given to horses and hogs. He truly says that the Scotch labourers would not be ' a bit less intellectual if they were to sit down to dinner every day to wheaten bread and meat, with knives and forks and plates, and a nice clean cloth every Sunday, as they get in a considerable part of the farm-houses in the southern counties of England.' ' I advise you to have your eye upon every man who has a Scotch bailiff ; for you may be very sure that his intention is to bring you down to the shed and to the brose ; to prevent you from ever

o

seeing knife or fork or bread again, and to have you considered as being nothing better than the cattle.' As his journeyings went on Cobbett began to appreciate the oatmeal somewhat more, and confessed to having made it, 'when well prepared,' the principal part of his breakfast. His own food he liked, but he observes with justice that 'everybody drinks too much.' As for saying with Dr. Johnson that there were no trees in Scotland, 'that lick-spittle Boswell' must have 'tied a bandage over his eyes'! Lanarkshire pleased him because of its smaller, less factory-like farms, and consequent comparative absence of his detested 'boothies.' Single horse carts also impressed him, and the excellence of the cows and sheep, and, of course, this was even more impressive when he reached Ayrshire and its dairies.

Cobbett's aspirations were quite different from those of the average Scot. He placed emphasis on simple homely living under decent conditions, where men were content with what they had, if what they had was sufficient. The Scot had also been rebelling against his lot, but he had different aspirations : he wanted to have new inventions and new methods so long as he had a hand in them. He did not hate big undertakings if he was given a chance of rising to the top. He did not mind the sort of uncivilized life that Cobbett describes as much as might be imagined, for he had never had the flower-embowered cottage and clean table-cloth Cobbett speaks of, and somewhat despised them in his heart as pertaining to wastefulness.

But that Cobbett had not much exaggerated the state of the dwellings of the married workers is made clear from an interesting book by Robert Somerville, a surgeon in Haddington,[1] though it was written some years earlier. The size given for the new cottages was much as Cobbett describes, *i.e.* 20 feet by 17 feet, and the height of the walls was 7 feet. They were of a single apartment and thatched. Somerville agrees that the cottage system in East Lothian has been criticized as being capable of improvement, and, allowing that the cottages were too few, he is convinced that a little thought would cause the critics to change their opinion and (as has so often been said before and after) ' they would learn to leave matters to find their natural level.' The cottages were numerous enough, he believed, for those in *constant* employment. He did not concern himself about the others. From Somerville's reports as to rent, it appears that the real rent in sterling for the county exceeded £168,878 and it was divided between 190 proprietors. He tells how a certain property of 626 acres purchased at £18,471 13s. 6¼d. in 1779 had in 1798 (after an expenditure on it of about £2,000) been resold at the price of £57,000, thrice the sum paid in 1779, and, being let on nineteen-year leases, now paid five per cent. interest. All this he tells in order to show how land had increased in value. It certainly makes present-day proprietors' mouths water, and explains the fact of the landlords of that day setting about the rebuilding of their mansions : more especially since the ' intelligent and active

[1] *General View of Agriculture in East Lothian*, 1813.

tenantry ' were ready to execute great improvements at their own expense. One would imagine that it might have occurred to landlord or tenant to do something for the houses and ' boothies ' of their workers, even though landlords had done a good deal to improve the farm-houses, as other writers state. And one also feels that there was not too great credit due to the prosperous farmers who were willing to assess themselves volun-tarily to relieve the great sufferings of the distressing years of poverty which occurred early in the century. The absence of a general Poor Law, such as England had enjoyed since the time of Queen Elizabeth, impresses other travellers as well as Cobbett. Failing a voluntary assessment, the money collected at church doors on Sunday was all the country folk had to fall back upon, and knowing how and where it was collected, they were most unwilling to claim it. The hatred of ' coming on the parish ' dates from these early days, and the great Dr. Chalmers did his utmost to have an organized voluntary system for good and all. His own Glasgow parish he organized with the prescience of the Charity Organization Society ; but there was then a Chalmers at the head, and that made all the difference. Many men and women starved in Scotland rather than claim sustenance from those they knew as possibly being not very much better off than themselves ; and this absence of Poor Law probably gave rise to the so-called independence of the Scottish people. Those who remember the feeling of the inhabitants of the Outer Hebrides not long ago when the potato crop failed, and their indignation over being made, as they thought, subjects for newspaper 'stunts' and national collections, will realize what the people of Scotland felt in the many lean years last century.

The Scottish point of view was well put by the Somerville just quoted. He considers that the English Poor Law was a dead weight on all agricultural exertion, and he hopes it may remain unknown in Scotland ; but he is inclined to allow that the poor ought to have some legal claim to support from the public, rather than have to depend on the goodwill of others, especially considering the temper which has sometimes been displayed when persons who happened not to be favourites applied for parochial relief. This throws rather a disturbing light on the lauded Scottish system. ' The character of the people must change before the support of the poor is likely to become a grievous burden here,' he says. And he points out also that as the people who lay on the assessment will be those who have to pay it, ' it will always be so moderate as to afford no encouragement to idleness.' No person, he says, will prefer the scanty pittance of the parish, barely sufficient to preserve life, to his own earnings if he is able to work at all. It is curious to see history repeating itself, with all its problems developing again ; but Somerville's views were practically adopted in Scotland long after this date, under the administration of Parish Councils.

It appears from what we are told that in the Lowlands at least wheaten bread had begun to be used. Somerville speaks of ' the infatuation of the lower ranks in persisting in the use of wheaten bread notwithstanding its high price,' as against that mixture of oats, peas and barley described as equally nutritive and a great deal cheaper. We all know that infatuation which is so easily detected by others in all our actions in such matters ! But however this might be, these luxuries did not extend to the northern counties in the thirties. A paean of gratitude should, however, be granted to the potato, brought in a small quantity from Ireland in 1740 as garden produce, and gradually introduced as ' a valuable article of food for the lower ranks and a substitute for bread at the tables of all superior ranks.' The reports of the Commissioners of the Annexed States give a doleful account of the poverty of the King's estates in Perthshire—a disaffected county, many of whose families had been attainted. The people often enough could not afford even oatmeal, but had to manage with coarse bear-meal. They were ' idle and unenterprising', and no wonder, for they were half-starved.

We ought now to turn to another Scotsman of a different class, who both travelled and observed in Scotland, and from whom we get an accurate and under-standing account of the conditions of his time. Henry, Lord Cockburn, was born in 1779, but he lived till 1854, so that he is a genuine representative of the nine-teenth century. He was an Edinburgh boy, and tells us of the incredible coarseness and roughness of the High School of Edinburgh, where, like Brougham, Scott, and many other great men, he was educated in nothing but weary Latin—and that even badly taught. Then came the time at the ' College of Edinburgh,' which was a degree better, for he studied under the Dalzell who is said to have, perhaps justly, blamed Presbyterianism and its engrossing interests for the Scottish lack of classical knowledge, compared to England. ' If it had not been for that confounded Solemn League and Covenant we could have made as good longs and shorts as they ! '

Cockburn remarks on the two vices which almost universally characterized the upper ranks of society—swearing and drunkenness. It was still, in the early part of the century and for some time onwards, quite common for gentlemen to get drunk after dinner and be unable to join the ladies, or else to join them in a far from agreeable condition. Swearing was not confined to one sex, we are always told, and it was combined with every sort of coarseness in expression. Stories were told by respectable people that in modern days would not bear repetition. The dinner hour in Lord Cockburn's youth was two o'clock, but in his lifetime it gradually got later till it reached the hour of six-thirty. On Sunday it had to be ' between sermons,' *i.e.* between one and two o'clock, for attendance at both services was common even in society not specially religious. At dinner parties champagne was never seen ; port and sherry were the usual drinks. Originally claret was the ordinary beverage, since it was exempt from duty till about 1780, but the horror of everything French drove it from all tables during the wars.

' Healths ' and toasts were real torments, especially to the young and shy; but it took a long time for them to die out. Every glass during dinner required to be dedicated to the health of someone; then there were ' rounds ' of toasts after the ladies left, and, worst of all, ' sentiments ' which had to be composed by the miserable proposer.

As dinner was early, supper played a large part in social life. Those who are old enough to do so can remember the familiar cry of the Newhaven fishwives about nine o'clock, ' Caller 'ou,' which meant that the fresh oysters in their creels were all ready for supper. Cockburn says that he doubts if from the year 1811, when he married, he went more than one day in a month without company at supper; and this was not in these times an unusual case. ' So far as I have seen social life, its brightest sunshine has been on the last repast of the day.' Cockburn goes on to relate that even the ministers had a good supper after their exertions on the Sunday, like the famous Sir Harry Moncrieff who walked home after preaching, his ' bands ' on, ' his little cocked hat, his tall cane, and his cardinal air,' and who, after holding family worship at nine, ' sat down to the roasted hens, the goblets of wine and his powerful talk.' The ' Moderates ' still reigned, but though people might be lax in conduct and easy, going in their beliefs, the French infidelity which was so much feared did not make much progress in Scotland. The horrors of the French Revolution were a general topic of conversation, and though the young men were keen to discuss Adam

EDIN. ROYAL VOLUNTEERS.

EDINBURGH ROYAL VOLUNTEERS
FROM KAY'S PORTRAITS

Smith and his political philosophy, as well as the views of Hume, Robertson, Montesquieu and the other great writers of the time, these new doctrines were considered dangerous by their conventional elders. It was a case of the young once more breaking in on the prejudices of the old, and the intolerances of a time of war, or of threatenings of war, are too well known to require description. The horror of everything French blotted out all the old friendship with a country with which Scotland had hitherto had so much in common; and later in the century it was to Germany and German Universities that Scotland looked for her culture.

Knee-breeches were still adhered to by the older people, for trousers were considered Jacobinical; and Cockburn tells us that loyalists thanked God that they had always ' stuck to the Constitution and buckles.' The French wore their hair short and undressed, and therefore the loyal laid on hair powder with profusion; but when a tax was put on powder their loyalty waned.

Public feasts were coarse and rough, and especially so was the official recognition of the King's Birthday, in which there was neither order nor decency, but ' roaring, drinking, toasting and quarrelling.' After such a feast the Parliament House, usually so grave and solemn, was left in a disgraceful state, full of broken glass and disgusting fumes.

As to defence, the ' Gentlemen Volunteers ' were patriotic but useless. Fortunately for them, however, there were few real Jacobins despite the efforts considered necessary to control them by an amateur army.

Toryism of the extremest kind existed, and as this party engrossed almost all the wealth and rank and public office of the country, every sort of ridiculous tale was told of those who professed different principles. The Whigs were but few till the Whig revival came with its outstanding men such as Henry Erskine, John Clerk, James Gibson, and, finally, Cockburn and Jeffrey. It is curious that it was the legal profession, perhaps the most conservative of all professions, that led the revolt against Toryism and the domination of Henry Dundas, hitherto the absolute dictator of Scotland. This revolt, when it took effect amongst the common people, made Scotland Liberal in politics for many a long day to come. The publication of the *Scotsman* newspaper was the beginning of the end. The appearance of such a paper was a portent, and many lawyers only ventured to subscribe for it in the names of their clerks. It had eminent writers and editors and soon made its way, serious and heavy as it now seems when one reads it. Before this time no paper had the courage to criticize even the mismanagement of the local institutions, much less political affairs.

A landmark in Scotland, as all intelligent observers say, was the first Exhibition of Scottish Art, which was held in Sir Henry Raeburn's house in 1809, and continued to 1813. Raeburn, Nasmyth and John Thomson were the best-known exhibitors; but excellent as was their work there was small encouragement for them, since there was little public taste for art, and, except for Raeburn's portraits, no market for its production.

This, however, was a beginning, and art in Scotland grew and flourished as time went on.

It was its literature, however, that made Edinburgh famous in the earlier part of the nineteenth century. *Waverley* was published in 1814, and it made a sensation such as it is difficult now to realize. The description of Scottish characters, Scottish scenery, Scottish language seemed to waken Scotsmen to the glory of their heritage, and to make them understand what they had never really understood, the manner of men that they were and the beauty and romance of their country. Of course there were plenty to say it vulgarized their country by bringing tourists in multitudes to its peaceful lochs and mountains ! It became very soon a known secret who was the author ; Scott himself had been famed not only for his poetry but for his talk, his stories, and sayings ' all graced by gaiety, simplicity and kindness,' and who else could have written these wonderful tales ?

One of the cases tried before Cockburn throws a dreadful light on the social conditions of the time. A poor little chimney boy, scarcely eight years old, was compelled by threats to go up or down thirty-eight new chimneys successively, without any interval for rest or food, though he was quite exhausted, cold, wet and excoriated ; he implored that he might not be sent down another, but was forced to descend the thirty-eighth vent, in which he died. The labour and danger was greatly increased by the vents being new, the object of descending them being to clear them by means of a chisel of the lime and rubbish that adhered to their sides, a task requiring time and strength. This crime, which seems to us so terrible, was only charged as culpable homicide, since the work was regarded as a necessary part of the operations of a brutal trade. It seems strange that as late as the year 1840 such terrible conditions should exist.

Transportation was still the punishment most in vogue, since, to Cockburn's disgust, public sentiment was turning against capital sentences for robbery and similar crimes; he considered this weak sentimentality not to be encouraged.

In the course of making his circuits Cockburn had, he said, occasion to blush for his country, so bad were the inns of which he had to make use. 'The pigs were as comfortably accommodated,' as he declares. For this, good Whig as he was, he rather unjustly blamed the ducal and other landlords. And he bewailed the condition of the cottages on the coasts, picturesque enough at a distance. ' It is,' he says, ' horrid that human life should be passed in these disgusting holes; until lands be civilized and cease to be all regularly and systematically bankrupt, it is vain to expect decency and comfort in the domestic habits of their people.' It is strange at this date to find the constant denunciations of the lairds, particularly the Highland lairds, who had been living through a time which should not have led to bankruptcy. There was, Cockburn allows, marked improvement in the houses between Perth and Blair, which used to be even worse than the ' pig styes of Luss.' On that

Great North Road between Dunkeld and Aviemore,
now so busy, the judge had met but two gigs, one mail
coach and not a dozen carts, and as he passed on his way
the tree lover regretted the planting of the ' abominable
larch ' instead of forest trees such as chestnut and oak.
Larch was a comparatively new importation and far
from popular ; one cannot conceive why.

Cockburn, like most other travellers in Scotland, had
none of the romantic admiration for the Highland chief-
tain that is presented to us by Scott.   In fact, nothing is
more strange than the contrast between the representa-
tions of the romantic novelist and those of the matter-
of-fact traveller.   He deplores the terrible condition of
the inhabitants of the Outer Islands in this time of stress.
He also deplores the way in which the ancient monu-
ments were neglected, for he was always concerned
about the preservation of ancient landmarks.   He saw
that tourists were already covering the land, filling
every conveyance and inn, 'attracted by scenery and
curiosity, superfluous time and wealth, and the
fascination of Scott.'   So much so that ' the mansions
of half our poor devils of Highland lairds are occupied
by rich and kilted southrons.'   By the forties the
influx from the South was beginning, and all hoped
that ' the English purses and English comfort of the
southern supplanters of our banished beggarly but
proud lairds ' would do something to help to abolish the
mud hovels and poor forms of humanity everywhere to
be seen.   But the great defender of its character and
beauties sadly realized that these new birds of passage,

who came in droves and flocks and had their uses, might accelerate the passing of everything that was peculiarly characteristic of his country.

Cockburn has many reflections as to churchyards, suggested by the disgraceful condition of the Priory of Beauly, then overgrown by nettles and full of rubbish. The Scots, he says, believe that if the soul is safe why misapply a sigh over the dust it associates with no more; and accordingly not one hundred modern tombs in Scotland are even decent; and amongst the dozen that are beautifully kept most belong to Episcopalians. He fears that though the Scots may be a pious race they are wholly regardless of their dead. This condemnation was justified long after the date at which Cockburn wrote, but others than lairds were responsible.

Another accusation against the Scottish lairds is their absence of sufficient sense or humanity to make the enjoyment of their places a source of enjoyment to others. This is a theme constantly dwelt on by Lord Cockburn. They seem, he says, to frown on every stranger as an enemy who was not to be admitted within their gates; and nothing provokes mischief so surely as the practice of stern exclusion from everything beyond the line of the highway. Examples of this can be remembered even after Cockburn's time, when lairds went so far as to threaten to shoot interlopers who were merely passing through their avenues. On Sunday, he says, any grounds for which permission to enter might on week-days be obtained are absolutely closed, and the fact that in Perth the beautiful surroundings ought to have caused the truly pious to enjoy God's works, instead of neglecting them, causes him to dwell on the wrongfulness of the Calvinistic grimness that reigned in Scotland. The old barriers were beginning to fall !

By 1842 the learned Lord deigned occasionally to use the railway, avoiding contamination with the common herd by travelling in a coupé, or private carriage. In the course of his journeys he played a useful part at Stirling in recommending that the public wells should each have more than one spout, having been struck by the rows of poor shivering people who had to wait for hours their turns to draw from the wells ! He saw, indeed, as many as 200 tubs, pails, pitchers ranged beside their owners in the street ! This bright idea had never occurred to the powers that be, and the truly Scottish Provost thought it might be carried out only ' if it did not incur material cost ' ! Such were the comforts of mid-Victorian town life. Victorian prudery is evidenced in the judge's condemnation of bathing for ladies excepting when conducted in extreme seclusion ; and Cockburn's feelings were shocked at what is now a commonplace arrangement. Portobello, where men's and women's bathing machines were adjoining one another, was bad enough ; but at Rothesay there were not even bathing machines ! He does not say how Rothesay divested herself of her garments ! And the railway mania greatly concerned this valiant Whig supporter of ancient ways and places : ' The country is an asylum of railways lunatics,' he says. ' The Inverness patients insist on having one by the Highland road from Perth, though there are no towns or even villages or chances of many passengers, and as to scenery, it meant nothing to these vandals.' The lairds, according to him, did nothing to help : ' They can dine off plate and build Puseyite chapels,' but ' not lay out one shilling in protecting a ruin that does them more honour than their title.' The charge for admission to Melrose Abbey was another evil, for it could be open to all ' if it received one thousandth the attention that the ducal kennel does.' The Abbey was not to be seen on Sunday, nor was the Free Church given a spot of ground, so that its adherents had to worship under the open sky. All these denunciations showed that the wind was veering in the direction which was for many years to be that which guided Liberal Scotland—Liberal but conventional too, with the conventionality of Victorianism.

Lord Cockburn was a considerable traveller, for he was able to look back on forty years of judge's circuits when he wrote his book in 1847. In the early days it was a serious business for his carriage to negotiate the fords. The mail coach, which went no further than Aberdeen, was a sort of chaise drawn by two horses, holding only three persons, and to go to Inverness from Edinburgh took four days by the direct Highland road, as there were neither public conveyances nor post-horses. The judges had four horses to convey their carriage, which made progress easier, but in earlier days it was necessary to ride the circuit on horseback, for carriage driving was not practicable. In Lord Cockburn's later days he always took ' the ladies ' with him ;

but that, of course, was impossible in early times, for the conditions were too rough. In 1808 and 1809 the Justice Clerk doffed his wig and reviewed the Volunteers ; for that was a time at which the fear of war caused volunteering to be in full swing, and it was enjoined on the Magistrates and gentry to attend the Circuit Courts in order to support the majesty of the law. The foot procession from every meeting or rising of the court was *de rigueur* up to about 1820, and the scene was illuminated by torches if these were required. Black bottles of strong port and biscuits were set beside the judges if they were kept beyond the dinner hour, which must indeed have made the mouths of the unfortunate counsel water ! Balls and feasts were given at certain towns on Circuit, so that the Judge's advent rejoiced the hearts of the young ladies in the country.

One of the Circuit cases which shocks modern minds was that in which an accusation of rioting was in 1849 brought against four respectable men in regard to a Highland clearing in North Uist. The whole population of Solas was ejected without providing the people with shelter or even with the means of emigrating abroad ; and these were people who had sown crops which they could never reap, who had no roof to cover them, or poorhouse to go to ; they had simply to lie down on the bare, wet beach. No life was lost by the so-called riots, so that this could not be brought against them. The men were convicted and imprisoned for four months, but on conviction a recommendation was added that they should be given ' the utmost leniency

P

and mercy of the Court, in consideration of the cruel, though it may be legal, proceedings adopted in ejecting the whole people of Solas from their houses and crops without the prospect of a shelter or a footing in their fatherland, or even the means of expatriating them to a foreign one.' In defence it was stated that preparations had been made for emigrating the people, but that they —reasonably enough—asked for delay till they could sell their stock at the summer market. Anyhow, there was no practical means of sending them abroad. The marvel is that greater bitterness has not resulted because of these desperate deeds not a century ago.

.   .   .   .

Southey made a journey to Scotland with Telford, the engineer, in 1819, and he tells us a good deal about the social life of the country as it appeared to him ; and it is always interesting to have accounts given from different angles and from those coming from another part of the kingdom.

As in the case of most English travellers, Southey was struck with the dirt of the inhabitants and of the ' windes, down which an English eye may look, but into which no English nose would willingly venture ; for stinks older than the Union are to be found there.' This reminds us of the account given of Edinburgh wynds in *Humphrey Clinker*, and of the primitive way in which impurities were got rid of not long before, when the cry of ' gardy-loo ! ' (*gardez l'eau*) warned passengers of what was coming from the high windows above them ! The houses seemed not to have been whitewashed since they were built, Southey says, and the windows of ordinary houses were in wooden frames instead of casements, and the panes were often broken and seldom mended but with paper or clouts. The girls he thought disgusting in their bare feet and hair in papers—the ' Medusa papers ' he calls them. To find bare feet in the case of otherwise well-dressed girls seemed to shock him terribly. This custom, however, was continued by servant girls for twenty or more years after Telford's visit, even in the most respectable houses ; and it always caused astonishment, if not exactly disgust, when observed by conventional Englishmen.

As we have seen, the country was still unenclosed and without hedges, but Lord Kames' work at Blair Drummond interested Southey, for that energetic laird was busy reclaiming the moss and otherwise effecting improvements. Southey was struck by what he regarded as a new invention, viz. an iron gate. Gates, indeed, of any kind were rare, so unenclosed was the land, but iron gates were unknown. On the other hand, he was very critical of the fact that, unlike other towns, Dundee was unflagged, though quarries were near at hand and stone could easily have been procured. The granite buildings then being erected in Aberdeen he admired, though the Town Council had apparently made themselves bankrupt through their improvements. Breakfasts he considered good and plenteous, as Scotch breakfasts always were, but there was but a ' poor Scotch allowance of water.' Of sanitary arrangements or commodities there at least existed some in the garden, ' the want of which was formerly the reproach of Scotland '; and the beds had ' every possible fault of bedmaking,' besides being hard and sloping in an inclined plane to the foot. We knew that bed, which existed a hundred years after Southey's visit in Scottish inns ! A satisfactory point is that he found to his surprise bookshops in most Scottish towns. They must have been of a humble sort, but still they existed.

Southey and Telford made their way to Inverness (where sixty years before there had been no shops but only booths) to inspect Telford's roads up Strathglass and to Loch Carron and Dornoch. Nowadays, he tells us, a ' Diligence ' went all the way to Thurso carrying three inside passengers.

James Haldane had an adventurous time in the first years of the century, when carrying on his ' Itineracies ' for the evangelization of the remoter parts of the country. When he went to Wick and Thurso his gig often enough could not negotiate the roads and he had to walk. Being a wonderful walker this did not, however, disturb him, especially as everywhere he met with a welcome and large congregations. Having been a sailor he was able to pass from island to island in an open boat, whose helm he had to take. He managed to go to Orkney and Shetland in this way, and to yet more remote islands in terrible weather, wrapped in the ' boat-cloak ' which had served him on his voyages to India when captain of an East Indiaman.

At other times he rode with his servant; thus his experiences were varied; sometimes he slept on boards and ate salted herrings and oat-cake, and at other times he was hospitably entertained in gentlemen's houses, but he took whatever befel him stoically and without complaint. On one of the occasions of the administration of the Sacrament those present were averse to coming forward, as was usually the case in the Highlands. Suddenly he heard a crack, which signified a blow on the bald head of one of the people, administered by the Ruling Elder with the view of hastening proceedings which were being unduly delayed !

Islan of Ar (handwritten marginal note)

The early nineteenth century must have been a very pleasant time for intellectual well-to-do people in Scotland. We are told that ' they formed an aristocracy that shone undisturbed.' It was a stationary society, for locomotion by private carriages or clumsy public coaches was slow. Lord Sands tells us that an Edinburgh citizen, who by leaving Cupar at 6 a.m. reached Edinburgh about 9 o'clock and had the best of the day there, considered that a century later such celerity would still be admired.

Cockburn gloried in the political changes that had come about. In 1830 he speaks of ' the last links of the Scotch feudal chains dropping off under the hammers that one may distinctly hear erecting the first Hustings our country ever saw ' ! . . . ' Happy are we who have been permitted to scent the " morning air ".' [1]   The

[1] *Letters of Henry Cockburn.* Introduction by Lord Sands. 1932. Grant & Murray.

Church appeared to be ' shaking in its gross temporal pillars and to be strengthening its spiritual foundations,' while the Press was making the world one audience. It was indeed a time of enthusiasm, anyhow for the prosperous.

. . . .

The journey to Scotland of William Wordsworth and his sister was another interesting visit paid very early in the century (1803), and it records a simple mode of living amongst the people with whom they and Coleridge (who accompanied them to begin with) often lodged for the night. They made their journey in a sort of Irish car, though they often went on foot, and one of the main objects of the journey was to see the Trossachs, apparently famous even then to the initiated, for it was before Scott wrote the *Lay* or the *Lady of the Lake*. The dirt and discomfort of the inns is once more a constant theme of remark and reproach, and even the gentlemen's houses and grounds had in the travellers' view an air of neglect and desolation. There were, as every traveller notes, hardly any enclosures excepting those around the newly planted woods of larch and fir, mostly surrounding the big houses. The village children and young women, of course, walked barefoot, and coming home from church they carried their shoes and stockings in a bundle over their arms. Some of the barefoot boys were, however, learning Latin and Greek at school, which seemed astonishing to the southern visitors. In Glasgow they were struck by the dulness and dreariness in the aspect and demeanour of the ' dim, common population.' There was certainly an appearance of business and bustle, but no coaches or gentlemen's carriages were to be seen ! In the Highland farmhouse all sat together round the fire, master and man, and the kitchen roof, walls and floor of mud were all black alike. There was again great criticism of the lairds who went to Edinburgh, leaving their own people and spending their money ' where they had no esteem.' The little walled-in burying-places of the lairds, ' like a pinfold with a stone ball at every corner,' were dismal spots, overgrown as they were with long grass, nettles and brambles. The Highland cottages were such as has been so often described, the cowhouse at the end, the kitchen in the middle with fire finding exit for its smoke in the roof, and then the inner room beyond ; the floors all of black mud, apt to be full of puddles in wet weather. The beds were of chaff and the food as usual, barley-broth, oatcakes, porridge ; and, curiously, it was said that umbrellas were used even by those whose clothing was of the simplest. This seems strange even in the wet Western Highlands, for umbrellas were only introduced about the middle of the eighteenth century.

. . . .

Mrs. Fletcher was a remarkable Englishwoman who, through her husband, who wrote for the *Edinburgh Review*, came into touch in Edinburgh with Brougham, Jeffrey, Francis Horner and James Grahame, author of *The Sabbath*, and Henry Erskine, all of the Whig party, and looked upon as Democrats by the Pitt and Dundas faction. Mrs. Hamilton and Mrs. Grant of Laggan were of those who had specially pleasant parties, and there were as guests Walter Scott, Jeffrey, Dr. Thomas Brown, Mackenzie, Prof. Playfair, Mr. Pillans and the Rev. Dr. Alison, all belonging to the literary coterie. Evening parties which took place from nine to twelve o'clock, with tea and coffee and light cold refreshments, were all the fashion. There was amateur acting, too, when the play of *Douglas* and some of Joanna Baillie's dramas were got up, and altogether the society was lively and full of interest. Sydney Smith and many distinguished men from London visited Edinburgh and made a pleasant society pleasanter. Lord John Russell was studying as a young man under the aegis of Professor Playfair. Later on we know from her delightful book *Mystifications* how the clever Miss Graham of Duntrune played pranks on Jeffrey by dressing up as an eccentric old lady and coming to consult him on her legal difficulties. From 1813 holiday time was spent by the Fletchers at Balfron in Stirlingshire ; here there was a weekly carrier who brought with him bread, groceries and letters ; the contents of the letter bag for the village were poured out on the road, whence they were supposed to be laid hold of by the proper recipients ! Smuggling was rampant in the Campsie hills ; the wives and daughters of the men who distilled the spirits used to carry them to Glasgow buckled around their waists as stays. A cotton mill was established in the village, and this brought a wild population with it, for all the industrial population in those days was apt to be lawless and undisciplined.

The visit of George IV to Edinburgh in 1822 affected everyone, Whigs and Tories alike, so well was the whole function staged, mainly by Walter Scott. The King responded nobly, for he told Sir Walter that he had always heard the Scotch were a proud nation and they might well be so, ' for they are a nation of gentlemen and live in a city of palaces ' ! Scotland was deeply gratified by these sentiments.

This royal visit indeed caused a quite extraordinary sensation, seeing that the principal actor in it was none too popular in his northern dominions. It is well described in some privately printed letters from the family of Grant of Rothiemurchus.[1]

The young ladies who wrote these letters tell us all about the preparations made for the occasion ; the caps which were to be worn ' gaily decorated ' ; the pearl white silk hats, the spencers to match the white feathers of the hat which had therefore to be ' dipped.' But above all they describe the Highland chieftains who were to appear with their ' tails.' The father was as keen about it all as the girls, though he deprecates the sort of Highland costumes which some of the visitors wore ' with as much propriety as if it had been Paris or Brussels,' and like all men jeers at the state of bustle into which the sedate citizens of Edinburgh had entered. He himself felt constrained, however, to do his part, and that was, as the possessor of the highest mountain

[1] The letters were written by Jane Grant, born 1800 (Mrs. James Gibson Craig), and Mary F. Grant, born 1804 (Mrs. Gardner), daughters of John Peter Grant of Rothiemurchus, during their visit to Edinburgh in August 1822.

in the King's dominion, to send his royal master ptarmigan, the birds that inhabit high mountains. A few ptarmigan might have been useful, though it seems doubtful whether King George would have greatly appreciated those not too appetizing birds; but the loyal retainers in the North dispatched no fewer than thirty brace for the King's consumption !

Mrs. Siddons' presence added much to the gaiety of the occasion and she drilled the girls in making their curtsies. The Edinburgh dressmakers were not quite up to the mark, and Jane Grant got her Court dress from London. This produced immense anxiety, for the mail coach, at a time when there was great demand on its capacities, refused to take bulky parcels. However, at length the much longed-for box did arrive, and with it full directions from those who knew London fashions as to how the hair was to be dressed and how the lappets were to be pinned in the middle of the bow; how the black velvet pad on which the feathers were pinned was to be covered with jewels well secured; and altogether the dressmaker in the metropolis was full of anxiety about her wares being shown to the best advantage. As so often happens, alas, in Scotland, on the first day the rain did sad execution on the ladies in white gowns and on the gentlemen in white trousers, which were splashed all over; on the yeomanry with their fine new coats, the lace all soiled; on the new liveries of the servants, tarnished with the wet. Suddenly, after all preparations were made, the news came that the King would not arrive till next day—'a pairfect wasterie' of good meat and jellies, as was said by the canny Scots. The next day came, and the ungainly King with his procession had mercifully lovely sunshine, and all went well, the bonnets being fortunately recognized as 'London.' Then the illuminations ; and Edinburgh illuminates as no other town. The walk to see the sights was made under the guardianship of Mr. Jeffrey ; another day brought the Levee, when all the gentlemen curled their hair, and fine bouquets were carried by the servants. Then Sunday arrived, marred by a 'disgraceful service' in which a great deal was made 'of the honour His Majesty did us in visiting this barren and inclement clime where the rays of the sun were never seen to penetrate,' and when the implication was made that the Scots were 'Nobodies' 'till their Union with a Braver Nation.' This was difficult to bear for loyal Scots.

Finally the Court : the Frenchman who arrived at 7 a.m. to undertake the young ladies' heads did them so badly that the wonderful Mrs. Siddons, a friend and connection by marriage, dressed the girls herself—hair, gown, train, everything—to their immense satisfaction. Jane and Mary consequently looked their best, and Mrs. Siddons was as pleased as they, and their father was delighted. Later on the great actress acted Portia to Kean's Shylock, which must indeed have been a delight. All past offences were forgiven to the King, and his dignity 'made you feel respect not only for him but for yourself.' He duly gave his kisses, though some ladies thought not sufficiently thoroughly, and Mary declared complainingly that she just felt him brush her cheeks ! Other dissipations followed, though rain poured, and as the King drank nothing but whisky a dozen of the best Glenlivet had to be sent from the cellar at Rothiemurchus.

There were many contretemps, such as the young would-be Celt who dropped his pistols on His Majesty's toe and lamed him thereby ; the young Dundas, who, when told by the lord-in-waiting to kiss hands, kissed his own hands to the King ! Then there was Lady Saltoun who said that if the King wore the kilt at the Drawing-room she did not know what the ladies would do, it would be shocking. And Lady Hamilton made the astute reply, ' Oh, if he's to be here so short a time, the more we see of him the better ! ' There was also the Review on Portobello sands, and so ended one of the greatest social events in Scotland during the early nineteenth century.

For Highlanders the visit was somewhat marred, indeed, by the stout King appearing at his Levee in Highland dress. Lord Aberdeen says that Peel and Melville tried in vain to dissuade him from doing so since he was the first King of Scotland who ever wore it since the times of actual barbarism. The Earl also highly objected to all being dubbed Highlanders, and, though the streets were finely decorated, the rain was trying and he longed to be back with his gardener, his forester and gamekeeper at Haddo.[1] That was where he did so much valuable service for his country, though it is

[1] *Life of George :* Fourth Earl of Aberdeen.

not remembered as is his work as a Minister of the Crown.

There were other functions that diversified life for the well-to-do during the century.

It was a real misfortune that in 1839 the rain spoiled what should have been a great mediaeval spectacle in the tournament at Eglinton Castle. It had been prepared for months before, and there was a crowd to see it from England, the Continent and America. The multitude was indeed overwhelming, and all promised well until the day arrived, when the sunshine was extinguished and the rain continued for hours. Thirty or forty thousand pounds of outlay was annihilated, though the undaunted Lord Eglinton at the head of his cavalcade did his best to carry out the programme.

Such celebrations in open air are dangerous in Scotland, as was also seen in a great Burns Festival on the banks of the Doon in 1844, where Lord Eglinton also figured, and which must have recalled to him in weather his unhappy experiences five years before. The Volunteer Review by Queen Victoria in the Queen's Park, Edinburgh, in 1881, was another national disaster as regards weather. The Scots have indeed to be inured to what Providence may bestow on them in this respect.

CHAPTER X

HOW THE PEOPLE MOVED ABOUT

IN the eighteenth century roads were far from being in a good condition. The idea was that six days' service should be given to roadmaking by tenants—three days after bear seed time and three days after harvest, but this was often commuted at the rate of sixpence per day. Tolls came into operation in 1714, and at first the turnpike duty was laid only on the industrial part of the community and others were exempted. However, this was so evidently unjust that in 1751 a new Act for the Edinburgh district made carriages of six or more horses pay sixpence, four horses fourpence, and so on. There were further Acts passed of a local sort, taxing gentlemen's carriages and industrial carriages alike. But the toll-bars were too few, and the statute labour was done without either will or method; there was no engineering excepting what was necessary through the desire to avoid hollows or swamps which became quagmires. Carts and carriages had often to half swim through these, and new tracks were then attempted; in the few cases where the track was confined within walls ' travellers were sadly beset, and had to float through or jolt through with all the patience they could muster.' Goods, of course, went mainly by horseback, especially such goods as meal, coals and peats which were in sacks. Straw and hay loads completely concealed the horses which bore them. The single-horse traffickers, known as cadgers, who carried fish, eggs, poultry, etc., were well-known characters both in the eighteenth and the next century. They were able to take the roughest tracks and had known resting places such as the ' Cadgers' Yetts.' The town carrier had a horse which dragged a rudely formed cart ' through dirt and through mire along these unshapely roads from one town to another.' The townsmen of the adventurous individual whose way took him along the channel of the Gala from Selkirk to Edinburgh turned out to take leave of him and wish him a safe return from the adventurous enterprise on which he was embarking, and which took nearly two weeks coming and going, though it was only 38 miles in distance. In 1758 a heavy coach ran between Edinburgh and Glasgow, drawn by five horses. It took twelve hours to do the journey, while in 1827 the distance was reduced to five hours because of the ' perfect state of smoothness ' in which the road was kept. Also by this time the drivers of stage-coaches had ' splendid liveries ' which betokened their high estate. In 1792 there was but one stage-coach—the one which once a month set out for London and took twelve to fourteen days on the journey of 400 miles—in addition to ' the Fly ' to Glasgow. It was said to be the use of wheels rather than horseback that made the roads so bad. Carts instead of sledges began to be used about 1750 by progressive landlords. One can realize the scene when the

migration took place of the great families on going to
and from town ; ' a whole cavalcade was mustered up
of it may be six or eight horses or more, among whom
was to be seen the tall sumpter horse, bestrode by the
butler, with a cargo of good things under him in pan-
niers—a component and most essential part of the
expedition.' [1]

The improvements in the making of public roads
went on apace as the eighteenth century passed to the
nineteenth. It seemed clear that a substantial stone
bottom was required for any good road ; but at first it
was thought that the bigger the stones the better for
their purpose ; small stones filled the interstices.
Thus was the turnpike or toll road made, and a jolting
road it was. Then came stones laid in two tiers—the
larger below and the small stone or gravel above. Unluckily the large stones always tended to come to the
surface, and the Macadam system of having all the
stones broken small (so small, it was said, that one
would go into a man's mouth), and the whole mass
of metal laid together so that it consolidated, was at
length adopted for the country, though causeways were
considered best for towns because of the dust and mud.
Then came the question of the better engineering of the
roads ; but the country gentlemen who were the Road
Trustees were much averse to the expense of carrying
out this improvement. There was also to be considered
the possibility of breaking in upon enclosures, and above
all on gentlemen's policies or pleasure grounds, the very

[1] *Rural Recollections*, by George Robertson, 1829.

idea of which was hotly resented. The large number of authorities dealing with roads was another drawback to good road-making. On the whole, however, the improvements were great : the roads went up and down still, but that was thought better than a dead level, and the wheels passed over them ' glibly.'

It seems curious to find the violent opposition that existed to new road-making on the part of various sorts of people. The gentlemen would not have a road near their mansion-houses ; the tenantry would not have it near their farm-houses, especially if they lived in proximity to a town, for they believed that it would probably result in vagrants and disorderly people coming to steal from them. ' Nobody above the rank of a coal-carter would like to have a road thrust upon his dwelling,' says Mr. Robertson.

Milestones and direction posts were introduced about 1765, but even in 1829 ' blackguards and idle boys ' marred and defaced ' these useful institutions.' Byeways and ' kirk roads ' were but tracks ; the only dressing which they received even in 1829 was the field stones thrown into them. Bridges were not numerous, and were usually formed in a single arch in the shape of a semicircle, so that they had literally to be climbed ; one sees these bridges still.

In 1780 there were no roads north of the Tay except those made for military purposes ; and George Dempster, M.P., a veritable ' improver ' and evidently a sort of pacifist, said that ' these roads are the first work the nation should undertake, long at least before it goes to

Q

war with France.' It was joyful news to him that the
Turnpike Act was passed in 1792. In 1799 he said
triumphantly, 'Already the mail-coach has reached
Inverness, and turnpike roads the extremity of Aberdeenshire.' By the Act of 1803 Parliament undertook
to provide half the estimated expense of necessary
roads and bridges, and only the other half had to be
provided by the landed proprietors.

Charles Cowan in his privately printed *Reminiscences*
relates that he had constantly to travel to and fro
to London in the twenties, and he gives a terrible
account of what happened in snowstorms. The time
occupied normally for going from London to Lanark
was seventy-two hours. The cost, with fees and meals,
was about £10. In severe weather, however, travellers
often got stuck in the snow, and in the severe storm
of 1831 the mail-coach to Dumfries was overwhelmed
by snow, the horses absolutely buried, and the bodies
of guard and driver were found a week afterwards cold
and stiff.

In road-making as in everything else private interest
kept interfering with public convenience. It was in old
days thought that independent persons with no private
ends to promote might be appointed to fix the great
lines of roads. We have had that principle reappearing
with railways and electrical transmission ever since, and
yet somehow the same difficulties always reappear while
human nature remains unchanged. Telford, who had
been a poor Scottish boy from Dumfries, and who from
being a stonemason managed to make his way to London

anyone could ever have settled there. And it had a sinister reputation between its witch-burning and slave trade ; for it is well authenticated that (about 1740) men were freely kidnapped there, driven with whips, and sold to the American Plantations as slaves. The city of Dundee had pleasanter associations, for it had a specially well constructed harbour which was much admired and which was completed in 1825.

It was the possibility of war — the French war in this case—that suggested the making of a canal across Scotland by the Great Glen, so that the stormy voyage round the Pentland Firth might be obviated. Watt had previously made a survey at the instance of the Commissioners of the Forfeited Estates. The work was carried out successfully by Telford but proved a financial failure, and this grieved him much, especially as he had been over-sanguine about its success. The Broomielaw Bridge in Glasgow and Dean Bridge in Edinburgh are other famous Scottish bridges built by Telford.

The Board of Commissioners had used their Fund well for North Scotland. They found it ' barren and uncultivated, inhabited by heritors without capital or enterprise . . . destitute of trade, shipping and manufactures.' They left it ' with wealthy proprietors, a profitable agriculture, a thriving population and active industry.' This happy consummation may not have been entirely owing to their efforts, but they had a great part in it, and Scotland owes a great debt to the Commissioners of the Forfeited Estates and to their intelligent policy.

One regrets that the work of this early ' Development Commission' came to an end on the restoration of the Estates.

Southey's account of his visit with Thomas Telford to inspect his roads in Scotland gives one a good idea of their condition in 1819, after a considerable amount of the latter's work was done. The Glencoe road, always a test road, the two did manage to traverse in their carriage, but that was by the help of the contractors who had employed their men in clearing the road for the Commissioner. It must, indeed, have been a difficult job, but in 1803 Wordsworth and his sister did just succeed in getting along it with their queer horse-shay, by walking a great part of the way. Southey says that no one could guard against the ' petriferous torrents ' that rushed down the mountains, and that the only remedy must be to look for a better line of road ; now done in a very effectual, if expensive way ! The road from Inverness to Dornoch appears to have been good, and with difficulty the Poet Laureate and Telford managed to drive from Dingwall to Strome Ferry, theirs being the first carriage which had ever got so far. ' To hear of such roads in such a country and to find them in the wild western Highlands is so surprising, everything else being in so rude a state, that their utility, or at least their necessity, might be doubted if half the expense were not borne by voluntary taxation.' After saying this Southey explains that the lairds (for whom he had no love) recovered their large arrears of rent by making their tenants work for them and so discharge a debt that would never have been paid in money. That is to say, when the expense of a road was £5,000 they got £2,500 from the Government and the tenants gave £5,000 worth of work, so that the lairds were ultimately the gainers by what they received and by the improvement on the value of their estates.

Perthshire alone would have nothing to do with the Commissioners and their projects, for suddenly the travellers came on the 'Devil's Bowling Green,' and when their bones and breeches had equally suffered they were told that it was 'only Perthshire'!

Telford was, however, a critical traveller whenever one of Wade's famous bridges was approached. Like all the General's bridges they were in his view badly constructed. However, despite his criticism, they seem to have stood the test of another century and more, and the Aberfeldy bridge is both strong and attractive to look at still. When Dorothy and William Wordsworth went through the Lowlands and the Perthshire and Argyllshire Highlands in 1803 they managed to negotiate most of the main thoroughfares with their horse and Irish car, making the poor horse swim the fords if to take it on a boat was impossible. They saw only one stage-coach during the two months of their journey, and that was near Langholm on their return home. The day of coaches had not yet arrived, and it was to prove a short one in Scotland.

Telford was a great engineer : he reconstructed under the Commission the road from Carlisle to Glasgow in 1816. The fact was that road-making in Scotland and

Ireland had been carried on to meet political necessity from the time of General Wade in 1725, and the well-made roads in both were better than the English turn-pikes. Others like Lord Dare, eldest son of Lord Sel-kirk, and Abercromby, a landed gentleman who had become a professional road engineer, gave their assist-ance in the process of improvement. In 1819 even the roads round London were disgraceful, and there were constant complaints about them owing to the growing postal business of the country. The influence of John Loudon Macadam, a Scot who was a Turnpike Trustee in Ayrshire, though he spent a good deal of his life in the South and was not a professional road constructor, did much to reform the whole system of road con-struction. He, indeed, revolutionized the system so far as surface making was concerned. His was an economical system, for a solid bottom was not required, and hence it appealed to the Turnpike Trustees ; but Macadam did a good work also in advocating the em-ployment of fully competent and well-paid labourers in road-making, for which hitherto unskilled labour had frequently been used and bad workmanship had ensued.

The General Road Act of 1845 made further great improvements in the matter of roads, and in the eighties tolls were abolished. Those who can look back so far will remember the annoyance of carrying and paying money at the toll bars, a shilling for two horses and sixpence for one, and the delay it caused in getting ' passes.' The drovers of cattle and sheep had also to pay, and consequently hill roads were used for conveying stock till tolls were abolished, after which they fell into disuse.

But one of the causes of the demand for good roads was the development of the bicycle about 1867 : the big ' penny farthing ' for men which developed into the low ' safety ' suitable for ladies in 1888. Bicycles only became really popular and fashionable, however, about 1895, that is, about the same time as the first petrol motor cars began to appear. In 1896 the ' man and flag ' Act of 1865 was repealed, and by the end of the century the new mode of locomotion asked for a new and better species of road. What served for the unfortunate horse was not enough for the elaborate machine. While horses and machines ran together there were difficulties. The considerate holder of the first Scottish licence used to carry with him carrots to propitiate the terrified horses ! But they as well as poultry (amongst whom there was terrible slaughter at first) became accustomed to the alarming apparition, as horses never did to trains. It was human beings who were about to suffer. But this is passing to the twentieth century, for the motor car Act that demanded that the new vehicles should be licensed and numbered was only passed in 1903.[1]

It was only a year after the railway made in 1825 between Stockton and Darlington by George Stephenson

[1] The holder of S 1 was the Rt. Hon. J. H. A. Macdonald, Lord Justice Clerk of Scotland, and the car was a noisy French one. The owner used to advertise that he and his car would stand at certain hours at certain cross roads so that horses might become accustomed to the noise of the engines running at full speed.

that the first Scottish railway running 'locomotives' or movable engines were completed. The road was a ten-mile line between Monkland and Kirkintilloch. Horse haulage by rail was, however, used till 1832; but soon locomotives were set to work and other railways were established in the same industrial vicinity. These schemes were amalgamated and became the nucleus of the North British Railway, while an extension westwards, authorized by Parliament to run to Glasgow, became the nucleus of the rival company, the Caledonian Railway. The tendency was to follow the course of the canals which already existed, but the rapid development of Glasgow demanded speedier and cheaper conveyance of coal than canals or canal routes could supply. The first train carrying passengers was propelled by a locomotive (named after him) by George Stephenson himself, and the terminus was St. Rollox. The train weighed over 100 tons; but it is recorded that the engine 'advanced under this prodigious load, not only with perfect freedom but at the speed of a stage-coach.' The train had four open trucks filled with passengers, two covered carriages on the model of a stage-coach, with the guards sitting on the roofs and a high open char-à-banc in the rear occupied by ladies. Three years later the system of purchasing tickets before a journey was adopted, to the great convenience of passengers and officials, and the increase in passenger traffic soon exceeded even that of goods. The word 'booking-office' reflects the custom of taking tickets, called 'check tickets', beforehand, as was, of course, done for the 'Limited

Mail ' later on. In 1837 a line running to Paisley and Ayr became eventually the South-Western Railway.

The Edinburgh and Glasgow Railway was opened in 1842, and there was great excitement in watching for the arrival of the first train. The second-class tickets cost six shillings, and the carriages had neither glass in the windows nor cushions on the seats. Third-class was four shillings with seats and two and sixpence without seats. Travellers speak of having to put up umbrellas to keep off the rain or snow. Third-class carriages were, indeed, little more than open trucks.

Seats were thus a luxury, and as is shown in the early Murray's Time Tables, there were what were called ' stand-ups,' and Mr. Alexander Hedderwick in his *Backward Glances* recalls the vehemence with which an unfortunate who had been placed in one of these un-seated tubs, and who was pinched and blue with cold, begged in a tremulous voice at the first station reached to be allowed to be admitted to an inside seat. A ' voluntary ' minister, however, who was asked how he travelled took it all as a joke and replied, ' I came in the congregation of the Upright ' ! It was at first incom-prehensible to passengers that they should not be put down and taken up at will as in the old days of the horse railways, and jumping out of a running train was not infrequent.

In 1850 the time occupied in the journey from Edin-burgh to London was $12\frac{1}{2}$ hours, but that was by a quick train : the slower trains took 15 to 17 hours. Lord Cockburn wrote to his daughter during the time of the

Great Exhibition of 1851 which she thought of visiting —' I hope you are not dreaming of going to London in one day. It is a great fatigue, though it be convenient— and only spines of steel can stand it ! ' Stone sleepers in some cases helped to make travelling rough, though poor springs and lighter coaches had most to do with it. The writer remembers a portion of a railway known to the children as the ' click-a-tick ' because stone sleepers still existed there. In 1840 Bradshaw advertises that the second-class carriages would be *closed* and protected from the weather in night trains ; usually they were open on the side. It was also decreed that there should be no smoking even in stations and no tips to officials. These decrees were soon given up !

It shows the improvement in the general behaviour of the people of the land that there were constant complaints in the early days of railways about the roughness and even violence of the passengers, especially in the industrial districts ; also of their efforts to cheat, and the consequent suspicious bearing and rudeness of the officials. Trains, too, were terribly unpunctual, and this unpunctuality continued in a less degree to the end of the century, as did the dirt of the carriages. The last was largely due to the lack of sobriety on the part of the passengers. The writer has seen a great station on the night of a market day strewn with bodies as after a great battle ! As to officials, there were those who were models of kindliness and uprightness—men who were beloved of all passengers, old and young alike—hard-working and faithful to the company whom they served, whose greatest sorrow was to doff their cloth or fustian uniforms.

It would be difficult to follow the course of the various Scottish railway companies, which developed quickly one after the other. The railway in the East of Scotland which began by horse-drawn carriages, when it took to self-moving locomotives and ran to Berwick, became the 'North British' railway company. It also made its way by coast to Aberdeen, and finally in 1889 to Fort William and Mallaig. The great engineering feats of the century were to be found in the erection of the bridges over the Forth and the Tay. The Tay Bridge, opened in 1878, was carried away along with its living freight by a gale which raged in December 1879, but it was replaced by a stronger structure. The Forth Bridge, a notable engineering triumph, was opened in 1890, and by its means communication between the North and South of Scotland was immensely facilitated.

The Caledonian Railway was incorporated in 1845 with a view to constructing a line from Carlisle up the valley of the Annan and over Beattock summit into Edinburgh on the one side and Glasgow on the other. There was a Scottish Central railway going to Perth ; other railway companies from Perth to Dundee and Perth to Forfar, and so on ; but by a series of amalgamations these companies were absorbed into the Caledonian Company, now absorbed into the London, Midland and Scottish. There were still, however, unabsorbed companies in the last century like the Great

North of Scotland, radiating from Aberdeen and never famous for its speed, though it ran the satirically named 'Flying Buchan'; the 'Highland' from Perth to Inverness and Thurso was also deliberate, but the Highland line had great engineering difficulties to surmount. The main competing lines towards the end of the century were, however, the North British and Caledonian. The railway 'Race to the North' which took place in August 1895 was a notable event in Scottish railway history, for then the highest average speed of a regular train was obtained. The race was between the West Coast route (North Western Railway and Caledonian), with its two bad gradients at Shap and Beattock, and the East Coast route (Great Northern, North-Eastern, and North British Railways). The East Coast managed to cover the $523\frac{1}{2}$ miles from King's Cross to Aberdeen in 8 hours 40 minutes, the fastest time attained over that route, on August 22nd. The West Coast night express accomplished the journey from Euston to Aberdeen in 8 hours 32 minutes, including all stops *en route*. No wonder that the engine driver was carried shoulder high! A run of 541 miles had been made in 512 minutes, with four intermediate stops, constituting an average rate of nearly 63 miles per hour, or 64 miles per hour without stops. There was great excitement at the time, but the race was run without accident, and less swift timing was subsequently adopted.

The West Coast trains reduced the run from London to Glasgow from 10 hours to $8\frac{1}{2}$, and this, or $8\frac{1}{4}$, became the normal running. The service can hardly be excelled in the present time; but in the eighties there was great advance in general comfort in travelling owing to the introduction of dining-cars, a better type of sleeping accommodation, lighting by gas, and heating of trains by steam instead of by foot-warmers, which were usually either so hot that they burned the boots or else were deadly cold. Scotland was early in the field as regards abolishing the second class, now almost universally done on all British railways: the queer anomaly now exists of there being only first and third classes.

The railways of last century made an enormous difference to the trade of the country, and perhaps as much to agriculture as to other industries. No doubt this was true of the whole of Britain, but the remoter parts profited more than those nearer the metropolis. The great development in the meat and fish trades, for instance, came largely through this means, especially as far as Aberdeenshire was concerned.

Until railways became established canals held the field, and most people thought that though railways would gain in swiftness canals would always excel in cheapness and comfort. The principal canals in Scotland in the nineteenth century were the Caledonian, the Crinan, the Forth and Clyde and the Union. The Union Canal, Sir Archibald Geikie says in his *Reminiscences*, had boats comfortably fitted up and drawn by a cavalcade of horses urged forward by post boys : ' For mere luxury of transportation such canal travel stands quite unrivalled.' The fly in the ointment was the delay at the locks. Despite their comfort, both stage-coaches and passenger-boats on the canal were soon disused after the opening of the Edinburgh and Glasgow railway in the spring of 1842. It was announced in the *Glasgow Courier* a few weeks after the railway was opened that all the stage-coaches were off the road except the six o'clock morning coach, which was kept running in consequence of its carrying the mail bags. For about thirty years after this, however, the Dunfermline coach ran regularly from Edinburgh via Queensferry. To watch for this picturesque vehicle was a joy to the children of the day. ' Swift Passenger Boats ' to Edinburgh, Stirling, Alloa, Perth and Crieff are advertised in the time-tables of 1844, as well as the regular mail- and stage-coaches. Of course, one helped out the other in reaching the desired destination. Both omnibuses and minibuses are also advertised for short distances.

The Caledonian Canal from Loch Linnhe to the Moray Firth has not proved the success that was expected in opening a highway for vessels between the eastern and western seas. The Forth and Clyde Canal had been suggested by the enterprising King Charles II, but it was not until the latter part of the eighteenth century that a body called ' The Board of Trustees for the Encouragement of Arts and Manufactures,' whose existence proved the presence of a new spirit of progress, seconded by the Convention of Royal Burghs, embarked on the scheme. The engineer Smeaton made the

OPENING OF THE GLASGOW AND GARNKIRK RAILWAY, 1831

survey and showed that it was feasible, and by the end of the century the canal was completed and the subscribers re-imbursed. A deep-sea canal has often been discussed but the scheme has gone no further. The non-success of the Caledonian Canal was discouraging.

. . . .

The sea journey from Edinburgh to London was popular because of its cheapness; before steam was introduced it was a slow and precarious voyage and the first steamers were small and primitive in their appointments. As mineral oil had not come into use, and animal and vegetable oils were dear, illumination in the cabins was by candles or dips which constantly required snuffing, like all the candles of the day. The grease also was apt to descend on sleepers during the night if the candles were left burning; and there is an amusing story of how an eminent divine woke thinking he was smitten by paralysis since he could not move the muscles of his face, whereas, when his anxious friends came to the rescue, they found that all that had happened was that the tallow had been dripping on his face and had there congealed!

The voyage from the Clyde to Skye, when done in sailing packets, took from ten to fifteen days, but the development of good steamboat services began before the middle of the century, though at first all the boats carried cargo and were loaded with cattle and sheep, and as at most of the places of call there was no pier, the comfort of passengers was not great. As to

R

time-table there was none.   There is a classic answer to
the request for one.   ' Weel, she'll be comin' sometimes
sooner, and whiles earlier, and sometimes before that
again ' !   Things, however, improved greatly as the
century drew to an end, and the islanders were less
cut off from mainland civilization.

CHAPTER XI
WORKERS IN THE TOWNS

IT is easier to find good accounts of working-class life
as it was a century ago amongst the more picturesque
rural workers than among the far more numerous town
workers. There are, however, various interesting books
of recollections of the early days in Glasgow and Paisley,
such as those written by a certain John Urie, a weaver's
son, who was born in 1820, and lived through the century. There is also a *History of the Working Classes of
Scotland* by Thomas Johnston, a book full of fire and
righteous indignation, which gives a side of working-
class life which the well-to-do and opulent are apt to
overlook. Paisley, Urie's birthplace, and always known
as ' The Suburb ' from being so near Glasgow, had
been prosperous and happy, making lovely ' Paisley '
and Chenille shawls with wonderfully attractive de-
signs until there came to pass a terrible time of distress, due to the introduction of the new machinery
and the rapid increase of child labour which it brought
in its train. In 1830 wages of 30s. a week had fallen to a
sum which meant poverty and starvation everywhere.
Many succumbed from actual lack of food in those post-
Waterloo days, whilst landlords were still flourishing.
Of all the bad years 1826 was probably the worst,

owing to the short corn crops—crops which were hardly worth cutting and were pulled up by the roots. The weavers were pallid creatures who worked in damp, ill-ventilated quarters ; and Urie tells us that the Glasgow tailors used to say they ' looked like churchyard deserters.' Things were so bad that Sir John Maxwell of Pollok introduced a Poor Board Bill, declaring as he did so that hand-loom weavers were not getting enough to keep body and soul together ; the Bill did not pass into law, and eventually the handloom weavers became a memory.

The food of the people in the towns was much as in the country, that is to say, oatmeal porridge morning and night, potatoes and bannocks and salt herring for dinner, and, of course, kail brose. The ' knee-breeks ' were going out, but the women still wore the jupe or short-gown, a drugget petticoat and plaid. Just as in the country, knives and forks were seldom seen. The townspeople were, however, always more literary than the country folk, and in quite early days book clubs were established for supplying really solid books ; these clubs usually met in public houses, for the Temperance movement for which Father Mathew had much credit, had not yet come along. The light was still derived from oil cruisies as in the country, but gas began to be introduced with steam factories, though it had to be used with discretion since inspectors perambulated the towns to see that it was not being burned after hours.

Urie's early life was passed in the time of the Radical

risings, when townsmen waved banners and sought to avenge the deaths of the ' martyrs ' of last century, Hardie, Baird and Wilson. Children were everywhere working in the factories where they could be very useful, and to get sufficient labour boys and girls were sent off to this work in gangs from poorhouses or hospitals for orphans and the destitute. The account given in evidence before the House of Commons of the child labour employed is almost incredible. In 1832 children were made to work for seventeen hours a day, and flogging and strapping were continual in order to keep the poor infants from falling asleep. The extraordinary thing is that in the *New Statistical Account*, written by Ministers, the system was supported. Even in country towns like Crieff it is said in 1837 that the occupation for which children received from 2s. 6d. to 3s. weekly was ' wholesome for children : those in a delicate state of health soon forgot their ailments.' Yet they worked thus for six days on end ! The Minister who reported deprecated giving alms, ' for the spirit of independence once so characteristic of Scotland is in danger of being completely lost'; yet he allows that ' people are alive to the necessity of education, but cannot afford it.' Another Minister says that ' there is no training of the volatile mind of youth equal to that which is maintained at the factories.' The result attained was a race apart, brown and haggard. In the fifties it was enacted that children had to be released for half-time education ; but that law was often evaded. Roebuck's account of the work done by children in the bleachfields in 1859 is terrible ; they worked from eleven to eighteen hours daily in heated chambers. The exertions of Ashley and others to pass satisfactory factory legislation are well known ; but it is matter of surprise that more was not done by common consent in a country which valued education, and should have appreciated the necessity of giving the opportunity for its being carried out amongst the poor. There seemed to be a feeling that on no account was industry to be interfered with. It was the period of *laissez-faire*, and as industry was apparently making a poor country rich by leaps and bounds it was believed that the methods adopted were essential to success. Even in 1874 it was said by an employer that a whole holiday once a fortnight to employees ' would lead to idle habits.' In England and Scotland alike the Industrial Revolution was brought about at great cost, and yet, in itself, it was a necessary process in social development, and if its operations could have been wisely directed it might have been wholly beneficial. Ignorance and lack of imagination more than ill-will were its bane.

The colliers had a bad time, too, as all will remember who have read of the work of the great Lord Shaftesbury and the Report of the Commission of Enquiry into the employment of children in 1840. The miners worked from twelve to fourteen hours a day, and carried heavy loads, as also did the women. The latter, indeed, were harnessed like horses to their bogie of coal, and continued in this work ' till the last hour of pregnancy.' The Bill to prohibit female labour was, of course, carried in 1842, but the women so valued the wage received that they sought to work still. One wonders, indeed, how they ever managed to do what is described, i.e. to carry coal from underground on their backs by a long turnpike stair. One day's labour was said to be equal to the carrying of a hundredweight from the level of the sea to the top of Ben Lomond. Metal mining was carried on at the mines of Leadhills and Wanlockhead alone, and it was an ancient and interesting industry.

It would be impossible to describe here all the disputes and strikes carried on by the Miners' Unions which were gaining strength, the attempted legislation and the laws finally passed to regulate miners' work. Even as late as the seventies the housing of miners was in many parts shocking, and it did not improve as it should. The inhabitants seem to have got accustomed to insanitary living, ashpits in front of their houses and bad water supply ; and even when they could get better houses, and were able to pay for them, they grudged the higher rent that was asked. Pit baths they had no use for. Knowing as we do that the Church was a democratic and national institution of great power it seems unthinkable that she did not raise her voice to protest against the evils that abounded, but left it to politicians and philanthropists like Shaftesbury and Bright to do so. As late as 1875 the *Glasgow Herald* gave terrible accounts of the state of the miners' houses—no closets for a whole row of houses, holes in the roof, roofs six or seven feet from the floor, and so on : a depressing tale.

Then the truck system was a great grievance to the miners, for men had to buy from the coal-owner ; wages went to the truck-store and from the truck-store to the pay office. Alexander Macdonald, the miners' leader, made a valiant attempt to get improvements effected, and his Union tried to look after widows and orphans, and to get a co-operative colliery started. But bad times came, and these projects fell through. There were occasional riots, of course, but they did not result in much. In 1881 Macdonald died, and Lanarkshire took an ' idle day ' in his memory. Then came Keir Hardie and the Socialist propaganda, which has kept its popularity in the congested areas ever since. The Trades Disputes Act of 1896 was an attempt at finding some means of conciliation in respect of trade disputes, and when we pass into the present century there has, of course, been frequent legislation. However, the Trade Union Act of 1871 was perhaps the most important Act of all, because it gave protection for the Unions' funds and property. This Act was thus the means of supplying the protection that was needed.

The introduction of an Irish population to Scotland was an element which did not help the rise in the social scale which might otherwise have been expected. The Irish were willing to work for low wages, and were, indeed, sometimes brought to Scotland by the employers for this reason. Their main reason for coming over was, however, the hope of finding better conditions than they had at home. The famine years of 1845 and 1846 were indeed but the beginning of a great

THE DRYGATE, GLASGOW

immigration of people of a different race and religion ; and the consequences are not yet fully realized. One-eighth of the population of Scotland has been stated to be of Irish extraction, but the number of those actually born in Ireland and now living in Scotland has steadily decreased since 1851. That year the Irish immigrants were 7 per cent. of the population. In 1921 it had come down to 3 per cent.

The agitation which characterized the days of the Reform Bill of 1832, and the Chartist movement of the forties, ended in the organization of Trade Unions in the form in which we know them. The history of the rise of the Unions cannot be told here, but they were found in other organized trades as well as mining, of which we have already spoken, and though strikes were often defeated the Unions were soon recognized by railway companies and other corporations, and that made bargaining easier for the men in the future. This power of striking and thereby gaining their ends justified to them what seems an out-of-date, expensive and senseless way of settling disputes. Along with the Unions there were all sorts of other organizations for the betterment of the people carried on by themselves. There was the wonderful rise of Friendly Societies and Benefit Societies of all kinds—some like the Gardeners on a craft basis—which enabled working people to face sickness and old age before Government schemes of doing so came into vogue. Their forms and ceremonies, their ' Courts ' and regalia, signs and passes, gave colour to that drab virtue, thrift. Then there were temperance bodies like the Good Templars and Rechabites, also with certain forms and banners that were attractive to the young, and enabled them to start along right paths. The mottoes inscribed on the banners such as ' Wha would hae a Drucken Man ? ' or ' Drucken Wife,' according to sex, and such like, many of us still remember ; and these bodies no doubt began the good work of the various temperance societies for men and women which was carried on at a time when it was terribly needed. To be present at a ' Feeing Market ' when farm servants were engaged for the year or half year in a country town was an experience not to be forgotten. At New Year's time the pavements were strewn with drunken men, and Glasgow Fair, the annual holiday, was an orgy. It seemed shameful that such things should be in a country whose professions of Christianity were higher than in most, and the worst was that drunkenness, if not constant, was not thought of much account. Things have changed in this matter now, but they changed after the end of the nineteenth century and for special reasons. Up to the end of that century, anyone expected to meet drunken men if he or she travelled third-class, and therefore did not do so if the extra fare could be afforded.

We must now come to some details of the actual life of the people as we find it in their personal records ; it is a strange and interesting tale.

A great horror, which was specially acute in Scotland, though it also existed in England, was that of the Resurrectionists or Body-Snatchers, who supplied anatomists with corpses dug up from graveyards before the passing of the Anatomy Act of 1832. Burke and Hare almost certainly murdered about sixteen people for the sale of their bodies to the anatomists. But the ordinary plan was to dig up recently buried bodies, and the heavy iron grids or mort-guards placed over the graves for protection are still to be seen in old graveyards, and patent iron coffins were advertised for sale. At Dundee a box full of gunpowder was placed on the coffin of a child for the purpose of blowing up anyone who tried to seize the body.[1] Bodies were also smuggled in from Ireland by boat to sell to the doctors. In Glasgow bodies were salted, hung up and dried like herrings, and when a portion only was required it was soaked in water. It was only after a body had lain in a grave for a month that it was supposed to be safe. Unfortunate and wholly innocent doctors who were accused of being abettors in the work had their windows smashed. Meetings were held in the towns in order to form clubs for the protection of the bodies of the dead, and within a year Urie tells us that in Paisley there were 7000 members each paying sixpence on joining and a penny per quarter thereafter. With the money thus collected big wooden boxes as guardhouses for each graveyard were obtained. These boxes were very comfortable, and it became a not wholly disagreeable task to sit by the fires which were lit in them and take duty as graveyard watcher for the night. Indeed, a bottle of whisky

[1] *Quarterly Review*, Jan. 1833. S. Wood.

was usually provided for the said watcher, as well as the necessary blunderbuss, which greatly added to the attraction of watching! However, the young people of the towns soon began to take advantage of the loneliness of the guard and the nerve-shattering nature of their business, and played all sorts of pranks on them, such as appearing among the tombs in white sheets, and letting out blood-curdling yells to startle them !

The clubs existed in Paisley till 1836, even though the Anatomy Act had passed ; but the boxes were left for any anxious relatives who might wish to watch over their dead, for there were thefts of bodies anyhow until 1831.

Burke was executed in 1829, and his body by a curious Nemesis was itself made the subject of dissection and lectured on. The mob threatened to burst in, and ultimately the body, stretched naked on a black marble table, was publicly exhibited to about 25,000 people.

In 1827 there was no such thing as a covered van in the streets, but in the following year the music sellers of Edinburgh had one built to be employed in the transport of their goods, without realizing what might ensue. For by 1829, when Burke was executed, the feelings of the populace were so excited that as the van passed through the villages the inhabitants insisted on having the door opened in order to be satisfied that no body was concealed inside ! If anyone cares to read an account of how the ghoulish operations took place at Dalkeith, and of how tricks were played on the unhappy watchers, these are admirably recorded in the well-known story

DR. ROBERT KNOX 1830

Dr. Knox was the Lecturer on Anatomy in Edinburgh
whose Porter received the bodies from Burke and Hare

Mansie Wauch, supposed to be the records of a Dalkeith tailor.

In the twenties and thirties of last century the town schools were numerous, but the majority were ' venture schools,' taught by someone who had picked up a certain degree of learning and wished to make the most of it. John Urie says that in his school in Paisley all the hundred scholars at all stages of advancement were taught by one master known as ' Wee Willie Aitken,' and none were neglected, though the brighter boys got most attention. The fee in these schools was usually at the rate of threepence a week, or three shillings a quarter, a good deal for poor weavers to pay. There were, however, some schools rather cheaper. As the boys got to be able for it they left school and were set to work as ' draw boys,' and then put to the loom itself, or to make shawl fringes. But the hand-loom was, of course, fighting a losing battle with the power-loom, which soon took all the trade.

It was in 1832 that the cholera plague broke out in Scotland ; it had been expected to arrive from Europe and, as usual, the cure which was essential, sanitation, only came along with the disease. Of drainage in the towns there was practically none, excepting a ' strand ' which ran down the town street. Public Health had not been studied much in those days, but something had to be done, and the bright idea developed in Paisley of fumigating the houses with diluted sulphurous acid and chloride of lime. No time was to be lost in carrying out the necessary measures, so six large tubs filled with the mixture were placed on barrows, and, preceded by torches, these were wheeled through the streets and lanes of Paisley. No wonder that this weird procession making its way through the narrow streets made a deep impression on the onlookers who opened their windows to admit the pungent fumes of chlorine.

With all that, and in spite of what we now call the 'psychological' effect that it might have, the people continued to die, and, as usual, the poor died faster than the well-to-do. The common ground in the city grave-yards had to be closed as being full up, and a part of the townland in the Moss was set apart for cholera victims whose relatives did not possess private lairs (as the individual sections in cemeteries are called in Scotland). This was the children's playground, and though warned off, the children continued to watch the constant pro-cessions from a safe distance. What was the horror of the town when it was discovered that the graves were being tampered with and that shovels and a cord with an iron hook attached to it had been discovered. The implements were brought to the 'Cross,' always the centre of the doings of a Scottish town even when no 'Mercat Cross' existed, and the dreadful conviction was borne in upon the people that not only had they ghoulish thieves among them once more, but that the doctors were responsible for the deaths of many of their patients. The hospitals in those days, and for many years later, were looked on with suspicion as being places in which the patients merely went to die.

Early next morning a large crowd assembled in the Moss, determined to discover the worst, and when an empty coffin was opened there was the greatest excitement. Exaggerated accounts arose of the number of graves violated, and a great procession of men who had not long since marched in support of the Reform Bill, walked to the town taking with them stobs and bars and stones ; and there was a regular riot when they arrived. The police, such as they were, were completely routed; 400 panes of glass, then a valuable commodity, were broken, and the Cholera Hospital was visited, its van seized, broken up and thrown into the river. It was only the reading of the Riot Act and arrival of the military that brought about peace.[1]

These accounts of the unorganized life of Scottish towns throw considerable light on the social conditions of the people, which seem to us singularly elementary ; but the efforts of the working men after their intellectual development are as interesting as any part of the story of their doings and their development. As there were no municipal public libraries till 1853, and hardly any circulating libraries of a private kind, the lack was filled by numerous book clubs, each member contributing one book to the common stock. We can imagine with what care and deliberation that one precious book was chosen, and how its donor followed its career. The books were exchanged monthly at the club meeting.

[1] *Reminiscences of Eighty Years*, by John Urie, 1909. A. Gardner, Paisley.

One club was named the ' Encyclopaedia,' because it owned the *Encyclopaedia Britannica*. Here men discussed James Watt and the steam engine, the Jacquard loom and the spinning-jenny. Sometimes the members had wherewithal to assist their discussions, and met in a public house ; sometimes they provided their own re-

THE PAISLEY ENCYCLOPAEDIA CLUB

freshment, and, if so, were not allowed more than one glass per member between eight and ten o'clock. The Burns Clubs began to be formed in the thirties, and at the Paisley Burns Club, Tannahill the poet and Noël Paton the painter, and other famous men began to show their powers in their different ways. But once the working men had got their liberty, politics was the main topic of discussion ; all weavers and industrialists generally were keen radicals and reformers, and loved

s

processions, attired in broad red sashes on which was imprinted the sacred word REFORM. Elections were, of course, great sources of excitement in days when money was often cast about by candidates to scramble for.

The other source of interest was of a morbid kind, connected with the executions which were held before the Glasgow County Buildings, or else, in the case of murder, in sight of the spot where it had been committed. A Glasgow execution, carried out on two navvies who had murdered their foreman, is vividly described by Urie as an onlooker. The crowd in the Jail Square collected at 5 a.m., and by 7 a.m. the Sheriff appeared, accompanied by a troop of cavalry and two companies of infantry, and rode to the prison. The streets were crowded as also were the windows. The procession consisted of a body of cavalry, then the Sheriff, Lord Provost and Magistrates, then the executioner, then the condemned men in their cart with their coffins beside them and accompanied by their spiritual advisers, and last of all the city marshals. The cart, in which the condemned men sat loosely pinioned, was guarded on all sides by strong detachments of cavalry, infantry and police, the infantry having their bayonets fixed. It appeared as if some important military operation was to have been performed, for the small army consisted of 1200 infantry, 600 cavalry and two guns. After the bodies had hung for forty minutes, the mournful and weird procession was re-formed and returned.

In those days the slaughter-house was near the place

of execution, i.e. behind the jail, but previous to its erection the cattle were killed in the street, and when an ox was knocked down the butcher called out ' Blood, blood, blood,' so that the poor people who gathered about might fill their cans as the blood flowed from the slaughtered animal. This, and the fact that the gallows, a large wooden erection on wheels ready to be drawn forward, was also standing there, gave a melancholy aspect to the scene, and a depressing view of the social habits of the city.

There was, however, a brighter side to life in town, for in those days the Fair was really a Fair and was held in Glasgow and not ' doon the watter ' (i.e. the Clyde) at Rothesay or elsewhere. There was an erection in the Saltmarket called Mumford's geggie, a penny show, Wombwell's wild beast caravans and Ewing's wax-works, jugglers, boxers and the rest. There were also other higher-class theatres, where famous actors made their début. Round the Jail Square were booths, and here queer characters of all sorts collected.

But this same spot was later on a scene of angry passion at the time of the bread riots in 1848, when men rendered desperate by hunger and want had the town at their mercy for forty-eight hours. It was just after the potato famine and potatoes were still dear, and it was before the repeal of the Corn Laws had taken effect. The power-looms were in full swing, and there was great unemployment and depression amongst weavers. The Chartist movement was going on, and, as always in Scotland, there was indignation at the idea of giving charity rather than work. There were deputations to the Town Council, and as the result of these was deemed unsatisfactory, shops were pillaged and gun shops raided, until at last the Riot Act was read, and the military arrived, and the streets were temporarily cleared. It was, however, long before peace was really established.

Prize-fighting was common, and the police did not interfere with it ; many of the smaller taverns had cock-pits and rat-pits in the backcourts ; for rat and dog fights and cock fights were ordinary entertainments. It is certainly true that there is more consideration for the feelings of animals in the twentieth century than in the nineteenth, and there is a probability that there will soon be more still; for we must remember that trapping, and hunting animals for pleasure, are still existent, though slaughtering, like hanging, is usually done in privacy.

Marriages were performed with great ease in Scotland and till 1855 registration was not demanded, and to this day it is not essential. Provosts and Principals of Universities used to be invited to perform the ceremony, as being people of importance, and there was a well-known character named Rab Steel, Provost of Rutherglen (then a little way out of Glasgow), and a toll-keeper, who was known as the ' Marrying Provost.' The ceremony in his case was marvellously simple, for he did not even require the candidates to repeat the Lord's Prayer as did Principal Macfarlane of the College. He simply thrust his head through the window and told them that it was ' *A' richt.*' These queer weddings were, however, often

more faithfully observed than the modern ones with the
'Wedding Marches' pealing from Cathedral organs
and hundreds of spectators.   Lord Cockburn tells in his
Circuit Journeys of a Justice of the Peace who in 1844
carried on a sort of trade of receiving declarations of
marriage, for which he was paid either in half crowns or
in drams.   From his register it appeared that he had
married 1200 people !   This is a curious fact in reference to the law;   but it was quite legal as the marriages
were duly attested.

One of the institutions which the twentieth century
man or woman would miss as much as anything, did he
go back a hundred years, would be any sort of tea-shop or
luncheon room other than a public house. This would certainly be the case not only for clerks and manual workers,
but also for the well-to-do and ' idle rich,' since there
was no place, for instance, for suburban ladies to take tea
after a strenuous day of shopping.   In Glasgow and other
large towns there were indeed ' pie-shops ' where pies
and porter could be obtained, but they were mostly
downstairs and in the busy parts of the town, and not
suitable for ladies.   Later on Glasgow became famous
for her tea-shops, just as she has always been for her
bakers' shops, the envy of other towns.

Those who can look back to a childhood spent in the
sixties or seventies remember the agonies of ' sitting
for your photograph,' and being screwed into a position
which had to be maintained for what seemed an endless
time.   Photography, or at least ' taking likenesses,' became a commercial pursuit in the fifties, though, of

course, it began earlier with the daguerreotypes, and earlier than that with black silhouettes. Once started as photography, it became a popular pursuit for amateur and professional, and had immense influence on the public prints when wooden blocks came to be used. One of the early Glasgow photographers gives an amusing account of his experiences. Once, in photographing a Highland piper in full costume with pipes in proper position, the man suddenly started off marching round the room to the tune of ' The Campbells are Coming.' When remonstrated with, he indignantly exclaimed, ' Tid you thocht I want tae be ta'en stanin' like a pig stookie ' !

There was always a certain love of music in Scotland, though it was not much developed excepting in the Highlands, where it was innate. There were always popular songsters like the Kennedy family. David Kennedy's concerts were crowded, and his daughter was Margaret Kennedy Fraser, who did so much good work in collecting and arranging, as well as singing, the *Songs of the North*. There was Grand Opera in Glasgow in the sixties, but for a few years only. The development of music through popular Festivals and otherwise came next century ; but admirable concerts have always been held, and were well patronized in Glasgow and Edinburgh, long before these others were developed ; and the hold Scottish folk-songs had on the people, through the songs of Burns and of Lady Nairne and of many others, is well known to everyone. It is difficult to say that church music had much part in this musical development, but at the same time the Psalm tunes were taught to every child, and crooned to the babes in the cradle. Music halls in the second half of the century were a part of the social life of the working class Glaswegians, and at times, and particularly during the seventies, they were rowdy places. There were many well-known songs, known to all, like ' The Captain with his whiskers,' which some still recollect, and others less select. Circuses were popular with everyone, but theatres were taboo with the religious, whose young people were told that it was indeed ' The way to the Pit ' ; and certain great fires like that of the Theatre Royal in Edinburgh, as already mentioned, were supposed to be a judgment emanating from a Divine Providence. Still all the great actors of the day made their way to Edinburgh and Glasgow, and even the ministers, especially those of the Moderate school, surreptitiously found the means of hearing and seeing the famous players. But as time went on and the Evangelical school took more hold, this was a forbidden joy, unless when an occasional visit was made to London and the clerical attire could be discarded. Playing cards, which were popular when used for whist, were to the religious the ' Devil's buiks,' and were never seen in a God-fearing house. Even music had to be treated with care in the earlier part of the century by a Secession or strictly evangelical minister ; and it was absolutely prohibited if of a light and frivolous sort, and of course on Sunday or the Fast Day, when even whistling was forbidden as well as singing any secular songs. On these days, indeed, the blinds were usually drawn down to betoken a serious frame of mind. Country walks, always a joy to a Scottish town-dweller, who kept love of the land in his heart wherever he resided, were unfortunately also discouraged ; since at least two diets of worship had to be attended there was indeed little time left even if they were approved of. However, people were occasionally brave enough to step forth by their back doors ! Books read on Sundays were absolutely confined to those known as religious, and children's toys to Noah's Arks. However, Mr. and Mrs. Noah, in their funny parti-coloured skirts, managed under the child's guidance to do some biblically unauthorized acts ; though the steamer that was said to be conveying missionaries to heathen lands was looked on with some suspicion.

An interesting thing that Loudon, the botanist, tells us is that in 1825 the operatives of Paisley were remarkable for their good taste and sense of beauty, as well as intellectual pursuits. Many of them composed verses. This characteristic, he says, was also found in the miners of Leadhills, who worked for six hours a day only, and devoted much of their leisure to the improvement of their minds. They had both a library and a reading club of their own. This is borne out by the account Dorothy Wordsworth gives of her conversation, when passing through the village, with schoolboys who told her that they were learning both Latin and Greek. The inhabitants of Paisley, however, Loudon says, specially devoted their attention to rearing flowers, and he believes that this contributed to 'improve the genius for invention in elegant fancy muslins' for which Paisley became famous. The florists of Paisley had apparently 'been long remarked for the peacefulness of their dispositions,' which was not always so in Horticultural Societies, as we have known them. Their 'Florists' Club,' a better name than the preceding, 'not only represses all irregularities at its weekly meetings which dismiss at ten in the evening; but would erase from its list any disreputable name.' And he concludes with satisfaction that 'the association of persons possessing this taste seems to be favourable to social order.'

There were various street cries early in the century, such as 'pease and beans' and 'rock partans' (i.e. crabs), 'wilks and buckies,' 'dulse and tangle.' But the very beautiful 'caller 'ou' was the best known. Oysters were always popular, and in 1817 they could be had from the fishwives for twelve a penny. In those days in Edinburgh a quarter of lamb was one shilling and sixpence and a four pound loaf a shilling; butter sixpence a pound and eggs sixpence a dozen! Good tea was, however, eight shillings a pound, brown sugar eightpence and loaf sugar one shilling. The best beefsteak was sixpence a pound and boiling beef fourpence and fivepence. The vegetable market was held in the High Street of Edinburgh till it moved to the site of the former Physic Gardens.

In 1823 there was no such thing as a cabman or cab in Glasgow or Edinburgh, but there were a few two-horse hackney carriages in Edinburgh which, of course, were expensive. Ladies of the higher circle used sedan chairs to carry them to theatre, concert, or assembly, and a long row would wait for hire near the Assembly Rooms. The bearers were mostly Highland and Gaelic-speaking, and were much given to love of their native moun- tain dew, which often caused great consternation to the enclosed ladies as they were swayed from side to side.

If we wish to get a good impression of life in a typical small Lowland town at this period we cannot do better than read the *Memoir of William Chambers by Himself*, for he lived in Peebles during the early years of the century.

His early recollections were of the minister of the parish wearing a cocked hat; a few men still wore pig-tails and went with top-boots or tassel boots (Hessians), i.e. boots with tassels suspended instead of 'Tops' or gaiters. And he describes vividly the pious chief elder who repressed all efforts at gaiety, and thought dancing sinful, so that his daughters learned it elsewhere than at the respectable dancing school then usual in all Scottish towns. The quiet of the little town was almost oppressive; the shops, such as they were, had 'half-doors' provided with bell-pull which might be rung by a would-be cus- tomer, if the owner were not leaning over his door arms akimbo. As elsewhere, the town herd blew the ox-horn; and then came out the cows in their deliberate way from their repulsive quarters and made their well- known journey to the hill. Tea-parties at six o'clock

were much in vogue and were followed by songs and
Scottish proverbs.

In these almost bookless days news circulated at
third and fourth hand, and the singing of ancient
ballads or telling of legendary stories by old female
relatives was greatly valued. Curiously enough recent
news, such as the battle of Corunna, was in Peebles
mixed up with digressions on the Jewish wars, taken
from an old translation of Josephus. The owner of this
much-valued book made a sort of profession of going
about in the evenings with his book, which he read as
the current news ! As he read only a few pages at a
time he kept up a constant anxiety as to what was
coming next. ' Weel Tam, what's the news the nicht ? '
would be answered by ' Bad news, bad news, Titus has
begun to besiege Jerusalem—its gaun to be a terrible
business.' When the conflict and destruction of the
city was arrived at, there was a perfect paroxysm of
horror !

Early in the century there was, as we have seen, no
Poor Law, but much human kindness ; mendicants were
everywhere, and each town had its two or three
' natural ' idiots, good-natured simple beings. And
these and all other poor people who deserved it were
in Peebles feasted on Hogmanay, the last day of the
year, and the great festival of the Lowlands. The town-
piper in red uniform and cocked hat was then in his
glory. At other times he played on his pipes between
nine and ten o'clock at night. Hogmanay was also the
day for tradesmen to call with their yearly accounts,

receiving payment and appropriate refreshment. This custom of yearly personal calls for payment combined with refreshment continued into the present writer's re-collection.

Handsel Monday, the first Monday in the year, and New Year's Day itself were other days of merriment, and in a sense days of cheer existed at other domestic festivities, such as births and marriages, and even deaths. For on the evening before the funeral there was the Lyke-wake, consisting of a series of services of refreshments presided over by an undertaker, who was required to say a fresh grace to each batch of mourners. One carpenter coffin-maker boasted of being able to say seven graces without repetition ! The consumption of whisky at these festivals was incredible, especially as the funeral was followed by a more cheerful entertainment called the Dredgy. The carpenter or wright could also paint signboards, make peg-tops and verses ; all useful in a little town. There were, of course, no police, but offenders against the law were captured by the town officer and brought before the provost, a shopkeeper, who ordered them to prison quite happily, in the midst of his dealings with his customers, keeping no record of what he had done. Superstition still existed here as elsewhere. No one could pass the cottage of a reputed witch without placing the thumb across the fourth finger, so as to form the figure of a cross, and salt was thrown on the fire as a guard against the evil eye. The postman carried with him a sprig of rowantree in his pockets as a preventative against

malevolent influences. The ' Drummer ' then as ever
made known the wants of the community, and he was
also jailer, constable and much else. But sometimes the
town was snow-bound, and then salt (always an important commodity), money and fuel alike fell short for a
fortnight, so completely stopped was all communication with sources of supply.

The characters which Chambers tells of are the
characters which are found in Walter Scott; for
instance, the bedesman, the ' blue-gown,' and in any
case the licensed wandering beggar, still existed. The
school to which the boys went was the Burgh school
attended by nearly all classes, but at least a third of the
scholars went bare-foot by choice. The master of the
school was none too sober. The grammar school was
the next stage, and it was attended at the cost of five
shillings per quarter. Here violence ruled everywhere.
The boys were flogged both at home and school, and
they fought one another, harried birds' nests, and
pelted cats, and even battered to death with stones poor
worn-out horses. After these boys reached manhood
the whole system was looked back on with horror.
Even the town officers were lent to assist in the barbarous floggings at school. And the education given
was slight ; no history, geography or physical science
was taught, only Latin and some Greek, and there was
not a map in the whole school. Yet there was a desire
for learning amongst the people, for a small circulating
library was established from which Pope's *Iliad*,
Gulliver's Travels and *Don Quixote* could be borrowed,

as also the *Encyclopaedia Britannica*, which was bought by the elder Chambers and proved a mine of wonder and delight to the boys.

As with all others of the weaving trade the introduction of the power-loom brought about trouble to the Chambers', and the father had to turn his hand to shopkeeping. At this time newspapers were handed round to subscribers, each having so many hours of reading, and by such means, or by others, it was suddenly learned that a large number of French prisoners on parole were arriving. These prisoners had but little money, though they were welcome guests, full of gaiety and interest ; a theatre was started in an old ballroom and the ladies lent their dresses to adorn the female characters. Chambers, as a shopkeeper, gave them credit, but, alas, none of them paid a sou after the peace; it would be charitable to believe that some of them fell at Waterloo. Then Chambers' family gave up their struggle for a livelihood in Peebles and departed on ' The Fly ' for the five hours' journey to Edinburgh with hardly anything in their pockets.

To take another example of a town-bred man— though this time of the middle class—the story of Nasmyth, the engineer, is interesting.[1] He was born in 1808 in the house of his father, the distinguished artist, and he tells us that one of his earliest recollections was the liberation of the French prisoners who had been kept for a long time in Edinburgh Castle behind palisades through which they handed out their handi-

[1] James Nasmyth, *An Autobiography*, 1883.

work in return for modest sums. At the Peace of
Amiens in 1814 the prisoners marched to Leith by
torch-light singing ' The Marseillaise.' Then came
Waterloo and the rejoicings for it, followed by hearing
of the killed and wounded, and then the enormously
increased taxation, and finally the return of the 42nd
Regiment, marching up the High Street to the Castle
with their tattered colours amidst the cheering of the
people. George Croal tells us that the soldiers had on
their way purloined largely from a field of turnips,
and that the turnips were waved aloft on the points
of their bayonets. Highland soldiers always have a
popularity at home and abroad which some consider
beyond their due, and attributable largely to a popular
dress !

One thing that Nasmyth emphasizes in regard to
Scottish life is the close association between children
and their parents and their servants. The latter were
usually fairly well educated and country bred, and the
children loved their tales as they sat sewing and bleaching the ' claes ' on the Calton Hill, while the young ones
played. As was usually the case, touch was kept up
with those servants after they married or moved on ;
indeed, the relationship was a truly human and natural
one, and in consequence there were not the sort of
difficulties that usually occur in a connection not
wholly normal. There were in Nasmyth's younger
days a number of ' caddies ' round the markets, i.e.
sturdy women, each with a creel on her back, who acted
as porters, which was convenient. When the caddie was

chosen out of the din the goods were then selected;
fish was put in first, after it had been bought from the
fishwives. These were an outspoken, healthy and handsome lot of women, who made and mended their
husbands' nets and then sold the fish, trudging about
with the heavy creels on their backs, their striped petti-
coats being well kilted up to show good, solid legs; and
legs were never then in evidence as far as females were
concerned. There was plenty of haggling before the
' haddies ' could be brought down to their market price
of about a penny apiece. After a stormy night the
answer was always the same to the question ' Well,
Janet, hoo's haddies the day ? ' ' Haddies, mem ? Oh,
haddies is men's lives the day '; sometimes true
enough. Herrings were twopence a dozen and crabs a
penny each, for there was little competition. Once the
fish were bought and a board placed on the top of them,
came the butcher's meat, poultry, and finally vegetables,
perhaps finally ' a floore ' (a bunch of flowers) on the top,
and marketing was completed for the day.

As usual Nasmyth was brutally used at school, and at
his first school his head was so hurt that he was kept in
bed helpless for a week. The High School was not
much better than his preparatory school as to learning,
and we cannot wonder when we remember that classes
were composed of 200 boys, none too well behaved.
Just as with Chambers, old Edinburgh and its his-
torical interest laid hold of young Nasmyth, as it has
done to generation after generation of boys loyal to
their Scottish traditions ; and the Nasmyths had plenty

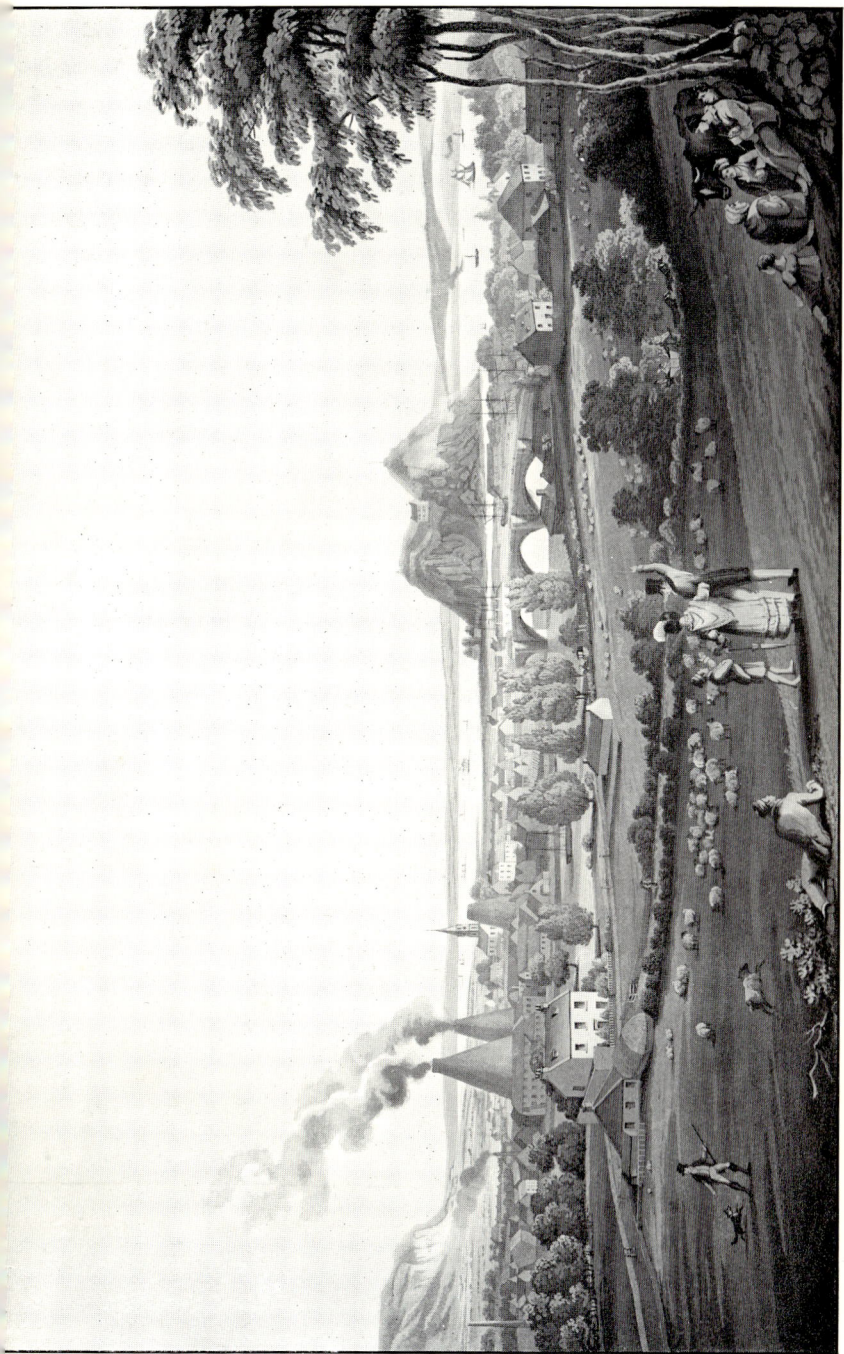

THE TOWN OF DUMBARTON.   FROM THE DRAWING ON THE SPOT BY J. CLARK ABOUT 1820

of these in their own family. Walter Scott was doing his best to make these traditions live, and he was often to be met showing places of interest to his visitors. He and young Nasmyth stood together while the great iron chest in the Tolbooth, in which those condemned to death had been kept, was with the utmost difficulty broken open by its narrow iron door. Another by-stander was John Linnell the artist, who had come with an introduction to the elder Nasmyth, and who kept a skeleton rat as a gruesome relic of the Heart of Mid-lothian ! Those strange experiences moulded the lives of the young Scots of the day as similar ones did young Louis Stevenson at a later date.

On another side there was the influence of James Watt, who visited the Nasmyths in 1817. He was an old man, but seeing him had a real effect on young Nasmyth's life. Nasmyth had a natural turn for mechanics, and already turned out spinning-tops known as ' Peeries ' by means of his father's foot-lathe. The tops had the steel shod or spinning point exactly centred, so that they spun better than other tops. Flying kites were also popular when made by Nasmyth, as were small brass cannon. The fire to light them was obtained by the use of a flint and steel and a tinder box, which every boy possessed. Nasmyth managed to elude his lessons by bribing the monitors with these desirable objects made by himself. Holidays were spent in foundries and in watching the process of hardening and tempering steel. Everything done by the boys was done by their own hands ; alcohol was distilled and converted into sulphuric ether,

T

and phosphorus was made out of bones, and so on. Anyone like Nasmyth, interested in natural science and physics, had in Edinburgh the encouragement which came from meeting Hall, Brewster, and Leslie, who used to discuss with him matters of interest, such as volcanic action as exemplified by the rocks and hills round Edinburgh.

Much work was at this time going on in Scotland. The walk under the Salisbury Crags was constructed by the unfortunate starving weavers who made their way to Edinburgh, endeavouring to find work. This road, like some others in Scotland made under similar conditions, is therefore known as ' The Radical Road.' The ironworks of Scotland were now developing, and Nasmyth visited some of these and became acquainted with the great industrialists like Napier, Nelson and Cook of Glasgow; and he also visited the celebrated Carron Iron Works, associated with the memory of Roebuck, Watt, and Miller of Dalswinton, the first two of whom began the first working steam-engine, while the last applied the steam-engine to purposes of navigation and invented the carronade gun.

Young Nasmyth, like Chambers, also owed much to the School of Art set on foot in 1821 by Leonard Horner, Francis Jeffrey, Henry Cockburn, and others. It was indeed the first technical college, and more thorough than the many (and very useful) Mechanics' Institutes that followed in its wake, though like them it was for the benefit of those who could only give time for such work in the evenings. The founders often attended, and a library of scientific books which was instituted was invaluable ; a queue of those desirous of borrowing books and getting a good seat at the lectures used to stand at the door in order to gain admission. Once started there was a run on scientific lectures, and on Nasmyth's models for illustrating them, so that he made a certain income by continually working at steam-engine models, etc. Gradually engines were made use of for agricultural and other purposes, and, finally, Nasmyth made a road steam-engine which went on trial trips for four or five miles out of Edinburgh ; but after that the engine was broken up. However, he constructed a complete working model of a high-pressure engine in order to send it along with drawings to Henry Maudsley of London, the great engineer of the day, hoping for employment from him. His father and he, with all his cumbrous packing-cases, made their way to London by sea, and, finally, after great discouragement because of Maudsley's experiences of previous ' gloved ' apprentices, the lad obtained the work he longed for. Then, as always happens when young Scots migrate to London, friends appeared. Henry Brougham the father and son accidentally met on the Duke of York's steps ; he provided an introduction to ' Mr. Faraday of the Royal Institution.' David Wilkie was next visited, and now young Nasmyth was fairly installed in England, where he spent most of his later life and made himself celebrated by his inventions, and more especially by his invention of the steam-hammer.

CHAPTER XII

HOW THE RURAL WORKERS LIVED

PART I.   LIFE IN THE LOWLANDS

BEFORE the nineteenth century opened the plan of enclosing land to keep in cattle was little practised, unless it was in the small extent of ground beforementioned round a gentleman's seat, and known as ' The Policy.' Later on the policies were increased and made more ornamental by plantations of wood and possibly of some rhododendron bushes ; but in the old economical days the policy did not exceed a few acres.   The fences were ' dry stone dykes,' occasionally ' harled ' with lime mortar on one side.   Properly constructed walks were few till the building craze came in.   The cattle were herded between sowing time in spring and harvest in autumn, but if not shut in they were at other times of the year allowed to roam at large by day and collected at night.   No wonder that there was constant warfare between tenants over the ' poinding ' of one another's cattle (i.e. the detention of wanderers), and the law-plea the Scot so much enjoys frequently resulted.   When artificial grasses were introduced, the cattle had, of course, to be herded all the year through.

The enclosures, when made general by the more enterprising and wealthy proprietors, often took the form of hawthorn hedges and ditches, which added to the beauty of the scenery and gave shelter ; but in many parts of the country, where stones abound, hedges are hardly seen to this day. This work of enclosing was for the most part done by the tenant ; but the landlord did the planting, if carried out at all. Until the new century brought in improvements the houses of the lairds were dingy enough ; roughly carved stones, always admired, adorned the gateways, but weeds infested the avenues ; trees were poor and badly chosen ; those selected were ash, alder, birch and Scots fir.

As to the ' farm-onsteads,' if quite small they were in old days of the simplest sort. The dwelling-house was in the middle, barns at one end and cattle-houses at the other, all low and thatched with straw. The one division called the ' but ' was kitchen and servants' apartment, where all assembled for food, and where the daughters and maidservants slept ; the second or ' ben-the-house ' was the master's quarters, where he and his wife and younger children lay, and where friends were sometimes entertained. There might be a low attic above used for lumber and stores, and possibly for putting up a young lad or a stranger. One wonders how the large families of the time collected in a room of perhaps sixteen feet by fourteen, the girls and gude-wife spinning, baking, kirning the milk and making the clothes, especially as, often enough, beggars were brought in to add to the population. But the same problem meets one in the tall, narrow lairds' houses of a short time before. The big ' lum ' or vent carried off

294 THE SCOTLAND OF OUR FATHERS

the smoke, or did not do so if wind was unpropitious. In future generations the same problems will be placed before those who gaze at our 'one-roomed houses' in the slums, and, after all, we can see it now in the remoter Hebridean islands. As in the Hebrides, the cow-house or byre opened out of the 'but-house' to afford easier access to the milking. Cattle and horses were tied up here without 'trevise' between them, and the poultry were supposed to thrive better in the warmth that arose from the animals' breath. The men servants, when there were such, slept on a platform above the horses, which were in a stable adjoining the byre, and a few sheep were put in a small cot at the far end of the stable. The corn-yard was beyond that, and then came the kail-yard, cropped with kail and a very few cabbages ; practically no flowers or berry-bushes grew, but generally there were some aromatics such as tansy, southernwood (appleringie), mint, etc., and possibly a few daffodils. The herbs were always taken to church on Sunday to help to keep the wearer awake and to disguise the damp smells that abounded in the ill-swept churches with their mouldy walls.

Cottars' houses were in a cluster near by and were mean hovels indeed, being not more than five feet high and twelve feet square, and composed of round land stones and turf or 'divots' in alternate layers. The fire was often on the floor, as in the black houses of the Hebrides, if there was no 'lum,' and hence the smoke escaped from a hole in the roof or by the door or shuttered window, which was often unglazed.

It is necessary to describe the state of matters in the eighteenth century to understand the task that confronted the ' improvers ' of the end of the century and the beginning of the next. With the developments of the new century the barns were separated from the house, the dwelling-house was improved, a square built on three sides was usually adopted, the dwelling-house occupying one side, while the dung-hill, pigs and poultry occupied the court. There was an upper storey and staircase, larger windows with one sash to move ; the walls were plastered as were the ceilings, and the height was increased. The plan of having cattle feeding in sheds, open or (as later) covered, did not come into vogue till well on in the nineteenth century. Slates or tiles took the place of thatch except in the offices, and kail-yards improved a little ; they were, however, still put at the back of the house. Cottar-houses were built of stone and lime, and were higher and bigger than before ; windows were of glass and a vent was placed in the wall ; in the kail-yard there even appeared a bush or two of gooseberries, some currants and a few onions, leeks and carrots.

The improved farms became what were called farmers' Mains. The barns had to accommodate the ponderous threshing-mill, and horses and cows had their own separate stalls. The house gradually betook itself to a little distance off, where it was free from the dung-hill, and trees were planted to give protection from the blast. If a year's rent was devoted to carrying on this work it was well repaid.

As to the furnishing of farmhouses early in last century, there were always in the kitchen one or two boxbeds of wood, enclosed on all sides and opening only in front with sliding doors, possibly an extra bed, some wooden chairs with long upright backs, a bunker, a long low chest on which several people could sit, a long table for meals, an aumry (*armoire*) or store press for provisions, a rack for displaying plates, a bakeboard for baking, an iron girdle for firing oatcakes, a heater for toasting the cakes, a salt-bucket set close by the chimney, and so on. Of course there were spinning and check or winding-wheels. The mattresses were well stuffed with oat chaff as were the pillows. Chaff they always pronounced ' cauf ' or ' calf,' and this often caused confusion, as when an astonished visitor from the south was asked for ' calf for a cod,' i.e. chaff for a pillow ! It is a pity that the plan of renewing the chaff, which was always done in old days, did not develop into that of teasing out the hair when hair mattresses came to be used, in the manner adopted abroad.

As to food in the farms in the beginning of the last century, there was porridge and milk for breakfast and supper, and this more or less continued up to the end of the century and beyond it. The kail-pot supplied barley broth intermixed with green kail, cabbage, pease or beans, and, in the old days, bannocks of barley meal or pease ; in later days flour scones took the place of the bannocks. In old days there was mutton in summer or beef in winter, perhaps twice a week. The beef was always salt, as the practice of feeding cattle in winter had not begun, and a store was laid in by killing one of the best cattle, known as 'the Mart,' at Martinmas to serve through the winter. The vegetables used prevented the ill consequences which might have resulted from the constant use of salt meat. Small beer existed as a drink before tea came into vogue, which it did by degrees until at last it became the common drink.

There was a curious mixture of religion and coarseness of expression in the conversation, which we see well exemplified in the life and writings of Robert Burns. We should probably find in a small farmhouse the works of Buchanan, Knox, Rutherford and Bunyan and Boston. Possibly, also, Wodrow and, for light literature, Hervey's *Meditations on the Tombs*. But above all there was the Bible, on which not a few could give chapter and verse for almost any quotation any one brought forward. This resulted, no doubt, from the teaching of the catechism 'with proofs,' which was done from earliest childhood. The family might dwell on such literature and even discuss theological questions, which seemed remote from their everyday lives of toil, but which, no doubt, kept the lamp of the spirit burning in their souls ; but otherwise it was hard and rough, unless in exceptional cases. One has just to read the Church records and see the sort of sins that were committed, confessed to, and dealt with by the Session, to realize what that life was. Drunkenness was constant where illicit stills were still existent, as they were in remote places until the middle of the nineteenth century. In any case spirits were cheap, and the pent-up life led by the young men and maidens naturally led to immorality. In many cases reputable marriages began in devious ways, but too often there was no possibility of, or desire for marriage.

The cottars' houses were poor imitations of the farmers'—a pot for boiling food on the hearth, a tub for washing and horn spoons were obviously necessary. There was always a certain allowance of oatmeal and usually milk, which ensured sustenance. As the century advanced improvements came. In the better class houses four-post beds sometimes supplanted the box-beds. A carpet was laid down and curtains put up, the usual pattern being the characteristically Scottish ' dambrod ' of squares which is still popular in Scottish linen. Pokers, tongs and fenders appeared as decorations of the firegrate. There were often china dogs with queer expressions and odd whiskers, beloved of the children, on the mantelpiece. Feather beds and looking-glasses began to be seen and used, and every farm-house had its old-fashioned grandfather-clock and hour-glass, though the presagings of the cat and ducks were thought more reliable, by the womenfolk at least ! China and stoneware 'equipages' soon became general, especially the cream-coloured stoneware invented by Josiah Wedgwood; and from this time forward there were but steps to go to reach the polished sideboard, the sofa and pianoforte. England, and more particularly Manchester, began to furnish stuffs of cotton and silk that replaced the home-made materials, but Scotland kept up its own fine linen and damask till the century was far advanced : it was sometimes made on hand-looms and hawked round the country, but the finest double damask was made in Scottish factories and designed by real artists. It is said by Mr. Andrews in his *Recollections* that though fictitious stories had come into vogue as ' book-entertainment,' or novels whose ' tendency was not always innoxious,' the farming class had not been guilty of reading much more than books concerning their own industry. In his time, 1829, the discursive tailor still made his rounds and dealt out his tales in the kitchen, and the webster appeared with his webs of sheeting, and prepared for the wefting and woofing of new commissions. He always received the bread and cheese and dram without which no bargain was made. The ' wauker ' brought his load of blankets on his switch-tailed mare, and the cooper his girds or hoops. Then there was the chapman who brought all sorts of finery, knives and needles, ribands and lace, even pamphlets and ballads; the tinker even, and the salt-man appeared; but, above all, the common beggars. These were a recognized class and were given a night's lodging in the barn and sent on their way. All this bevy of visitors kept a certain liveliness anyhow in the farm-buildings and took the place of the day's shopping in the county towns of later days. Those who can remember the relics of this life cannot forget the enjoyment of the visits on the part of children and servants. They also remember the tales of the old days when the system was universal.

Of course all this happened before the invention of

labour-saving appliances, and while wages were low a number of men and women were employed on a good-sized farm. The old knocking-stone, resembling an apothecary's mortar, seen so often in a farm-steading, was the implement originally used for grinding barley. It went out of general use soon after Andrew Fletcher of Saltoun brought the idea of barley mills into Scotland from Holland, i.e. about 1710; and barley mills were soon erected all over the country. But as to the plough, it always required its gadmen or plough-drivers till the new swing-plough came in. There would be a ' haflan callant ' or sturdy boy as cowherd, and possibly two married ploughmen living in the cottages. And female servants were also numerous compared to later days, especially as one might be kept continually at her wheel. For amusement there was often a fiddle, always songs; of games there might be the dambrod (draughts), but work was continual, for even in the dark nights the horses and cattle had to be suppered, the cows milked, and the guidman amongst decent living people ' took the book ' and conducted family worship after the supper was over. Artificial light was poor and dim. There were few general holidays, but Hallowe'en, when ' a' the witches are to be seen,' was always kept as in a degree it is even now. In old days there were many more guizarts or lads dressed up in queer garb, visiting the houses, and apples were ducked for ; but the great holidays (since Christmas Day was not kept) have always been Hogmanay, the last day of the year, and Handsel-Monday, the first Monday of the year. The first again was kept by gysers or gyzarts going about and chanting their rhymes, asking for cheese and oatcakes or wheaten loaf, saying, ' Get up guid-wife and gi' us a penny,' or ' Huigmanay troll-al-ay, gie us some of your whitebread, and none of your grey.' Then, in the village street—for Scots villages are usually one long severe-looking street, very likely on a hill—the ' futyers ' who lived at the foot of the town, armed with their flambeaux or torches, met the ' headers ' or those who lived at the top, similarly armed, at the centre or Cross ; and, throwing their flambeaux into a pile, they made a bonfire of them all. Handsel-Monday, as its name betokens, meant the giving of ' handsels '—a feast and a true holiday when everyone who could go, went to their own homes. Long before the day the gyzarts were prepared for ; money was collected for tar for the flambeaux, and the lads sometimes got up a sort of play which included a sham fight. ' Fause faces ' were usually worn. It is not so long since the gyzarts ceased ; indeed in a mild fashion they continue to this day.

Penny-weddings are now no more, but as everyone contributed they were an excellent way of setting up a young couple of farm servants in their new homes. They meant a dinner and dance in the barn : as in all barn dances there was always a master of the ceremonies, and in old days the dance was followed by the ' bedding ' of the young couple. The Harvest Home was usually held early in November (when the belated harvest was at last gathered in), often on a bright frosty night, and the barn was decked up for the occasion while the gudewife got plenty of tea and cakes and other good things ready in the adjoining house. The ' Maiden,' the last handful of corn brought in, was tied up in ribbon and set over the mantelpiece. Then the M.C. announced ' Take partners for " Triumph," " Rory O'More " or " The Flowers of Edinburgh," ' or, best of all, an ' Eightsome Reel,' and there was fun and noise enough. Most young Scots were and are taught to dance, and dance well; the older men are often the best dancers, but that is perhaps on the principle of the survival of the fittest, for a considerable number drop out and take to quieter amusements. The Whist Drive became a popular entertainment at the end of last century, and it usually ended in a dance for the younger folk, but it is a comparatively recent institution. Cards were played a century ago, but they had sinister associations, and for religious church-going folk the ' devil's buiks ' were anathema almost until the Great War, when laxer manners and more cheerful forms of entertainment came into vogue even in the Highlands. The Drama was not altogether unknown half a century or more ago, though frowned on by the Church, for many villages in the Lowlands had their Dramatic Societies even then, and excellent work was done, if of a crude sort. There was a small repertoire, since suitable plays for amateur representation did not seem to exist, but *Rob Roy* and *Colleen Bawn* were constantly produced; and occasionally actors who began in these simple ' play-actings ' found their way to larger spheres of action in the south.

New inventions combined to make employment scarcer, and, though the towns were suffering too, there was always the off-chance of finding good work there, while there was none in the country. Even the elementary change of the plough from what was called the Scots home-made wooden plough of the eighteenth century to the English plough, and then, in the nineteenth century, the change to the new plough of iron which enabled a ploughman to manage it easily with a pair of horses and no driver, made a difference in employment. Carts grew from being sledges on wheels of solid timber, such as were used in the eighteenth century, to being real wheeled carts, the wheels being made in three parts with the axle made fast to the under part of the cart body. Later on the wheels revolved round the axle ends, and in the nineteenth century the axles became iron instead of wood, which effected an immense improvement in progression. All this tended to reduce labour, as also did the ' coup ' cart, so made as to admit of being unloaded without unyoking the horse, thereby greatly relieving the carter. The consequence of better carts and better roads meant that one horse could draw a cart of a ton or more in weight and one man could drive two carts. So thoroughly were these advances established that in the early quarter of the nineteenth century there used to be a turning of tables on the neighbouring country, and there was much criticism of the English waggon drawn by six or eight horses. These uneconomical and clumsy and cumbrous vehicles accomplished about half the work, horse for horse, of

that done in Scotland. All these improvements, however, meant less human toil and less employment for
human beings.

PART II. RURAL LIFE IN EASTERN SCOTLAND AND THE UPLANDS OF THE SOUTH

It is characteristic of the Scotland of last century that
there was a great diversity of customs and speech
throughout its different parts. This strangely enough
continued even when means of communication through
good roads and railways came to exist, but it was
very marked early in the century. The speech of the
North-East was hardly comprehensible in the South-
West, and the manners were very different. Life in
counties such as Aberdeen and Banff was incredibly
hard and rough, especially for those who had no external
advantages of family or fortune. Indeed, visitors from
the South always found it difficult to believe in the good
stuff that existed below a forbidding exterior.

It is difficult to describe this life exactly, as it varied
in detail though not in essentials, and it seems best to
take an instance of what may be regarded as a typical
lad of very poor parentage who yet made good. So
many, alas, fell by the way.

John Duncan, who lived to be a well-known botanist,
was born in Aberdeen in 1794, and thus at the end of the
eighteenth century, but his life belongs to the nineteenth.
Like so many of his time he was born out of wedlock, in
his case under specially trying conditions. His first
introduction to nature-study was that he was employed

to search for rushes such as would produce the pith required to make wicks for the crusies—these crusies, the triangular lamps of former days, used to be suspended from the walls. At ten years of age he went like other country lads into farm service, and there he was treated with the greatest harshness, for the East Coast farm servant was rough and coarse and poor John was a shy, backward boy. Despite the vaunted educational systems of the country, John had never been taught to read, so nature had to take the place of art, and he used while acting as ' gairdsman ' to goad and guide the horses in the old-fashioned plough, to watch, like Burns, for the little wild flower that he displaced.

He wearied of his strenuous work, and made for a village or ' toonie,' as it was called (for in Aberdeenshire diminutives are popular), composed of rural weavers who made unbleached linen and wincey. He there found what was almost always found with Scottish weavers, a taste for a general reading of the news. Newspapers were few and dear, and as many as twenty men often joined in the subscription for one valuable print.

Private stills were, of course, illegal, but they not only existed but flourished. John's master ' made malt ' in a loft over the workshop and carried on a trade in the spirit there produced and in the gin that was landed from abroad on the rocks of the East coast. When other means failed for getting rid of the officers he used to take the mare into the kitchen and place her with her heels toward the door. The hoofs of the mare and fists of the smugglers had small difficulty in beating

U

off the gaugers ! There was nothing then to prevent a
boy apprenticed to his master from being worked from
early morning to late at night and cruelly treated, as
poor boys apprenticed to weavers—sometimes waifs
and strays—often were; no holidays excepting Sunday
were given during the whole long year. In 1811 came
' the bad harvest,' when the perpetual wet caused the
meal to be almost uneatable. John was sixteen before
he learnt to read, and then he was taught by a kind
neighbour to say in Scots Ay, Bay, Say, and to conclude
the alphabet with Ized and 'Eppercy And,' which signified *et per se*, And.

Duncan became really happy when he settled as a
weaver on Donside, near the famous hill of Benachie,
where he lived a congenial rural life. His time of
misery had passed. There he used to make soap, then
so expensive, with the outside husks of corn (when
ground) known as ' seeds,' which when rubbed in
water made a sort of lather. These seeds also make a
sort of gruel known as ' sowens,' very frequently used,
particularly in times of scarcity such as the Scots were
so well used to. One marvels to think how such men as
Duncan grudged themselves every comfort, slept in
ill-lighted, unventilated rooms, in box beds, or ' stockit
beds ' as they were called, and yet took the pains to
study Latin and even Greek. The thrifty neighbours
thought Duncan was ' losing his time instead of working
at his loom,' and yet he was respected and liked.

The usual plan of a weaver's house in Eastern Scotland
was to have a kitchen with earthen floor, a ' ben-house '

within and a 'weaving shop.' The kitchen was usually open to the thatch, made black with the peat smoke of years. Breakfast and supper were, as usual, porridge and milk; for dinner there was 'kail brose,' which consisted of oatmeal with perhaps a little butter and the broth of green kail—but sometimes only 'water-brue, that is, oatmeal softened by boiling water. Tea was ill thought of as a beverage, and it was besides expensive. The club which bought a newspaper spent on it the great sum of a guinea a year. The *Aberdeen Journal* was taken till 1843, the Disruption year, and then the *Aberdeen Banner*, the organ of the Freechurchmen and Liberals.

There were wandering tailors in those days as well as websters, and known as 'whip-the-cats.' These, when employed, received two shillings a day and their food. Tailors were also keen debaters, and the Church questions when the Disruption came in view gave plenty of opportunity for defending the 'auld kirk,' as the Established Church was always called, or championing the new or Free Church. There were amusements, too, for there was always someone who was the professional fiddler at weddings and dances. The little change-house which had 'entertainment for men and horses' was a simple public-house; but often a grocery shop was added—a 'shoppie' as Aberdonians always affectionately called it. A hearse was added as a further attraction when such was to be procured.

During the forties John wandered about the country following his botanical pursuits, and, being a gentle creature, found kindness almost everywhere; never was he charged more than sixpence for his night's lodging. He tells how when there was no food in the house his host went out and cut with the sickle a sheaf of corn ; the oats were held over the great pot and in a short time set on fire so that the chaff was consumed and the grains dropped into the pot where they were dried as in a kiln. The bellows blew away the charred portions of the husks, and then the ' quern ' or hand-mill, often to be seen still in farm steadings, was used to grind the hard, dry grain which had been poured into a hole in the centre. This process was carried on in Scotland till the thirties in remote districts, and in the very early years of the century the distaff was still made use of. In Banffshire, indeed, the work was done in peculiar fashion, for the young damsels used to give the requisite rotary motion to the distaff by rolling it on the bare thigh, since it was said that it would not spin half so well over their clothes ! These things are, no doubt, matters of convention, as were the fording of rivers in primitive attire and washing linen with the feet instead of hands—the usual plan for many years after this. Duncan soon learned to make winceys (linen warp and woollen weft), blankets, carpets, and so on. There was great art in the ' broad loom ' weaving, where the pattern was produced by means of the Jacquard machine.

John Duncan was one of the last of the websters who wove home-made material, though the trade went on in the villages in the East and middle of Scotland till the eighties ; the work was varied by harvesting in autumn.

There was a dread in rural Scotland which weighed on every mother. In the early part of the century every able-bodied man between the ages of eighteen and thirty-five, with certain exceptions, was liable to be drawn for the militia ; this was done by ballot—the ballot-boxes may still be seen—and Duncan was ' drawn ' as a militiaman, not that this concerned him much. In every district associations were formed to buy out (by getting a substitute) all those who wished for any reason to be relieved from duty ; the sum required to pay the substitute varied from £5 to £40. By offering himself for others Duncan twice got the bounty, and served the requisite month in spring and six weeks in autumn, that being the period required in times of danger. Militia-men were a rough lot very often and flogging was frequently resorted to, though Duncan never was a victim.

In Aberdeen there was a riot in 1831 (which had to be quelled by the militia), when the populace burnt down Dr. Morris's Anatomical Theatre, one of the first to be made in the North, and known as ' Burkin' House.' This showed how the prejudice that had arisen against the medical profession after the Burke and Hare murders in Edinburgh extended even to Aberdeen.

In the course of his peregrinations Duncan came into touch with the ' tinklers,' as they were called, who were a recognized community in Scotland, and in their way kindly enough. There are in Scotland still a certain number of well-known tinkler or tinker families who prefer wandering and living in tents to dwelling in stationary houses of stone and lime, and who have some virtues as well as a good many minor vices. They present constant problems to the educationalists, but manage to elude most of the laws and regulations of social life.

The villages in Aberdeenshire and Banffshire were famous for their 'Mutual Improvement' Classes. Sometimes the man read, and sometimes the woman was the best reader, if she had a strident voice : if so, she was chosen to read aloud to the weary weavers and out-door workers by the peat fires. As to books, there were plenty of theological volumes, and many discussions took place ; sometimes moral problems presented themselves, such as whether the webster was entitled to keep the 'thrums' or refuse of his client's wool ! Matthew Henry's Bible, *The Scots Worthies* by John Howe, and Foxe's *Book of Martyrs* were found on the shelves of many 'well-doing' cottagers in the land. In later times there was almost certainly the *Ten Years' Conflict, recording the events leading to the Disruption of 1843,*—that is, if the family had 'come out' on that occasion. Everyone subscribed to their church, how-ever poor, and especially did those who had 'come out,' and who had not only to support their minister and build their churches, but also to subscribe to missions, home and foreign ; for these were practically all dupli-cated by the new organization. These collections were 'gathered' every four weeks by volunteer collectors, and in the early days varied in amount from four-pence to four shillings and sixpence a month. There was often difficulty in getting a site for the new church, and sometimes a bad one had to be taken because of the opposition of the lairds. Thus a great deal of the energy that would otherwise have been expended on politics proper went in the direction of Church administration. What was very remarkable was the immense amount of money expended on their Church and its 'schemes' by quite poor men and women, who felt it a privilege so to contribute.

The Mutual Improvement or Instruction Classes formed themselves into a 'Union' to promote this form of Adult Education, which had also a Female Section; classes for artisans and farm-servants, and a library of a simple kind, were likewise set on foot. The Union lasted only till 1857, but after that classes were still carried on, and, of course, after a time the work was done, though in a different way, by other organizations, and finally by statutory methods. But these early societies of working people are not to be scoffed at, for they produced many men who later on became eminent in literature and politics. The unfortunate thing for the societies was that the best of their members kept moving away to the towns, which discouraged those who remained.

John Duncan's trade failed him in 1870, when hand-loom weaving in his part of the country was practically extinct, and, to his infinite grief and sorrow, he had to apply for parish relief—an unspeakable shame to him, as it was to other men who were poor but proud. In 1874 he was awarded three shillings a week by the parish, and he felt himself, as he tells us, stamped with the brand of Cain when he received his card. But when his distress was known a public subscription was set on foot to which Darwin sent a gift as to a ' fellow botanist.' So that Duncan, when he died in 1881, was free of all pecuniary anxieties and honoured by his fellowmen, and, above all, by a great contemporary scientist.

This story has been told in detail because it exemplifies the struggles of Scottish countryfolk in the nineteenth century, and the fine way in which they overcame almost insuperable difficulties.

Conditions seem different when viewed from different angles, and the next account concerns the more civilized, but less strenuous, men of the Southern Uplands, as taken from the records of certain ministers who lived there early in the nineteenth century. As far as rural life is concerned, indeed, a great part of our information is derived from the records of parish ministers such as those who wrote in the two Statistical Accounts published respectively in the eighteenth and nineteenth centuries. There is also an interesting book by Dr. James Russell, the minister of Yarrow, describing the ecclesiastical and social life in that lonely upland country. His father was originally minister of Ettrick, close by, and then at Yarrow itself, so that their joint recollections extended for about a century. He tells of that very characteristic event in early days in Scotland, the parochial examinations on the catechism which in the first half of the century took place from time to time in a schoolroom or barn. It was, indeed, a formidable trial for the farm-servants and young people to attend these gatherings, since the answers to the questions had to be repeated by heart. It is, however, related that an unfortunate woman who had been found deficient in knowledge by the eminent divine, Sir Henry Moncrieff, and therefore sent back till she was sufficiently instructed to receive the Sacrament, was yet found to be reading her answers from the printed page. She, however, got her own back; for, when reproved for this misdemeanour, she exclaimed, ' Oh, Sir Harry! You that read your sermon every Sabbath, winna ye let a puir body read her Carritches?' Sir Harry had, apparently, contrary to what was then approved, been convicted of reading the sermon that ought to have been delivered *extempore* !

The elder Dr. Russell was chaplain to the Lord High Commissioner from 1805 till 1842, so that he had great experience of the annual Church meetings that play so large a part in ecclesiastical life in Scotland. Originally the Lord High Commissioner and his Purse-bearer went about in sedan chairs, each carried by two footmen in livery. The meetings of Assembly were then held in the old Assembly Aisle of St. Giles' Church, a narrow, confined place, and there were constant disputes as to precedency between the ' esquires,' or lairds, and the doctors of divinity. In the beginning of the century, before the revival in interest on such matters, there was little religious work to do at Assembly times; there was no missionary zeal nor even ' schemes ' supported by the Church, or deputations from other

Churches, such as later on were so engrossing. When the discussion on Non-Intrusion began it was, of course, very different. In the earlier days, as we saw, the ceremonies were elaborate. There were two tables for dinner, one presided over by the Commissioners, and another, less distinguished, taken charge of by purse-bearer and chaplain. The Town Guard was in attendance on the representatives of royalty, and the Captain of the Guard was a daily guest and never retired without a bottle of port under his belt.[1]

Cases of inebriation were rare ; but on one occasion at least Dr. Russell had hard work conveying a minister unaccustomed to much wine safely down the High Street, and committing him to the care of his wife ! St. Giles, where the Assembly met, was the first church to have a choir, and the innovation was much disliked by the Earl of Haddington, who remarked to Dr. Russell : ' I come here to praise my Maker, and not to hear a concert ! '

As regards the working people in these upland regions the life was characteristic.

Early in the century the big and little spinning wheels were still ' birring ' in every parlour and kitchen, and home-made clothing was the order of the day. Webs of linen were spread out to bleach, and in Dr. Russell's parish an old woman had learned from Dunfermline the art of making table-cloths. The farmhouses were thatched, small and low-roofed, all on the same plan, with a room at one end and kitchen at the

---

[1] This trait is illustrated in Kay's Portraits.

other ; and through the kitchen another room, generally used as a bedroom ; or perhaps two attics above which were reached by a trap-ladder and with a few small panes placed in the thatch for light. This was the usual construction of any such house, and was that of the house in which Mungo Park, the traveller, was born. There was usually a ' loupin'-on-stane ' as an adjunct to any house, or church, to assist the gudewife in mounting on a pillion behind her husband when the two went on horseback, as they so often did.

The hinds' and shepherds' cottages were such as we have met with before, dark smoky hovels, the walls of stone and sods alternately, the floors of earth and the roof of coarse timber, covered with turf and rushes. A hole in the middle or end of the roof, surrounded at the top by a wicker frame, widening as it came down, plastered with a mixture of straw and mud and supported by a strong beam, was the only chimney. People sat round the peat fire, and the hams were smoked by it. The window was a single pane of glass, but it was sometimes without glass, and stuffed at night with old clothes. The cow-byre might be on one side of the entrance, the family apartment, which served alike for eating and sleeping, on the other. Box-beds were convenient receptacles for all possible odds and ends, while potatoes in heaps were stored beneath.

Of course the difference between these primitive hovels and the stone and lime cottages at the end of the century was immense. In these early days the only fuel was that of peats carried on horseback from the hills, before

roads and railways existed. Leases were almost unknown, and this was a barrier to permanent improvement by the tenant on farms partly arable ; also there
were tiresome obligations of service for the landlord,
of which we are always reading, kain-fowls, a ' darg ' or
day's work, and so on, all latterly abolished. ' Thirl-
ing ' to a particular mill was one of the most trying of
these conditions. The distance of the mill from the
farm might be great and the rates charged for milling
unduly high.

The advances during the century are too great to
be enumerated : artificial manures, rotation of crops,
improved implements and machinery followed one
another so quickly that the nineteenth century became indeed famous in agriculture. The cultivation of the high hill ground by means of which the
cultivator was raised above the boggy ground, and all
the work that was carried on by cheap labour and rude
implements, are only known now by the marks of the
plough that we see upon the hills, and the remains of
the ' feal ' or ' fail,' i.e. turf, dykes. Any new-fangled
idea, such as that of using bone-dust as a manure, was
in these early days looked at with distrust, just as was the
iron plough. There were usually several tenants on one
farm, amongst whom there was not always agreement.
The hill-pasture was a common, but the arable land was
on the run-rig system, and each tenant tried to cut his
patch with his sickle faster than the other. Winnowing
was carried on from an elevated spot where the wind did all
that was required. All those who know about hill farm-

ing know the terrible effects of many ' drifty days ' on the stock, and of the anxiety sometimes about the shepherds themselves, when they went to dig out their sheep. This dread was always present, and is so even now.

As we have seen, the usual custom for farmers was to kill a ' Mart ' at Martinmas for the winter's supply of butcher's meat. The ox was cut up and well salted—too well before it was finished. The profane suggested that the long graces then *de rigueur* might be obviated by having one very long grace over the beef-tub ! Tea was a luxury little dreamt of ; and salt, up to 1825, owing to the tax, was a dear commodity and kept carefully in a salt-box or bucket by the fire. Hair powder was taxed out of existence. Oatcakes and bannocks of barley meal with an admixture of peas were the ordinary table fare, wheaten bread was hardly known until toward the end of the century, when spring carts plied daily in the valleys of the Ettrick and Yarrow. Postage from London to Yarrow was 1s. 1½d., from Edinburgh 7½d., and the manse letters came once a week with bread and butcher's meat by a weekly carrier. The penny post introduced in 1840 made a marvellous change in the lives of the people, as did the removal of the tax on papers and journals. One paper, *The Courant*, served all Yarrow when Dr. Russell first came there.

In 1812 the first gig was introduced into Yarrow lanes, and such a luxury was only excused in the case of a farmer because he was lame. It was a large yellow gig, hung on leather springs. It was years after this that the minister was persuaded to have a spring carriage on four wheels with a patent leather dickey or coach box. Rivers were crossed on horseback or mounted on stilts, until bridges were built. Town Councils seem, at one time, to have had the power to exact compulsory contributions of labour from people quite outside their bounds, and thus they succeeded in constructing some of the bridges, greatly to the advantage of the community.

Vaccination, though introduced in the end of the eighteenth century, was little practised in the remote country districts, and then often at the hands of non-professionals. The minister of Traquair used to come over to Yarrow on the day before the Communion service armed with lymph which he proceeded to insert if needed; and the writer remembers the same ceremony in a far-away parish, though whether, as alleged, it is the fact that the clergyman vaccinated first and then stated, ' and now let us proceed to the other ordinance,' i.e. baptism, she cannot say! Bleeding was another operation often done by the rural clergy.

The feeling between the Seceders of the Meeting House and the Parish Church was such that the former used to walk twelve miles or more to attend their own conventicle, and refused to enter the church by law established; but this feeling tended to diminish. Still the Seceders felt that they were suffering for righteousness' sake and were quite conscious of the sacrifices they had made in building their churches or meeting-houses, often with their own hands, and stinting themselves and their families to support their ministers and the ' schemes ' of their churches.

In pastoral districts like Yarrow the dogs were constant attendants at church, for each plaided shepherd took his dog with him as a matter of course. If by chance a couple of these fell out there was apt to be a regular collie-shangie, till the owners brought about peace by forcible means. A strange dog had short shrift, and the going round of the elders with the ladles for collections, which signified the approaching conclusion of the service, put all the lower creation on the *qui-vive*, so that the human congregation were forced to keep their seats during the Blessing (when, in Scotland, everyone stands) ' to cheat the dougs.' In these quiet regions the Fast Day and the subsequent days of the annual Communion Season appear to have been observed with decorum and seriousness, differing thereby from certain other parts of the country ; or perhaps the minister gave a happier account of what occurred. The services on Communion Sunday were long, for they began at 10.30 and ended at 7 p.m., with an hour and a quarter of interval. There were, indeed, seven full Communion Tables, and refreshments of a material sort were provided from the kitchen of the manse ; bread and ale in the barn, and food for the farmers and their families in the manse dining-room. No public-house refreshments are mentioned.

Poaching, which was common in the Lowlands, was never thought ill of in nineteenth-century Scotland any more than smuggling—that is, if the poaching were done in a gentlemanlike fashion and for personal use. Sheriffs did not forget that time was, not so long ago, in which wild game was free to all. The writer remembers talking to an old bedridden man about the hills he was gazing at. 'Do you know them?' she asked. 'Aye, fine that.' 'You were a shepherd then?' she said. 'Na, na, I was just seein' what was to be seen.' And, with a twinkle in his eye, 'They ca' that poachin', I ken, but we were the richt sort o' poachers, we aye gae the gentlemen twa three days sport afore we began!'

PART III. THE SCOTTISH GARDENER

One of the best-known Scottish rural workers is the gardener, who has been famous for centuries and yet had little opportunity of exercising his talents in his native land until the beginning of last century; and even then only within a limited range. Tobias Smollett, brought up a Scotsman though he early made his way to England, following in this practice Dr. Johnson's famous dictum that 'he found the noblest prospect in Scotland to be the highroad to England,' tells us in *Humphrey Clinker* that though the gardens and parks in Scotland are not comparable to those in England, nor are the pleasure-grounds so well laid out, almost all the gardeners of South Britain were natives of Scotland. This remarkable testimony is given on the assurance of the 'ingenious Mr. Philip Miller of Chelsea.' Gardening was clearly not so well developed in the eighteenth century as it became later on; but we have plenty of testimony to the virtues of the Scottish gardeners through the next century. George Eliot says, ' A Gardener is Scotch as a French teacher is Parisian,' and Louis Stevenson in his paper on *An Old Scots Gardener* says that a gardener was a man whose very presence could impart a savour of quaint antiquity to the baldest and most modern flower-plots : ' To me he stands essentially as a *genius loci*.' Then again, even earlier, Voltaire wrote that ' to-day rules of taste in all the arts, from epic poems to gardening, came to us from Scotland.' Thus from every side is his high reputation supported.

The advances made in the nineteenth century were fostered by distinguished amateurs. In early days these advances were made, no doubt, by those who had undertaken the ' Grand Tour,' and who came home anxious to carry out schemes for forming Italian and Dutch gardens under skilled supervision ; or in later days by those who were enamoured by the quaint beauty of the gardens of Japan. But the real progress was of native origin and derived from the liking for, and the desire to have, genuinely Scottish gardens such as required no foreign influences but were characteristic of the land. Scottish gardens, however, always had a utilitarian side, for they were founded on the kailyard, and consequently vegetables and flowers were never far removed from one another. If you peeped over the yew hedges— the ' teased yews ' of many shapes—you saw the onions and leeks as well as the various berries growing in happy proximity ; and whatever they may be as food, leeks present a noble appearance in their blue-green foliage !

x

322 THE SCOTLAND OF OUR FATHERS

As usual in our country, societies were everywhere formed to promote the study and practice of Horticulture. Not only did these societies, which flourished in almost every village, draw attention to the scientific side of gardening, but they also drew attention to the value of vegetable food, and this in Scotland was specially needed. Consequently market gardens grew up around the towns, and in the latter part of the century the mercantile side developed immensely through the growth of fruit farming on a large scale. It was discovered that strawberries flourish in Scotland, and as both they and raspberries are indigenous, they formed good subjects for growing on a large scale and utilizing for jam-making and canning. But it was the little local flower-show that did most to help to give the country good amateur gardeners amongst the poorer folk, though in Scottish villages the tendency was always to place the garden well hidden behind the house, so that the passer-by had no conception of the beauties or treasures so effectually concealed. The uncompromising severity of a Scottish village street strikes every traveller, and it is sometimes considered that this is a reflection of the Scottish character !

One reason for the reputation of the Scottish gardener was undoubtedly his passion for education and knowledge of Latin, and another that the craft insisted on a regular apprenticeship being observed (probably derived from Flanders) and a regular system of promotion from apprentice to foreman being carried out.

In the early nineteenth century Mr. George Robertson in his *Rural Recollections* reports that however poor the houses in Scotland were, there was always a well-stocked garden, with straight walks and flower borders laid out on a consistent plan, and a great supply of ordinary orchard fruits and ' berries of all descriptions, together with a superabundant supply of kitchen vegetables of the best sorts and qualities.' No hot-houses, greenhouses or conservatories were, of course, to be seen, but instead there were neatly clipped edges of boxwood, square-cut yews and holly hedges. Mr. Robertson was drawing somewhat on his fancy when he says this garden was common, but he was describing a laird's house such as it was at its best. Farmhouses had in their gardens for the most part kail, a few cabbages, currant and gooseberry bushes, and some—but not many—flowers. Somerville of Haddington reports that the ' residing nobility and gentry ' all have gardens, hot-houses, greenhouses and ' the usual appendages of a modern garden,' and also notes that the farmer and cottars have gardens, but that the county was not suited to growing fruit owing to the cold easterly winds. As a matter of fact East Lothian has always been famed for the gardens attached to the great houses, and one would imagine that they need not have been confined to them. Somerville goes on to tell how these ' gentlemen's seats ' were ornamented with plantations, though few of them were extensive, and that some experiments have even been made in the direction of hedgerows ' after the English fashion,' and also in osier planting, which had been tried successfully in damp meadowland. Probably in this rich county the damp meadowland was soon drained and made more profitable, though osiers were usually planted for basket-making.

The necessity for having gardens had been impressed on the people of Scotland even in the eighteenth century, for Lord Kames, always forward in such matters, in his *Hints to the Commissioners of the Annexed Estates*, says about 1778, that now that meal has so advanced in price that the poorer people cannot buy it, every tenant on the King's estates should have a kitchen garden for vegetables, kail, cabbage, potatoes, etc. He thought that in every ' tack ' (i.e. ' let ' through a tacksman), there should be a clause obliging the tenant to have a kitchen garden of one acre at least : the rewards for doing so should be the grant of a good spade, shovel and hoe. This unfortunately was never carried out.

Even before these days gardeners were recognized, for they were allowed to be members of the Society of Improvers, founded in 1743, *gratis*, and there are in the Society's *Transactions* most elaborate descriptions of how best to grow hyacinth beds. Probably the tulip mania of the seventeenth century was known of, but it would not appeal to a thrifty Scot. It is not stated whether the bulbs were imported from the Low Countries, but it is explained how to perpetuate them. This was done by James Crichton, a Fellow of the Royal Society, and one of the Principal Clerks of Session.

Both on the medical and instructional side Scotland had a distinguished career so far as gardening was con-

cerned. Two eminent physicians, Andrew Balfour and
Robert Sibbald, obtained in 1670 the use of a small
portion of ground to the south of Holyrood House
usually let to market gardeners, and James Sutherland
was appointed to the ' Care of the Garden.' This was
the foundation of the Royal Botanic Gardens of Edinburgh, which is therefore, after that of Oxford (founded
in 1632), the oldest in Great Britain. Dr. Balfour and a
certain Patrick Murray had been collecting medicinal
plants, and they helped to stock the garden. Subsequently the Royal Garden to the north side of the
Palace became a Physic Garden, and the first one was
given up. Later there were two other gardens called
the Town's Botanic Garden and College Garden, so that
there were three gardens under the same custodian
Sutherland, who was by royal warrant made Botanist
to the King, and even empowered to set up as a Professor
of Botany. Then the Town Council made Sutherland
Professor of Botany in the Town's College, now the
University of Edinburgh. This showed the keen
interest taken in the subject, though all the gardens
were on a very small scale and Professorships in these
days were far from lucrative. There were troublous
times before the Botany Professors, one of whom was
implicated in an unsuccessful Jacobite plot to seize the
Castle in 1715 (and naturally lost his job), and many
changes took place in the Gardens up to the time when
the present Botanic Gardens were established at Inver-
leith in 1820. They were extended in 1845 under the
distinguished Curator, John Hutton Balfour (popularly

known as ' Woody Fibre '). Since then they have grown apace.

The interesting point is that gardening was acknow-ledged as a science to be studied in days of great turmoil and poverty. By the time Loudon wrote his famous *Encyclopaedia of Gardening*, first published in 1825, Scottish gardening was most prosperous, and rather oddly he ascribes the taste for it to the French weaver refugees of the seventeenth century who came to what is now called Picardy Place in Edinburgh and taught Scotland how to manufacture silk and linen. Then he believes that the great landowners took it up in their policies (a word which he derives from the French *polir*, to level and improve). Lord Kames did wonders at Blair Drummond between 1710 and 1774, and wrote an essay on gardening in his *Elements of Criticism*.

Writing in his *Encyclopaedia*, Loudon considers that the country residences in Scotland generally, setting aside the dreary mountains and moors, excelled those of England in the prominence of their natural features, but are inferior to those of the South in magnificence and even in taste, both as to architecture and landscape gardening. ' The gardeners of Scotland have long been known for skill and assiduity in their profession ; they excel in culture and general management of the kitchen garden.' Apparently these ' were kept in much better order and at less expense by the thrifty Scot than were the gardens of the same kind and rank in England.' The gardeners, he says, ' are better educated in their youth and more accustomed to frugality and labour.'

Hence they were found not only in England and France but also in Russia and Poland. These countries, however, could be arrived at by sea more easily than one might imagine.

Planting was what most distinguished Scotland early last century, which, Loudon said, 'is beginning to assume a new and sylvan character.' But dessert was rare among the middle classes, and fruit pies and cider quite unknown to the operatives, so that in fruit Scotland did not excel. The cottage gardens had but, he says, the common vegetables, and the farmers' gardens were neglected. This seems to give a very true account of how matters stood.

Market and commercial gardeners appear however to have been doing a good trade, according to Loudon. In 1760 there were about 60 or 70 acres so cultivated in Scotland, and 'now (1825) there are 700 acres.' The making of British wines with currants, gooseberries and raspberries, was very popular in Scotland, while Scottish strawberries were even then famous. Garden seeds were still obtained from London or Holland rather than from home.

Arboriculture seems indeed to have been growing apace early in the century, for one house alone, in Edinburgh, shipped over two millions of seedlings. Even Aberdeenshire had gone ahead and planted some hundred thousands of trees and sent seedlings to the South. Perhaps this was owing to the influence of the young Earl of Aberdeen and his improvements.

The Scottish gardeners often wandered off to France.

Mr. Blaikie of Corstorphine went there as a professional gardener in 1776, and remained till 1828, when he died at the age of eighty-nine. The gardens at Versailles were partly reconstructed by him in English fashion. Perhaps in this the Scotch were merely returning what they had received from France in days gone by, a taste for French architecture, cooking and furnishing.

The Caledonian Horticultural Society was established in 1809, and thereafter all sorts of gardening (including that of cemeteries, hitherto certainly neglected) were set on foot, and associations for gardeners came into being. In Edinburgh Lord Cockburn tells us the establishment of the Horticultural Society was chiefly the work of a printer called Patrick Neill, whose ' little acre garden at Canonmills put many a grander establishment to the blush.' It had one of the first of the many exhibitions of the kind in Scotland which have done so much to promote the love of flowers and interest in vegetables.

If we revert back to early history, the most famous writer of former days on Scottish gardens was the *Scots Gard'ner* of the seventeenth century, who was actually John Reid, gardener to Mackenzie of Rosehaugh, Avoch. The book went through several editions, but was first published in 1683, and has been recently republished with an introduction by the late Lord Rosebery.

Greenhouses are mentioned by the *Scots Gard'ner*, but they must have been different from what we now envisage as such. Frames, of course, came into use early, but the first greenhouse of wood and glass was put up in the Oxford Botanic Garden in 1734. These greenhouses were lean-to erections with steep sloping sash-lights, and no doubt when these came into vogue they would be welcomed in Scotland, where the climate was rigorous. As a matter of fact they had existed in a certain form since 1670 in England, for at the Physic Garden at Oxford there was then 'A fair Greenhouse or Conservatory to preserve tender plants and trees from the injury of hard winter.' It was a solid building, afterwards converted into a library, and heated in a curious way, as Sir Arthur Hill tells us, 'by means of a four-wheeled "fire-basket" filled with charcoal which was drawn backwards and forwards by a gardener.' [1] Evelyn also mentions the greenhouse and hot-house at Chelsea in 1685 as well as Loader's Orangery in 1662. As to Scotland, we are told that James Justice had the only Pine Stove in Scotland in the eighteenth century. It was in his house at Crichton near Edinburgh. He was a great reformer of Scottish gardens and had lived for long in Holland.

Though there were garden 'fans,' as they would now be called, at all times in Scotland it does not appear that in early days garden products were everywhere in use, for Southey in his *Tour to Scotland* in 1819 remarks that 'garden-stuff is of late introduction into Scotland.' He, however, adds that 'the Scotch now excel as gardeners,' which is satisfactory to Scottish pride.

[1] Sir Arthur Hill in *Annals of the Missouri Botanic Gardens*, Vol. II.

Wesley was never complimentary to Scotland, and he declares that when ' he was first in that country they had only one sort of fleshmeat even at a nobleman's table, and no vegetables of any kind.'

The fame of Scottish gardeners, such as it was, brought its own Nemesis upon it, for it drew to them the jealousy of their Southern rivals. Four young Scots set up as nursery gardeners between 1760 and 1770 in different parts of the suburbs of London (probably in land now densely crowded) and their success was such that they excited the jealousy of the native commercial gardeners. These last took the drastic resolution of forming a sort of trade protection society, inasmuch as they formally passed a resolution not to employ any young men from the North. They went indeed so far as to publish about 1760 an essay entitled *Adam Armed* to prove how they might ' bring themselves to such a degree of good order that they might become incorporated as Professors in the art ' so that the rude invaders could be repelled. They had the more reason on their side in that King James I had apparently once granted a Charter to the craft, though it had never been enforced. Had it been so, they could have had a monopoly in the profession, and as it was, they claimed that only licensed practising gardeners should be allowed to take apprentices, and so on. For a time these valiant Adams were successful in keeping out the forward Scots, but not for long, for they did not know their men if they expected their tactics permanently to succeed.

Gardeners' Lodges, too, became established in early days, especially in Aberdeen and Banffshire, and they developed into the various societies of later days which promoted gardening. Paisley, a town always to the front, was, as has been recorded elsewhere, famous for its ' Florists' Clubs ' and general love of flowers. The culture of pinks was its speciality between 1785 and 1790, and these originated from seeds procured from London, some of which to the cultivators' delight came out *laced* and not plain. These laced pinks were carefully propagated, and plants reared in Paisley were in demand in London as superior to any grown in England. Other improvements were made in flowers, and this resulted in an ' Annual and Amicable Competition.' Competition flowers ' were eight in number, viz. Auriculas, Polyanthus, Hyacinths, Tulips, Anemones, Ranunculi, Pinks and Carnations.' Some cultivators could show 70 or 80 of the choicest varieties of pinks; others 200 varieties of tulips, others 60 or 70 named varieties of carnations. There were elaborate rules for judging the flowers at the weekly meetings and for appointing judges; this last was done with the greatest care to obviate any favouritism in adjudicating as to the prizewinners. One knows how necessary this precaution is in flower-shows! At the first adjudication ' forty to a hundred manufacturers and tradesmen of the place dined together, and everyone who had formerly received a medal was expected to wear it.'

One of the many remarkable young Scots who made his name famous in gardening and arboricultural circles

was David Douglas, born at Scone in 1799, the son
of an intelligent stonemason. He had a tumultuous
school life, being more addicted to bird-nesting and
rambling than book-learning. He spent the money he
had for his luncheon in buying food for his owlets.
His master used, however, to say of him, in spite of his
misdeeds, ' I like a devil better than a dult.' He served
his seven years' apprenticeship in the Earl of Mans-
field's garden and after a time went to the Botanic
Gardens at Glasgow, and from thence as Botanical Col-
lector to the Horticultural Society of London. Then
he travelled extensively in North America and other
places and thereby made his famous collection of trees
and plants.

Charles Black, born in 1813 at Pitcaple in Aberdeenshire, was another well-known gardener. He had been
a herd-boy like most of his compeers, after leaving
school, and then a farm worker, but subsequently became an apprentice gardener without pay at Cluny
Castle. The shilling his father gave him every fortnight was spent in the purchase in parts of Mackintosh's
Practical Gardener, a great book that cost the large sum
of two pounds. He went on to study Botany with
Rattray's *Botanical Chart*, which expounded the Lin-
nean system. He and his friend Duncan worked together identifying plants and making collections, and
this though Black had long hours of work and no
holidays, so that the two occasionally used Sunday
for their walks, a thing unprecedented in those days.
They would start on these walks before daybreak and go

ten miles and even further before breakfast to get a precious plant. They managed to get a sight of a precious ' Hooker,' owned by the father of a studious young gardener then dead, only by free potations of whisky ! Such was the character of Scottish gardeners in Aberdeenshire, so no wonder they advanced in their profession. In 1838 Black got employment for a time at the Botanical Garden in Edinburgh at the colossal wages of ten shillings a week, and then returned home to complete his herbarium. The lives of men like Black and his botanical friend Duncan show the passion for information and education that existed in Scottish working gardeners.

CHAPTER XIII

THE HIGHLANDS AND THE HIGHLANDERS

EVERY traveller in the Highlands last century begins by denouncing the Highland black houses, inhabited, as Southey assures us, not by 'ignorant ferocious inhabitants such as are the Irish' but by a 'quiet, thoughtful, contented, religious people.' Dorothy Wordsworth says much the same, but Southey includes in his denunciation the Highland laird, whom, with his usual vehemence, he declares to have brought whole districts under the heinous system of rack-rent 'even to a sixfold augmentation.' A few landlords, he says, really desire to improve their estates, but many only to increase their revenues by converting their estates into sheep farms and expelling the unfortunate inhabitants from their homes and burning them.

The housing conditions in the Outer Isles were especially deplorable, many of the houses having no fireplace or chimney and sometimes being built into a bank. These houses were also often crowded together, and the cattle were housed under the same roof as the human beings, so that one had often to go through the byre to get to the living room, and the manure in the byre was removed but seldom. There was a fire in the middle of the living room round which the inhabitants sat, and there might be a very small window, which was probably unglazed. It is no wonder that tuberculosis had been rife in the worst of the ' townships ' where such houses existed. But the strange thing was that even in these conditions comfort and cleanliness might be found. There was sometimes an inner bedroom where the girls slept which was often beautifully tidy, and as there was plenty of peat there was always a bright fire, though the smoke escaped as best it could, and terribly hurt the eyes. This type of black house lasted to the end of last century, and in a manner still exists though it is fast disappearing; the Great War brought new ideas and for a time it also brought new prosperity. All through the latter part of last century the population tended to diminish, and large numbers went to make their homes in Canada where there were so many of their fellows. The islands were over-populated, and when emigration took place voluntarily it had the best results.

The attraction of life in the remote islands was and is the independence of an almost class-less population. The minister was the chief person where lairds were seldom or never seen, and he was of the people's own election. So in a sense were the doctor and the teacher, and there was a truly educated aristocracy founded on democratic principles. Hence there is still a wonderful courtesy of demeanour without subservience that is noticed by all visitors. There was always an unusual interest in education; in the present day the only means of advancement is to obtain bursaries to the secondary schools from which professional life for boys and girls takes its origin ; in old days the same process took place in a less regulated manner.

Perhaps the most melancholy part of Highland history, however, concerns the ' Clearances ' made in the end of the eighteenth century, and yet more in the nineteenth century—more especially in the first half of the century—when the evictions were carried out on a huge scale. The main evictions took place in Sutherland-shire, between 1811 and 1820, when Hugh Miller says fifteen thousand people were turned out of their homes ; and earlier than that there were evictions in Inverness-shire.[1] Indeed, right up to the thirties and forties, when there were clearances in Ross-shire and Sutherland-shire, this policy was carried on. In 1846 there was another misery in the potato famine, which left 300,000 people on the verge of starvation, though on this occasion Scotland arose and through its ' Destitution Fund ' sent relief. But the greater evil proceeded from the evictions. The remoter islands suffered as much as did the mainland, and a great population was decimated, many of whom had been good soldiers in the French wars and all came from a country that was to do good service in the Great War a century later. There was something to be said on the other side, but not a great deal. The people were leading a miserable existence ; they were living on a land which no longer gave them the subsistence which others equally placed possessed now that trade had developed in the industrial areas.

[1] *The Highland Clearances*, by Alex. Mackenzie.

THE TOWN OF INVERARAY. FROM THE DRAWING ON THE SPOT BY I. CLARK ABOUT 1820

Famine might come to them at any time when weather was bad and crops failed ; there was no future for the young people at home and they wished to go off and seek their fortunes. The land was only fit for grazing at a time when sheep-farming was flourishing, and this was inconsistent with a mass of little crofts uneconomically distributed, with little patches of cultivated land or grazing rights. But the people loved their land and the old people clung to their poor shanties with deep affection. They were offered holdings by the sea, where they were assured that they would not only have land but the power of improving their economic condition by fishing. Many went there, but unfortunately the sea to those who had never seen it, much less been trained to the fisher life, had no attractions. Many emigrated, and they and their descendants were most fortunate assets to Canada ; they did well and encouraged others voluntarily to follow in their footsteps. But even they had much to endure before they settled in their new homes. There are books, like Mackenzie's, telling of the hard times that the evicted people went through that make one's blood boil ; and they appear to be virtually correct, for they are supported by responsible people like Hugh Miller and General Stewart of Garth, as well as the many records of travellers in Scotland.

The whole inhabitants of some parishes were rooted out and the parish made a solitary wilderness ; some died from exposure in childbirth. The crofters doubtless had previous orders given them to quit,

Y

338 THE SCOTLAND OF OUR FATHERS

but no one had believed that the event would follow the threat, and that their homes would be burned before their eyes. Even the parish church, no longer needed, was in one instance razed to the ground. It is easy to imagine the results in the alienation of the peasantry from their superiors. No doubt the large sums expended on enclosing, clearing and draining for agricultural purposes made the land economically more valuable ; but the bad feeling remained for many a day, especially as it was held that the tenure was as under a chief, not as to a proprietor, and that the claims of the chief were rather for service than for private possession.

The main population, however, remained, though spread over the sea-coast and poor enough ; the emigrants at first were few. But ever since these days emigration has grown—emigration to Canada and emigration to the great cities, and now there is but a fraction of the old population in the Highlands. There was nothing in the way of serious riot because the ministers took the side of the proprietors. The ministers of that day in the Highlands were none too spiritual, and their stipends depended on the lairds. They told their people that the evictions were to be regarded as from the Hand of God and must not be withstood by force, since they were the punishment of sin by a Divine Providence ; and apparently the people accepted the strange doctrine. A new attitude of mind came with the rising of the evangelical movement of the Free Church, as well as that of other yet stricter faiths, and these took such a hold of the Highlands that the

Parish churches were practically deserted. The feeling against this new faith was so strong on the part of some of the lairds that even sites for the new churches and manses were refused, and the very sheltering of a protesting minister forbidden.

The famous Dr. Norman MacLeod in his book entitled *A Highland Parish* bemoans the clearances like everyone else. Especially does he deplore the removal of the ' tacksmen ' (who were a sort of middle men), including the ' gentleman tacksmen,' often men of education whose sons rose to be distinguished officers in the army and who helped their poorer dependants, neighbours and friends. Probably his experiences were personal ; some of the tacksmen are not so kindly spoken of.

The people, no doubt, were near starvation. They had to live on broth made of nettles, thickened with a little oatmeal, or had to bleed their cattle and mix the blood with oatmeal which made a cake which was then cut into slices. On the coast they lived on shellfish. But they should have been dealt with more gently. For long after these events the deserted fields and grass-grown foundations of Highland cottages razed to the ground, could be seen to remind people of a population now disappeared. The land once over-populated is now deserted. Later on there were disturbances amounting to riots, but they were speedily put down.

The consequence of these latter troubles was the appointment, under Lord Napier's chairmanship, of the Royal Commission of 1883, which heard evidence of a most interesting and surprising kind, and on its re-commendation the Crofters' Holdings Act of 1886 was passed. There have been many subsidiary Acts since then, but that Act gave the crofters what they wanted as regards the fixity of tenure and reduction of rent, and in 1897 the Scottish Congested Districts Board was set up to enlarge old landholdings or create new ones. The Board of Agriculture now takes the whole matter in hand and most of the grievances are no more. Land Courts were instituted by the Small Holdings Act of 1910.

The Napier Report of 1883 is a striking and unusual one amongst Government documents ; for it not only gives a clear view of the conditions of the crofters, but also deigns in ' Appendices ' to let those who loved the Highlanders, and especially the Islanders, tell of their love-songs and customs. The townships they say, were like communes ; each elected his constable who, on accepting office, stood barefoot, bonnet in hand and a handful of earth on his head, to take the solemn oath of fealty. Another constable was appointed by the factor and was subservient to him. It was clear that the many crofters probably paid more rent than the large farmers, but crofters were notoriously poor farmers and there were naturally high poor and school rates where they existed in large numbers. It is interesting to read in the Evidence of the hard work of the crofter women, who carried the manure in creels on their heads and then dug it into the ground ; and of how the milkmaids sang their lullabies to the cows : without their lilt the cow would not milk, and she had, so we are told, very often to be encouraged by hearing her favourite air ! The salt-tax had been special grievance as it came hardly on those who had to salt the herrings.

It must be remembered that acute discontent did not exist everywhere, for there were many estates on which the relations between landlords and occupiers were friendly and happy. Bad treatment makes bad blood, and last century there certainly was in the South a sort of distrust of the Highlanders as being a grasping and unsatiable person who had to be kept in bounds. This no doubt dated from the days of his poverty and degradation, and of the old practice of cattle stealing. Once the feudal relationship ended in 1748 (when the Government took from the chief his heritable jurisdiction and almost regal power), a new relationship came in, which became in the eyes of the proprietor similar to that of laird and tenant in the South. No doubt real progress followed, but many of the proprietors got into financial difficulties from their own fault. This happened in the case of Rothiemurchus, where there were immense forests to fall back upon, but when these failed to provide funds on which Mr. Grant could run his expensive English elections he tried to live by farming, and when again that failed him and he was on the point of being imprisoned for debt, he discovered, what all the Highland lairds gradually discovered, that their estates had another sort of value in that he could let them to great advantage to English sportsmen. In earlier days there was no preservation of game, and men could shoot and fish as they willed, but gradually game preservation came into vogue, and as sheep runs became less profitable and wool less valuable, deer and game provided the revenue which nothing else in mountainous districts could give. In 1900 it is said that there were 2,287,297 acres in deer forest, an increase of 575,605 acres since 1883.

From one cause or another the character of the Highlands has changed, and now it seems as if the remaining population was frequently dependent on the advent of tourists in the autumn. This was less so in the end of last century, and it is not true of a large portion of the Highland area. There are, as there were, very many crofters and fishermen who carry on the old traditions and who have the native qualities of gentle manners and love of learning : in the West a certain indolence may result from the soft Western breezes, but that is not everywhere, and those Highlanders who go far afield, as so many do, whether into soldiering or into other adventures, give an excellent account of themselves.

A very interesting account of Highland life last century from the laird's point of view, is given by Mr. Osgood Mackenzie in his *Hundred Years in the Highlands*. He was the son of the laird of two Highland properties, and was born in 1842, and therefore his life fell in the second half of the century, when lairds were of a somewhat different stamp from before. In his childhood there was still compulsory labour given by the tenants, and when a journey had to be made from the family estate on the East of Scotland to the more remote one on the West a troop of people appeared, with a mob of ponies, and men who packed and managed to convey the family party and goods as best they could by a bridle-path, taking the babies wrapt in sheepskin and deerskin. The fords were a matter of great difficulty. A small fleet of boats conveyed the cavalcade down Loch Maree, and the company stopped at one of the many islands to hunt for gulls' eggs.

In the old days there were no sheep on the property, but herds of black cattle. The sixty cows belonging to the estate were milked in the open, and the calves fed by their mothers at the same time. So that the calves had to be kept separate till they were allowed to come and have their share of the spoils along with the troop of milkmaids !

In the middle of the century all the letters for the island of Lewis, with its population of 30,000, as well as the 6000 people in Gairloch and Torridon on the main-land, were carried on one man's back. The Lewis letters met a sloop which crossed the Minch once a week. The walk that the postman (Big John the Post) had to take over precipices and moors was indeed an alarming one. An inspecting official from London, who on one occasion had the temerity to come and see that all was well, fainted by the way and had himself to be carried as well as the heavy bag !

The houses of the crofters were built in clusters, end to end, like a street, and were miserable hovels ; but Lady Mackenzie had them rebuilt on separate crofts, abolishing the run-rig system and giving each croft four acres or so of land. She herself, being a woman of great courage and skill, inspected the road-making on horseback, and built new schools. There had been great poverty amongst the people on the West Coast, especially before the potato was introduced, when they lived largely on shellfish boiled in milk in order to keep alive at all. Limpet and whelk shells around the sites of the houses told their tale.

The black houses had depended for light on the roaring fires of peat in the centre of the rooms, and an open barrel in the roof served to let out the smoke. Candles were used only in the great houses : in the black houses there were no lamps burning oil, excepting some tiny tin lamps made by the tinkers and fed by oil made out of the livers of fish, which were allowed to get rotten before they were boiled down. If better light were needed to see sufficiently well for the women to card and spin, or the men to make herring nets, the lighting was done by having a big heap of carefully prepared bog-fir splinters full of resin ready in a corner; and a small boy or girl did nothing but keep these burning during the evening. It was known as a ' Puir man,' probably because an old man often tended it instead of a child. The hemp for the herring nets was at one time home-grown, but not in Mr. Mackenzie's time, and the flax also came from the East, for flax spinning at home had ceased. To make candles, the wicks were put in metal candle moulds and these were placed in frames holding about a dozen, then the fearfully smelling tallow was poured into the moulds. The best candles for the chandeliers were, however, made from the spare suet; everything was made at home, if it were in any way possible, but of course vast stores of food were kept on hand. It all reads like Robinson Crusoe.

Nails were scarce, and heather roots were sometimes used as a substitute in fixing slates. It was a common thing for a man who had been to Inverness to bring back a few nails for his own coffin in case of need! The manner of interment was for the body to be swathed in blue homespun and carried on an open bier to the churchyard.

A pail of clean water made an excellent looking-glass as it has done so often before. Sacks were made of sheep-skin, as jute sacks were non-existent. Ropes for thatch were made of heather, and that for boats of twisted birch twigs; the best ropes of all were made of the fibre of bog-fir roots. Riddles for riddling corn were made of stretched sheepskins perforated with holes made by a big red-hot needle; trout lines were of horsehair, so that a pony's tail was never safe; and the only spoons were those made of the horns of sheep or cows, and melted down by the tinker, who also made fish-hooks when required. Knives and forks were never known in crofters' homes, for everything was eaten with the fingers and thumbs: herrings and potatoes were supposed to taste better eaten in this manner. The Highlanders had no pot-barley, turnips or carrots, onions or cabbage, as had the Lowlanders, so that supposing they got a bit of meat and made broth of it, it would be thickened with oatmeal, and each person would help himself with his horn spoon out of a dish placed in the middle of the table.

Coal was rarely imported before 1840, and all the oak had been cut down and turned into charcoal long before this, for, as we saw, there had been charcoal furnaces in 1727 at Invergarry in Inverness-shire and at Taynuilt or Inveraray. These furnaces were used to smelt iron ore into pig-iron, it being more economical to transport the compact ore to the wood than the bulky wood to the ore. Peat charcoal had therefore to be used by the Highland blacksmith. Sage tells us the method used for converting peat into charcoal. A large pit was dug in soft friable ground and dry peats were placed in it, tier above tier. This was kindled and allowed to burn almost to a cinder, when it was covered with earth till the fire went out. Tar for the boats was sometimes obtained by boring holes in the boles of the old Scotch firs.

Women had hard work on small crofts. In summer they migrated to the shieling-huts in the high ground, taking with them their cattle, sheep or goats (for goats were kept considerably in old days, pigs never). These had to be herded by the children all day to prevent the lambs or kids from being carried off by the eagles and foxes : at night they were driven into bothies. The women slept on heather beds and carried the peats on their shoulders in creels as they still do, kneeling down to cut short grass for hay, standing out in the sea collecting shellfish, or rounding up and chasing the goats barefooted amongst dangerous precipices. They loved their lives in the shielings.

No one who has been present at a Highland Communion service will ever forget it. It was held in different places at various intervals ; early in the century it might be only once in three years at any given spot. When held in summer or autumn all work stopped, however pressing it might be. Every hole and corner had to be got ready for the incoming hordes who assembled from many miles around—sometimes fifty or sixty miles—walking or riding as the case might be. These were not, of course, all communicants, for communicating is held to be a serious matter, only to be undertaken by those who are fully prepared for so solemn a sacrament. Barns and stables were made use of for holding the people. If the services were out of doors, as they usually were, they were held in an open grassy space, sloping upwards, with the minister's preaching box at one end, thus giving him shelter from sun and rain. Three thousand people often congregated together, and all chanted together the ancient Gaelic psalms. There were services for three days beforehand, when the tables were ' fenced ' to prevent the unworthy from coming forward, and a thanksgiving service was held the day following the Communion day. In some places there were mundane tables of gingerbread and kebbucks to tempt the hungry outsiders ! No one was permitted to carry a parcel on Sunday, and as for putting in a stitch it would be unpardonable. Shaving was also forbidden, so it had to be done on Saturday night if at all, and to use a wheelbarrow was unthinkable, so that turnips had to be carried by armfuls to the cows. A lantern could be carried lighted on Sunday, but by no means taken unlighted, even though necessary for the return journey.

Highland funerals were too often scenes of drunkenness, and Mr. Osgood Mackenzie gives a terrible account of the funeral of a laird early in the century where at a dinner following the burial most of those present were drunk, and as outsiders took the opportunity of pressing in, a real fight ensued. Every farmer and crofter that could attend for miles around had done so, and in those days that meant a crowd of thousands, so that the matter was serious. Mr. Mackenzie also gives a wonderful account of a very different funeral, when the body of the young wife of the laird, who had died in childbirth, was carried on foot in silence all the long way through the mountains across Scotland to her family burying-place. In this case where all was decorous and solemn.

Since smuggling was never deemed a crime, the lairds never tasted anything but smuggled whisky: every caller received a glass. Very often indeed people distilled on the Saturday what was needed for the following week. Even the clergy did not condemn the practice of drinking smuggled whisky, so unpopular was the law against it. Indeed, excisemen were often said to have found the whisky they said they had discovered in their own peat stacks! Thus the resident gauger was not disliked until the 'riding officers' came with their long iron-pointed sticks and all comfort in smuggling departed. Before that time barm (yeast) was got by housewives from smugglers as a matter of course.

A man named John Kennedy who lived pretty well through the nineteenth century in Aberfeldy gives a good account of life in a village in the less remote Highlands.[1] He was born in a manse, not a grand manse belonging to the Church of Scotland but in a small house belonging to a little chapel, for his father was one of the evangelists placed in the Highlands and remoter districts by Robert Haldane of Airthrey Castle with the view of preaching the Gospel in a time of spiritual deadness. The laird, or his factor, would not at first allow a chapel to be erected in the village, though the nearest church was a mile off.

The villagers were mostly Gaelic-speaking but the kilt was proscribed, not by law through its Jacobite associations, but by the feeling of the people; by one party it was associated with Highland fierceness, and by men like Kennedy it was connected with a lack of genuine religion. As a matter of fact one man, and one only, wore the kilt in Aberfeldy; he was a carpenter. Such was the elder Kennedy's feeling about the garb that when at length the laird's consent had been obtained to build a chapel the minister persuaded the carpenter to don the trews whilst on work upon the sacred edifice. His success was short-lived, for next day the kilt reappeared, the excuse being made that the trousers made the wearer catch cold! Whether from one reason or another the kilt was not a popular garb in

[1] *Old Highland Days*, by John Kennedy.

Scotland excepting with those who rightly considered it a becoming costume, and for Highlanders one to be encouraged. For the ordinary population it was and is associated with Southerners on a holiday. As a military uniform it was preferred to any other, but it was hardly ever to be seen on a normal working man either North or South. In his *Circuit Journeys* Cockburn says that at Inveraray in 1843 not a single kilt, bonnet or plaid or even a yard of tartan was to be seen in church.

All the villagers in Aberfeldy grew their own lint, sunk it in a wet pit till disintegrated, cleaned it and sent it to the lint mill at the burnside. The lovely white 'pund o' tow' thus came out ready for the young wives to spin. Then there were the village handlooms to weave the thread, and after that it was beautifully bleached and made into shirts and sheets. Cotton in those days was unknown in the North, but a sort of linsey of linen and wool mixed came to be used for sheets. Boots and shoes were also made in Aberfeldy, but of course neither shoes nor stockings were worn by children in summer (except on Sunday) till quite late in the century. The girls went bareheaded, but the elderly women wore the neat white 'mutch,' goffered in front by goffering-irons just like the caps of French women whom in many ways they resembled. In 1806 only one woman in Aberfeldy owned a bonnet.

The food partaken of in the manse, morning and evening, was, as usual, porridge made over a peat fire in a pot hung by a chain or 'sweigh,' or else a mess of potatoes mashed in milk. For dinner there was in-

variably good barley broth with perhaps some mutton
in it, and plenty of oatcake. There were no butchers
or ' fleshers,' as they were called, in the small villages,
but people bought a few sheep jointly and shared them
out, making ' mutton hams ' of some of the meat.
There were few changes of diet in Scotland, and in
much later days it was difficult to get children at their
school dinners (when such were instituted) to appreciate
vegetables beyond potatoes or kail, whether in soup or
otherwise. Sugar was a rarity, never being less than
ninepence a pound ; and much later on, where servants
were kept, their pound of sugar and quarter of a pound
of tea were carefully weighed out every week. Donald
Sage (who will be quoted later) relates how he was
spending his holidays with neighbours at Dornoch and
was given as a treat a pound of tea put into a pot with
nearly a gallon of burn water. This was treated as a
stew and seasoned with butter, pepper and salt. The
leaves were kept for a further decoction !

Tea was often, however, given to elderly ladies,
taken dry with butter and not too much appreciated.
Wheaten bread, if required, came from a town, but
everything else was to be purchased from the ' merchant '
of the village, who usually had everything in hand from
rat-traps to wheelbarrows. A ' piece,' i.e. a barley-
meal bannock or oatcake, was a special treat, and most
small Scottish children thought that there was a special
and just Beatitude for the ' Piece-maker ! '

Early in the morning the herd-boy used to take his
stand on the village square and blow a horn, when out

came all the cows from the byres behind their respective owners' houses. They were taken to the common ground that every village possessed, and brought back to the mustering point every evening from whence each animal contentedly made for its own byre. In Aberfeldy the herd-boy left an ox-horn at the house at which he was next coming to receive his supper. Peat was practically the only fuel, and each family had its own bit of peat-bog; the casting and collecting of the peat was a great undertaking, and the villagers used to be led up to the peat moss on the opening day of the peat harvest, accompanied by the skirling of the bagpipes.

The schools in Aberfeldy were much like other Scottish schools, held in an ordinary cottage, which was heated by peats, one of which, according to the usual custom, each boy brought under his arm to help to keep up the fire. The Shorter Catechism, the Book of Proverbs, and a primitive spelling-book, along with *The Collection*, a reading-book containing many of the stock pieces, served for text-books.

Ever since it was made an offence, efforts were made in Aberfeldy as elsewhere to deal with smuggling, for in old days people had distilled their own spirit and it was not thought wrong to do so still, even by the religious. It was argued that no profit could be made by selling Highland barley, since the freights to the Lowlands were too high, and also that it enabled the Highlander to pay his rent; besides—and this was a clinching argument—the illicit whisky was so much better than that on which the King's duty had been paid!

GRANNY GIBB'S COTTAGE

A Lodging House for Drovers from the Highlands, from Drawing by Sir D. Y. Cameron, R.A.

General Stewart of Garth, who wrote on *The High-landers*, tells how, when the glens were raided by the dragoons, the Highlanders showed true courtesy by inviting the raiders to partake of refreshments ! A raid was the occasion of great commotion in the villages, for everyone sympathized with the offenders. Kennedy tells how illicit malt was even hidden in the chapel garden, and taken to the school where the boys were made to sit upon it in the darkest part of the school-house ! The excisemen entered, but soon departed empty-handed. Even ministers would have their annual brewst of malt whisky for family use, and there was often a cowhouse of stone and turf near a burn that served for this as well as other purposes. Whisky played far too great a part in the lives of the people. In Perthshire the great Sacramental gatherings were, as we have seen, often held in the churchyards, the crowds being too great to be accommodated in the church, and there used to be a constant stream of people flowing between churchyard and the village public-house. Not only was there sometimes a melancholy scene in the inside of the public-house where the crowds were enjoying whisky and oatcakes only too well, but in the preacher's ' tent ' in the churchyard it was occasionally the case that the minister had clearly taken his share of the whisky that was flowing. It was a disgraceful scene, but an occasional one, to have ministers drunk not only at the Holy Fairs but at baptisms and weddings; and we cannot wonder that when religious feeling developed there was a breakaway

z

from a Church that had come to permit such things to exist; in parts of the Highlands, at least, the parish church in those days was consequently neglected. When a notorious offender, the father of illegitimate children, had been sentenced to sit on the cutty stool and be admonished from the pulpit, he had been known to buy himself off with a keg of whisky. This event had actually occurred at Aberfeldy, and it caused such indignation that one of the elders left the Established Church and joined the new sect. Such behaviour was fortunately rare, but the preaching of the Evangelists undoubtedly helped to rouse the people to a sense of a truer type of religion than the Moderates of the time supplied. Kennedy's converts were many, and people came fifteen or twenty miles to hear him, starting at four o'clock on a Sunday morning to be in time for the moving Gaelic sermon; neither snow nor rain, he says, prevented them from ' listening to the Word.'

Games in Scottish villages, Highland and Lowland, were not very numerous. Dancing was, of course, carried on in the barns or farm-steadings. There was a sort of shinty played in the village schools with bent sticks : the sticks were home-made and had to be very carefully chosen in the woods. The ball was made by taking yarn unravelled from an old stocking and winding it tightly round and round a bit of cork. Shinty, in different forms, was played in all boys' schools. For a long time football was a specially Scottish game, just as was golf with those who lived near the links by the seashore. Golf was very little played on inland courses, and in old records like those of Lindsay of the Mount it is not mentioned as an amusement of the ordinary laird as are bowls and hawking ; cricket was, of course, unknown. Curling in winter was for very long a purely Scottish amusement, belonging rather more to the Lowlands than the Highlands, and it had every virtue and no draw-backs ; for it was played with great good humour and fun by all classes and ages when no outside work could be done.

The Royal Caledonian Curling Club, started in 1838, has since held Bonspiels when weather permits. That between Highlanders and Lowlanders at Carsebreck causes great excitement. Each rink has its ' skip,' who directs the ' sooping ' of the besoms and the play gener-ally. A beautifully polished stone intended for the Prince Consort was sent to the Exhibition of 1851, but was unfortunately taken to be a model for a cheese !

The ' smiddy ' in a village was always a delightful spot—warm and pleasant—for boys and men to meet in. Until the middle of the century there was usually some such place where tales were related about fighting clans, witches or ghosts, for though officially the two last were disbelieved in, it used to be said mysteriously that there was something in them that could not be explained, and then terrible tales came about dogs that ' luck luckit ' at the corpse (as though licking the blood) when it had been ' streakit ' and was being watched, thereby betray-ing the fact of its having been murdered ; of the hare that had something to do with the cows going dry, for it could not be shot but with a silver bullet, i.e. a valuable threepenny bit; and much else that even the writer has heard told in bated breath from an aged lady.

Writers narrate how a raid was made by ministers and elders in the Highlands against the fiddles so much beloved by their owners. They made the people break and burn their pipes and fiddles and ' forsake their follie, playing with a cold hand without and the devil's fire within.' The singing of Gaelic songs was most general in the Catholic islands of the Outer Hebrides, where there were fewer restrictions of a religious sort. There were many such songs, each having a marked rhythm to which the motions of the limbs in working were adjusted, e.g. grinding corn, ' wauking ' the home-spun and home-woven cloth, etc. There were also herding songs for the time in summer when the crofters went to the common ground and lived in shielings on the hills.

Donald Sage is another interesting writer about the Highlands.[1] He was the son of a minister at Kildonan in Ross-shire. The most curious part of the narrative concerns the school and games. Donald and his brother rode to Dornoch with their father to be put to school there. It was the nearest country school, but it had as its master one who was famed for learning but a great disciplinarian, so much so that he had been cited before the Sheriff for cruelty to the boys, and only escaped punishment by promising never to inflict punishment himself but only doing so by deputy, the deputy being the pauper or janitor of the school. This 'pauper' had to

[1] *Memorabilia Domestica, or Parish Life in the North of Scotland.*

perambulate the towns with his post-horn to waken and summon scholars to school, then to sweep the school and light the fire, and all he received for his many and disagreeable labours was a free education.

Shinty was the game universally played by boys, and it was also played by men on New Year's Day, when the whole male population turned out to the links, each armed with his club : this game continued till darkness fell upon the combatants, and it was a dangerous affair when, as often happened, it was keenly contested.

Then there was the pancake cooking on Pasch Sunday, a relic of Catholic times such as is continued in at least one of the great English Public Schools ; and the universal cockfight at Candlemas. This last was considered so important in Dornoch that the Sheriff gave over the Court House for the occasion, and there the unfortunate cocks did battle. The Council Board and Sheriff's Bench was occupied by the schoolmaster and his friends, and highest honours were given to the bird which gained the greatest victories. He was declared King, and the next bird in order was the Queen. The ' fugies ' or non-fighters became the property of the master. On ' Coronation Day ' so-called, the master sat in school with two crowns made by the ladies of the town who surrounded him, and the owners of the royal birds were crowned when they appeared with the ' lifeguards ' they had chosen, and addressed in Latin on their duties in the high places they occupied. The ceremony concluded with a march headed by the town drummer and a ball and supper in the evening.

Markets in Dornoch were held in the churchyard, as being a convenient centre. Merchants' booths were set up, and as they were covered with canvas they had to be erected on poles inserted in the ground far enough to reach the coffins. Ginger-bread, ribbons and whisky were the principal commodities sold at these markets. Frays of one kind or another frequently happened amongst the Highlanders, when cudgels did yeoman service, and strangely enough they frequently occurred at funerals when different family or clan feuds were remembered, and when few people were quite sober. Occasionally, however, the fights were political, particularly when during the agitation for Reform the corpse represented the unpopular party. But this more often happened in the South than in the Highlands. In many parishes there was, however, ' battery and bloodshed ' for various reasons, and if it happened that the minister was unpopular (or even possibly given to drink) the ' heritors ' were also disorderly and wild. On the other hand they were often prosecuted by the minister either for failing to augment his stipend or for failing to pay the fines laid on them in course of parochial discipline.

It was while Mr. Sage was at Achness that the Clearances of 1819 took place, and almost a thousand summonses of ejectment were dispatched all over the district. Every home and hovel, ministers, catechists as well as cottars, he says, received them. The extraordinary thing was the spirit in which many of the people regarded what they looked on as the chastisement of God. The ejectments took place in April, and some patches of ground on the shore were doled out, but without the poorest hut or shelter; and the people could not fish, nor had they ever set foot in a boat. Mr. Sage gives a pathetic account of his last sermon before the evictions : all restraint at last gave way and the whole congregation lifted up their voices and wept together. Many parted never to meet again. The inhabitants had half an hour in which to pack up and carry off their furniture and then the cottages were set on fire. The widow of a soldier, a much respected old lady, begged in vain for delay till her neighbours could give her help, and she had to do her best with her own hands till the torch was applied ; but unluckily the furniture also took fire and was burned to ashes. Another decrepit and pious woman had, he says, to be carried on a blanket and she died soon after. The scene afterwards was a terrible one ; the mission was ended after the Strathnaver Clearances, for there were few people left to minister to.

The best account of life in the Highlands as it appeared to the wealthier classes is to be found in the delightful *Memoirs of a Highland Lady*, written by Elizabeth Grant of Rothiemurchus. She describes the journey made to Speyside in 1803-4, the miserable crossing at Queensferry, and the three-days' journey between Perth and her home. The fording of the rivers was a terror, except where there was a ' carriage boat ' to take the party over. At the end there was, however, a great welcome from their people. The Highland servants were strange, ignorant creatures, who simply ran in one

another's way, and the piper declined any work uncon-
nected with whisky ' for fear of spoiling the delicacy of
his touch.' Whisky flowed everywhere, and there was
plenty of dancing, the lessons in which took place for
servants and gentry alike, all learning their flings and
' shuffles ' together. Many of the Highlanders played
the fiddle, and the house was filled with guests who
danced away, old and young, rich and poor, whisky
punch always at hand.

All this sounded cheerful, but the treatment of
children in those days is almost incredible. The little
Grants were plunged in a tub of water in the kitchen
court, the ice on the top of which had often to be broken,
and to this ceremony they were brought down covered
only with a cotton cloak. Then they were dressed in
cotton frocks with low necks. Cold milk the writer
detested, and when she refused to take it her father
stood over her with a whip and gave as many sharp
cuts as were necessary to make her empty the basin.
Whatever was given had to be eaten : fat if not easily
managed had to be taken under the lash, recalcitrance
ended in being shut in a dark closet. What was not
eaten was kept for next meal, and one child went thirty
hours without food rather than partake of the hated
dish. On ' rhubarb mornings ' the breakfast was water
gruel, thick and black, and seasoned with salt, and if
it was refused starvation followed. At their parents'
dinner the children sat still, seeing and smelling but having nothing till dessert came with its fruit and a little
wine. Boys and girls were flogged alike for every error.

Though young Grant was sent to Eton, where he was miserable, most lairds' sons had tutors who sat at the side table with their charges, and ate their porridge, broth and boiled mutton with them. When there was fear of invasion a volunteer company was formed and the officers used to come to dinner after inspections. In the year 1809 it was recorded that for the first time some of them came to the drawing-room for tea sober !

In Morayshire illegitimacy was constant in all classes alike. In the upper circles these 'accidental' daughters, as they were called, were often helpful in the house, and their fathers acted as their guardians, and as regards the boys saw to their schooling. Indeed, as the children bore the paternal name, there was no attempt at concealment or idea of impropriety.

In 1812, after a stay in the South, an unfortunate governess was brought to the Highlands from London to teach the Grants, and one can imagine her tears over the dreariness of the moors and the poor fare she found she had to partake of. For in the inns there were no clean tables, though hotch-potch, salmon, good mutton and grouse, bad bread but excellent wine, seemed good enough for most people as food. When the party arrived they found the garden moved a quarter of a mile from the house, and the vegetables far from the cook : the kitchen department of the garden being considered the reverse of ornamental. This inconvenient arrangement was universally admired by visitors, being the fashion of the day. The work of the house was easily done. There was a small army of retainers who purified the water, brought in the wood and peat, bottled the whisky, etc., besides supplying the food and wearing apparel of the household, which involved spinning, weaving, dyeing, and so on. There was a fox-hunter to kill foxes, bow-man to guard the cattle, sheep-herds for the sheep, also the universal ' orra man ' for odd jobs.

A property which was really a great forest of sixteen square miles was prosperous, especially during the French wars. That is to say, when there was a high duty on foreign timber all was well, but when the price of wood fell there was nothing to turn to but the black cattle of olden days. In some ways the life was simple, but not as simple as that of earlier generations. At every house whisky was offered; every gentleman began his day with a dram, and a bottle of whisky on a silver salver full of small glasses was always placed on the side table in the morning. In the pantry a bottle of whisky was the allowance per day for those who came on errands, along with bread and cheese.

The kirk was filled to overflowing, but neither doors nor windows fitted; plaster, fallen from the roof, lay in heaps about the seats, the graveyard was overgrown with nettles, and the path choked with weeds. It was a small church in which service was conducted only once in three weeks, for there were other parish churches not many miles off. But the people attended most regularly, the women with their white caps, and men in their red plaids. As usual there was a laird's pew, with a wooden canopy over it, and a servants' pew behind. The Psalm given out, the book was handed to the precentor below,

who called aloud the tune and began a recitation of the
first line on the key-note, which was then taken up by
the congregation. The tremolo, remembered by those
still living, had just come into vogue, and was thought
very effective. Everyone stood for the long prayer. The
women were plaided as well as the men, but the wives
wore a large handkerchief under the plaid; a bonnet
was not to be seen. No Highland girl ever covered her
head, but had her hair braided or plaited and bound by
a snood, a bit of velvet or ribbon placed rather low on
the forehead and tied beneath the plait at the back. Few
wore shoes or stockings, and the material for the gowns
was home-dyed linsey-woolsey. The girls used to wash
their hair in a decoction of the young buds of birch
trees, which agreeably scented the church. The men
snuffed vigorously, using quills fastened by strings to the
lids of their mulls, spooning up the snuff in quantities;
the old women snuffed too.

Harvest-homes were scenes of happy mirth and much
food; there were roasted fowls, mince-fowl, apple pie,
haggis, singed sheep's-head and trotters, black and white
' puddings,' sowens and curd, and plenty of whisky and
dancing, the lasses ' footing it ' and the wives more
demure; but all classes dancing together in the barn.
At Belleville, once the home of Macpherson of Ossian
fame, and now of his son, was a delightful centre for
neighbouring friends. Dinner was at five o'clock, card-
playing was seldom over till midnight, and a well-filled
tray came during the interval.

For the ' Floater's ' Ball the hay-loft was gay with

tallow dips ; punch was made in washing-tubs, an ox
and some sheep had been killed for the occasion, for
those employed in the forest, lopping the branches and
floating them down, were many. There were also
workers in the saw-mills to be considered. The process
of getting the wood down the river was wet and difficult;
but, as usual, in order to help it, a lad went round with a
small cask of whisky on his back and a horn cup in his
hand three times a day. Even the children were given
whisky. 'The dram,' it was said, 'was the Highland
prayer, it began, accompanied, and ended all things.'
In a town of 3000 or 4000 inhabitants there might
be fifty ale-houses. No wonder there were tragedies !
But the food was simple, because when in bothies on
the hill and quite alone shepherds often did not trouble
to have a fire, but took their brose of meal milk or water
cold. With hot milk it was thought to be excellent, and
with the skimmings of the broth pot it was considered a
special treat.

Elizabeth Grant 'came out' in 1814, at seventeen
years of age, the usual age for such an event, and she
gives an account of her trousseau, which was an elaborate
one. One can imagine the joy of the Highland girl, so
far equipped merely in cloak and hood of home-spun
and home-dyed tartan, that is to say, the red dress
tartan of the clan and riding-habits of green tartan,
the tartan of the 42nd Regiment or Black Watch.

The Northern Meeting, now famous in the Highlands,
had been set on foot at the end of the eighteenth century by the famous Duchess of Gordon, who got people

from the northern counties to collect for the best part of a week's entertainment.   After her time no one arose quite to replace her, but the gatherings went on success-fully, and Miss Grant set off gaily in the family barouche (now come into fashion) which was to carry her to this scene of pleasure, fording the river and rest-ing at a desolate dirty inn *en route*.

We have spoken of the superstitions of the Highlands, of which there are many descriptions, but which would need a book to themselves, so numerous and interesting are they.   Holy Wells and Fairies are known through-out Scotland : large green mounds are always known as fairy dwellings, not to be disturbed.   There is also often enough a live trout in a stream aged hundreds of years, and held sacred.   But in the Islands we have much greater mysteries, such as the water-horse or 'each Uisge,' which had a special fondness for young women and would seize them and carry them off to the loch or tarn from which they never would return ; indeed, in the Outer Islands most of the spiritual apparitions were terrible, as were spells exercised on innocent people ; but there are some less gruesome folk, such as the 'green men,' and other sorts of fairies whose associations were less evil.   The very names in Gaelic are impressive. Gaelic became less common last century amongst the younger people, and at the end of the century it was only in the Islands that English was not understood by the ordinary man or woman met in travelling through the country though Gaelic might be the language ordinarily spoken.

CHAPTER XIV

EPILOGUE

WE have reached the end of a great period in history, and we must try to remember what it has meant to us and to the world. As the nineteenth century dawned Scotland found herself a poor, rude, and little-thought-of nation, though with the promise and beginnings of better things. She was, in the belief of her rulers, very near to the Revolution which had burst over a neighbouring country, and therefore required to be kept in severe control. They did not see, because their eyes were blinded, that this Revolution had already taken place in the minds and characters of the people, and that both the dull political outlook and the dead Religion —not really dead but only sleeping—were emerging into something living, real and insistent.

This came to pass after much tribulation, and then came success—success in the arts and sciences and in almost every phase of life; but, above all, material success undreamed of before. And Scotland learned through her writers to have that confidence in herself and her qualities that formerly had been lacking to her. And with that pride and material success came self-sufficiency, and the idea that if men were left to work out their own destinies without interference from outside all would be well, and they would be prosperous and happy. Hence resulted the *laisser-faire* doctrine that encouraged people to disregard what did not minister to their prosperity.

The result proved to be disastrous, and ever since there has been a continual struggle to put wrong right and to get conditions improved, inasmuch as it was made clear that men counted more than money, and that a nation where human beings were neglected could not be a truly prosperous nation. It was also realized that the inhibitions and limitations of the Victorian age were part of the self-sufficiency of the time.

These lessons had begun to be learned, but much was left to be done; and the twentieth century opened with hope, all unconscious of the terrible trials that awaited it. But it had much to be grateful for inasmuch as it inherited a wider outlook on the part of its rulers, and more humane standards of living on the part of its people, than existed in the ruder and less tolerant age a hundred years before. It had also got a religion with less logic but more soul, and a sense that somehow the ordinary comforts, luxuries and leisure of life were not necessarily the privileges of the few but the birthright of all—men and women alike.

SOME OF THE BOOKS CONSULTED

COBBETT'S TOUR IN SCOTLAND, 1833.

LORD COCKBURN'S MEMORIALS AND JOURNALS.

SOME LETTERS OF LORD COCKBURN. Harry A. Cockburn, 1903.

Wordsworth's JOURNAL.

SOCIAL LIFE IN SCOTLAND IN THE EIGHTEENTH CENTURY. H. G. Graham. 2 vols.

THE ANNALS OF THE PARISH. John Galt.

EVERYDAY LIFE IN OLD SCOTLAND. I. F. Grant.

A SHORT HISTORY OF SCOTLAND. George M. Thomson. 1930.

THE HISTORY OF THE WORKING CLASSES IN SCOTLAND. Thomas Johnston.

A HUNDRED YEARS OF THE HIGHLANDS. Osgood Mackenzie.

THE COTTAGERS OF GLENBURNIE. Elizabeth Hamilton.

REMINISCENCES OF EIGHTY YEARS. John Urie, 1908.

BACKWARD GLANCES. James Hedderwick. 1891.

MEMOIRS OF A HIGHLAND LADY. Elizabeth Grant. Edited by Lady Strachey. 1911.

RISE AND PROGRESS OF SCOTTISH EDUCATION. Alex. Morgan. 1927.

A CENTURY OF SCOTTISH LIFE. Charles Rogers.

A FARMER'S FIFTY YEARS IN LAUDERDALE. R. Speirs Gibb.

HISTORY OF SECONDARY EDUCATION IN SCOTLAND. John Strong.

THE SCOTS GARD'NER, TOGETHER WITH THE GARD'NER'S KALENDAR. John Reid.

AN ENCYCLOPAEDIA OF GARDENING. J. C. Loudon.

REPORT OF ROYAL BOTANIC GARDENS, EDINBURGH.

SOCIAL AND INDUSTRIAL HISTORY OF SCOTLAND. James MacLennan.

THE INDUSTRIAL REVOLUTION IN SCOTLAND. Henry Hamilton.

THE STORY OF THE KING'S HIGHWAY. S. and B. Webb.

THE SUTHERLAND EVICTIONS. Craig Sellar.

HISTORY OF HIGHLAND CLEARANCES. Alex. Mackenzie.

RURAL RECOLLECTIONS. By George Robertson. 1829.

THE PRESENT STATE OF HUSBANDRY IN SCOTLAND (1778).

GENERAL VIEW OF AGRICULTURE IN EAST LOTHIAN. From papers of Robert Somerville. 1813.

A HIGHLAND PARISH. Norman MacLeod.

LIVING MEMORIES OF AN OCTOGENARIAN. George Croal.

REMINISCENCES OF YARROW. Dr. James Russell.

MY SCHOOLS AND SCHOOLMASTERS. Hugh Miller.

REPORTS of the Scottish Board of Health, the Board of Agriculture, and many others.

MEMOIRS AND LIVES of Adam Black, James Nasmyth, William and Robert Chambers, Thomas Telford, Francis Jeffrey, John Duncan, George fourth Earl of Aberdeen, George Hope of Fentonbarns, Robert Dick, Sir Archibald Geikie, Dr. Alexander Whyte, Robert and J. A. Haldane, Charles Cowan, and others.

INDEX

376 THE SCOTLAND OF OUR FATHERS

PRINTED IN GREAT BRITAIN BY ROBERT MACLEHOSE AND CO. LTD.
THE UNIVERSITY PRESS, GLASGOW

62

W/.

20

8/6

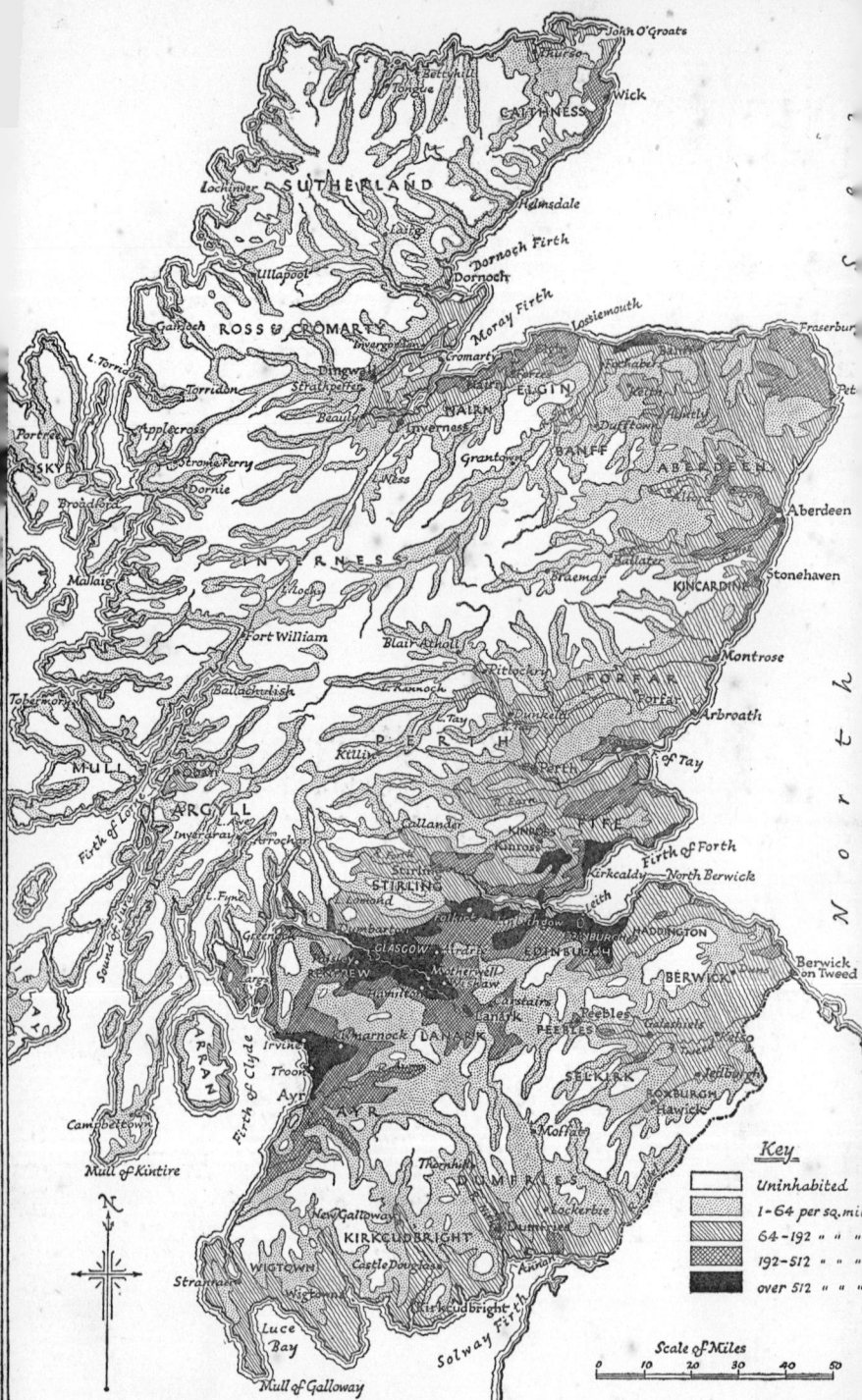

MAP SHOWING THE DISTRIBUTION OF THE POPULATION OF SCOTLAND